CAR CHASE
LONG LENS — TRACKING

 2nd UNIT

ALL SAME SHOT as BOND rockets into frame crossing L. to R. (to the correct side of road) .. A BEAT & XENIA sweeps R. to L. into frame — starting to draw level again ..

50.

XENIA — BOND

DIAGRAM TO ILLUSTRATE ABOVE SHOT

 2nd UNIT

51.

AERIAL SHOT.
HELICOPTER crabbing L. to R.

GOLDENEYE

This Storyboard must be returned to the Production Office at the end of your involvement with the film. It is made available to you only and must not be divulged to any third parties. Should it become mislaid, the loss must be reported to the Production Office immediately. This Storyboard and all rights therein are owned exclusively by DANJAQ INC.

© DANJAQ INC.   MCMXCIV   DATE:..........................

BOND CARS
THE DEFINITIVE HISTORY

BOND CARS
THE DEFINITIVE HISTORY

Jason Barlow

BBC Books would like to thank Meg Simmonds and Debi Berry for their kind help with the production of this book.

BBC Books, an imprint of Ebury Publishing
20 Vauxhall Bridge Road,
London SW1V 2SA

BBC Books is part of the Penguin Random House group of companies
whose addresses can be found at global.penguinrandomhouse.com

2020 © EON PRODUCTIONS AND DANJAQ, LLC. ALL RIGHTS RESERVED
007 AND RELATED JAMES BOND INDICA © 1962-2020 DANJAQ, LLC AND METRO-GOLDWYN-MAYER STUDIOS INC.
007 AND RELATED JAMES BOND TRADEMARKS ARE TRADEMARKS OF DANJAQ, LLC. ALL RIGHTS RESERVED.

First published by BBC Books in 2020

www.penguin.co.uk

A CIP catalogue record for this book is available from the British Library

Standard hardback edition ISBN 9781785945144
Slipcased edition ISBN 9781785945137

Senior Commissioning Editor: Yvonne Jacob
Design: Elliott Webb
Project Editor: Steve Tribe
Cover design: Two Associates
Cover credits: Aston Martin DB5 image courtesy of Aston Martin Lagonda Global Holdings plc.
Lotus Esprit image courtesy of Lotus Cars Ltd.

Quotation from *Casino Royale* reproduced with permission of Ian Fleming Publications Ltd, London
Casino Royale copyright © Ian Fleming Publications Ltd, 1953
www.ianfleming.com

Printed and bound in Italy by L.E.G.O. S.p.A.

Penguin Random House is committed to a sustainable future forour business, our readers and our planet.
This book is made from Forest Stewardship Council® certified paper.

DR. NO © 1962 Danjaq, LLC and Metro-Goldwyn-Mayer Studios Inc. FROM RUSSIA WITH LOVE © 1963 Danjaq, LLC and Metro-Goldwyn-Mayer Studios Inc. GOLDFINGER © 1964 Danjaq, LLC and Metro-Goldwyn-Mayer Studios Inc. THUNDERBALL © 1965 Danjaq, LLC and Metro-Goldwyn-Mayer Studios Inc. YOU ONLY LIVE TWICE © 1967 Danjaq, LLC and Metro-Goldwyn-Mayer Studios Inc. ON HER MAJESTY'S SECRET SERVICE © 1969 Danjaq, LLC and Metro-Goldwyn-Mayer Studios Inc. DIAMONDS ARE FOREVER © 1971 Danjaq, LLC and Metro-Goldwyn-Mayer Studios Inc. LIVE AND LET DIE © 1973 Danjaq, LLC and Metro-Goldwyn-Mayer Studios Inc. THE MAN WITH THE GOLDEN GUN © 1974 Danjaq, LLC and Metro-Goldwyn-Mayer Studios Inc. THE SPY WHO LOVED ME © 1977 Danjaq, LLC and Metro-Goldwyn-Mayer Studios Inc. MOONRAKER © 1979 Danjaq, LLC and Metro-Goldwyn-Mayer Studios Inc. FOR YOUR EYES ONLY © 1981 Danjaq, LLC and Metro-Goldwyn-Mayer Studios Inc. OCTOPUSSY © 1983 Danjaq, LLC and Metro-Goldwyn-Mayer Studios Inc. A VIEW TO A KILL © 1985 Danjaq, LLC and Metro-Goldwyn-Mayer Studios Inc. THE LIVING DAYLIGHTS © 1987 Danjaq, LLC and Metro-Goldwyn-Mayer Studios Inc. LICENCE TO KILL © 1989 Danjaq, LLC and Metro-Goldwyn-Mayer Studios Inc. GOLDENEYE © 1995 Danjaq, LLC and Seventeen Leasing Corporation. TOMORROW NEVER DIES © 1997 Danjaq, LLC and Eighteen Leasing Corporation. THE WORLD IS NOT ENOUGH © 1999 Danjaq, LLC and United Artists Corporation. DIE ANOTHER DAY © 2002 Danjaq, LLC and United Artists Corporation. CASINO ROYALE © 2006 Danjaq, LLC and United Artists Corporation. QUANTUM OF SOLACE © 2008 Danjaq, LLC and Metro-Goldwyn-Mayer Studios Inc. SKYFALL © 2012 Danjaq, LLC and Metro-Goldwyn-Mayer Studios Inc. SPECTRE © 2015 Danjaq, LLC, Metro-Goldwyn-Mayer Studios Inc. and Columbia Pictures Industries, Inc. NO TIME TO DIE © 2020 Danjaq, LLC and Metro-Goldwyn-Mayer Studios Inc. All Rights Reserved.

CONTENTS

CHAPTER 01.
DR. NO
08

CHAPTER 02.
FROM RUSSIA WITH LOVE
20

CHAPTER 03.
GOLDFINGER
32

CHAPTER 04.
THUNDERBALL
54

CHAPTER 05.
YOU ONLY LIVE TWICE
68

CHAPTER 06.
ON HER MAJESTY'S SECRET SERVICE
76

CHAPTER 07.
DIAMONDS ARE FOREVER
90

CHAPTER 08.
LIVE AND LET DIE
102

CHAPTER 09.
THE MAN WITH THE GOLDEN GUN
114

CHAPTER 10.
THE SPY WHO LOVED ME
134

CHAPTER 11.
MOONRAKER
154

CHAPTER 12.
FOR YOUR EYES ONLY
164

CHAPTER 13.
OCTOPUSSY
180

CHAPTER 14.
A VIEW TO A KILL
190

CHAPTER 15.
THE LIVING DAYLIGHTS
202

CHAPTER 16.
LICENCE TO KILL
212

CHAPTER 17.
GOLDENEYE
220

CHAPTER 18.
TOMORROW NEVER DIES
234

CHAPTER 19.
THE WORLD IS NOT ENOUGH
248

CHAPTER 20.
DIE ANOTHER DAY
260

CHAPTER 21.
CASINO ROYALE
274

CHAPTER 22.
QUANTUM OF SOLACE
282

CHAPTER 23.
SKYFALL
292

CHAPTER 24.
SPECTRE
304

CHAPTER 25.
NO TIME TO DIE
314

ACKNOWLEDGEMENTS & LIST OF CARS
330

What elements define a great Bond film? The glamorous locations, the action, Bond's female co-stars, the villain… And, of course, the car.

In the first Bond novel, *Casino Royale*, Ian Fleming set out his stall pretty clearly – the author was a car fan and his fictional spy would be, too: 'Bond's car was his only personal hobby. One of the last of the 4½-litre Bentleys with the supercharger by Amherst Villiers, he had bought it new in 1933 and had kept it in careful storage through the war … Bond drove it hard and well and with an almost sensual pleasure. It was a battleship-grey convertible coupé, which really did convert, and it was capable of touring at ninety with thirty miles an hour in reserve.'

Casino Royale was first published in 1953, and Bond's transition onto the big screen took some time. The first two films were terrific, but the series didn't achieve full cinematic blockbuster status until the third entry, 1964's *Goldfinger*. And *Goldfinger* is, of course, the film that brought us what's widely regarded as the first true Bond car.

While it was not the first automobile 007 drove in his movie incarnation, the Aston Martin DB5 looked right, it sounded even better, and it had the gadgets, a confluence of factors that influenced the generation who saw the film at the time, who enjoyed it on television ever after, or who owned the famous toy version. This was pretty much everyone on the planet.

The DB5 features prominently in the 25th Bond film, *No Time To Die*, and many pages are devoted to it in this book. But it's far from the only Bond car, and just as these wonderful films reflect the times in which they were made – 'it's not just the politics, it's the attitude of the movie,' as Daniel Craig told me – the cars tell a story, too. Sometimes they're literally driving the action along, personalities in their own right, as carefully cast as every other participant. On other occasions, they help provide context, as important an indicator of the era as the costume design or the cinematography. And if they're at the heart of a big chase, they're also players in cinema history, stars of sequences conceived, designed and executed by the most talented people in the entertainment business.

So this book isn't just a forensic examination of all the key cars to feature in the James Bond film series (as well as some of the lesser-known ones), it uses them as a way into the creative process. We've also had complete access to the EON archive, so the stories of each film are amplified by many rarely seen images and previously unpublished documents. Some of these are absolutely priceless, and it's an honour to be able to share them here. Whether shaken or stirred, I hope you learn something new…

Jason Barlow

THE FIRST JAMES BOND FILM!

IAN FLEMING'S

DR. NO

007

A UK advance poster
for the first Bond film,
from October 1962.

CHAPTER 01

DR. NO

1962

STARRING Sean Connery as James Bond

EON PRODUCTIONS LIMITED

CALL SHEET Loc. No.1

Production: "DR. NO"
Director: TERENCE YOUNG
Set: INT/EXT. AIRPORT
Scs: 39, 40, 41, 42, 43, 44, 45, 46, 47, 48.

Date: Tuesday, 16th January '62
Unit Call: 7.30 a.m. Leave hotels (See Movement Order attached)
Location: PALISADOES AIRPORT

ARTISTE	CHARACTER	Costume No.	M/U	Hair	W/Robe	Lv Hotel	On Set
SEAN CONNERY	JAMES BOND	2	7.15	7.30	7.00	8.00	8.30
MARGARET LEWARS	GIRL PHOTOGRAPHER	1	6.00	6.45	–	8.00	8.30
REGGIE CARTER	CHAUFFEUR	1	6.45	–	7.15	8.00	8.30
JACK LORD	FELIX LEITER	1	As Available				
JOHN KITZMILLER	QUARREL	1	On Set	–		8.00	8.30

Stand-ins:
Michael Borota For Mr. Connery — At Airport at 8.00 a.m.
A.N.Other For Mr. Carter
A.N.Other For Miss Lewars } Stand-ins for these Artistes to be selected from Crowd.
A.N.Other For Mr. Lord
A.N.Other For Mr. Kitzmiller

Crowd:
  2 Stewardesses
  20 Passengers
  35 Relatives } Direct to Airport arriving at 8 a.m. or as arranged by Danny Ennevor.
  4 Children
  2 Taxi Drivers
  2 Porters
  2 Customs Officers } From Airport staff – On set 8.00 a.m.
  1 Police

Driving Double: A.N.Other For Mr. Kitzmiller - To S/By if required.

PROPS: BOND's personal props, holster, Walther, wristwatch, cig. case, lighter.
BOND's luggage, black hand case, Press Speed Graphic (Flash attach bulbs and repeats), accessories case, luggage for crowd, handbaggage for crowd. Toys for children, Porter's barrow, flight bags for stewardesses, telephone and dressing, coins for 'phone, tip for Porter, newspaper and cigarettes for LEITER.

VEHICLES: To report to Car Park, Kingston Airport at 8.00 a.m. (Please ensure vehicles are fueled and in mechanical order).
LIMOUSINE – LEITER'S CAR – 2 TAXIS (As arranged by Chris Blackwell)

CONSTRUCTION: Telephone Alcove
Ropes for crowd control

SPECIAL REQUIREMENTS: Police control
Flight (Arrivals & Departures) Schedule
CATERING: As arranged – in Old Airport Block.
CROWD: Lunch will be taken in the Airport Canteen.
M/U & HAIR: Block 72-74 Courtleigh Manor.
ELECTRICAL: Please ensure that all cable runs are as far as possible clear of public thoroughfares.
PRODUCTION OFFICE: Block 68-70 Courtleigh Manor Hotel. Telephone: 69642
AIRPORT LIAISON: Mr. Eric Williams, Asst. Airport Manager
Contact: Miss Byles. Tel: 81109
BREAKFASTS: Breakfast served at all hotels from 6.45 a.m. PTO

The call sheet for the very first day of shooting on Dr No, Tuesday 16 January 1962. Vehicles were to be fuelled and in mechanical order.

This rarely seen contact sheet documents the scene in which Strangways meets his fate at the hands of the Three Blind Mice. A British agent is duly summoned to investigate.

Harbour Street, Kingston, Jamaica. Three men make their way gingerly along the road, white sticks tapping out a rhythm that they alone can understand. In fact, we've already met them, animated in silhouette at the end of Maurice Binder's spellbinding credits sequence, the colour palette of which betrays an immersion in modernism, op-art and jazz.

This is a new kind of film, all right, and it still zings off the screen almost 60 years later. (Now imagine it's October 1962, and imagine you've just heard 'Love Me Do', the first single by a promising new band from Liverpool called The Beatles, on sale the same day that *Dr No* premieres in London. Maybe this was the moment the era we came to know as the Sixties actually started.)

Back to Jamaica. The soundtrack has segued from Monty Norman's soon-to-be immortal subverted surf rock title theme into 'Kingston Calypso' by local musical stars Byron Lee and the Dragonaires. The Three Blind Mice tap-tap-tap their way across the screen, apparently inviting our pity but hiding a deadly secret. A blue Ford Consul Classic appears briefly in the background, while a cream Ford of the same model is much more visible in the foreground. It's categorically not a Bond car, not as we'd come to know them anyway, but it does have the honour of being the first car to appear *fully* in a Bond film. There's one for a pub quiz. More background colour: we pass a Ford Anglia, while a red 1959 Chevrolet El Camino and yellow '58 Pontiac are also in shot.

The trio manage a surprisingly long walk given their visual impairment, and eventually they arrive at the Queen's Club, where the car quotient rises substantially. Barely five minutes into the first Bond film and an important precedent is being firmly established: the supporting cast is just as worthy of our attention as the leading characters. A burgundy Jaguar XK140 sits alongside a beige Hillman Minx Series III – a feline British classic versus a faded and now largely forgotten sourpuss, although the Minx is referenced in Fleming's *Dr No* novel.

John Strangways is playing bridge with friends – these scenes were filmed at the Liguanea Club, located at 80 Knutsford Boulevard – when he's called away. Pausing only to slip a coin to the first of the three 'mice', he passes another (pink/peach) Hillman, before being shot point-blank as he climbs inside his Ford Anglia 105 E.

While this is the car that most remember as the first to appear prominently in a Bond film – or at least to be featured in a major plot pivot – diehard fans might want to ponder the presence in the background of a 1956 Studebaker Sky Hawk. Studebaker is now a footnote in US automotive history, but many were the work of Raymond Loewy and Associates, one of *the* visionary and versatile designers of all time (he's widely known as 'the father of industrial design').

Presumably the Sky Hawk is also the last thing Strangways sees before he collapses into a heap, having set in motion the film's primary narrative, and gets dumped unceremoniously in the back of the LaSalle Funeral Coach. LaSalle is another, even more obscure American footnote, one of the name-plates dreamt up by General

Above: Assassins and a Hillman Minx. Below: James Bond and a 1959 Ford Consul Mk II. His transport would become more glamorous.

Motors' forward-thinking CEO Alfred P Sloan back in the 1920s when he envisioned a revenue-generating hierarchy of brands at escalating price points. LaSalle sat at the top, above Buick and below Cadillac, but it didn't last: the 1939 Series 50 which featured in funereal form – a 'combination' body by AJ Miller that doubled as an ambulance – in *Dr No* was one of the last.

Two other fabulous pieces of trivia: Tim Moxon, who played Strangways, was too tall to fit in the back of the hearse so his feet dangled dangerously beyond the tailgate as the vehicle fled the scene; and one of the blind mice was played by his dentist.

Checking out the background isn't as geeky as it sounds. Bond's producers would become expert at conjuring a milieu, and if you subscribe to the theory that automobiles are as powerfully redolent of an era as the clothes, hairstyles, and music, then the 25 films that make up the 007 canon aren't just movies, they're matters of record and documents of fast-moving trends in popular culture.

So it is with *Dr No*. Interestingly, Jamaica would achieve independence in 1962, but its status as a British colony and strategically useful location meant that, despite its balmy climate and distinct local customs, it had a curiously familiar feel. It was also a desirable bolthole for post-war celebrities, and the likes of Errol Flynn, Noël Coward, Alec Guinness, Clark Gable and, of course, Bond's creator Ian Fleming all made it their home. Look at *Dr No*'s call sheets and you'll see that a young Chris Blackwell – who would later found Island Records and introduce the world to Bob Marley, Grace Jones and U2, amongst others – was hired as a location manager, at the suggestion of family friend Ian Fleming.

Jamaica's colonial status also explains why so many of the cars in *Dr No* are British, their ubiquity assisted by the omnipotence of the UK's car industry in this period: it was the second largest producer of motor vehicles in the world at the time. We see Bond in several local taxis during the film, including cars that are ever more wreathed in the mists of time as the years go by. That boxy black

CIA man Felix Leiter (Jack Lord), his local contact Quarrel (John Kitzmiller), a Chevrolet Impala and background Austin A40 Farina, in a rarely seen image.

Right: The villainous LaSalle mysteriously transforms into a Humber as the hearse heads to its own funeral. Opposite page: A previously unseen archive contact sheet.

car with the yellow roof is an Austin A55 Cambridge of which almost 150,000 were made (it's a badge-engineered reworking of the more common Morris Oxford), and its dowdy appearance couldn't be more evocative of 1950s Britain if it smoked a pipe and wore slippers rather than tyres. Amazing to think its design was the work of the famed Italian *carrozzeria*, Pininfarina. A Standard Ensign taxi is also glimpsed. A 1959 Ford Consul Mk II used by the government is marginally less fusty, while we see the traitorous and saturnine Professor Dent driving somewhat raggedly in a Vauxhall PA Velox ahead of his meeting with Dr No (and a tarantula, in a scene that was an early showcase for the genius – and frugality – of production designer Ken Adam. He would later get to spend more on a single set than the entire budget of *Dr No*).

Perhaps more obviously appealing, then and now, is the retinue of American cars that feature. CIA man Felix Leiter stakes out the airport in his Chevrolet Impala (one of two used in the film, one a Sport Sedan, the other not, and there are continuity issues), Ford Galaxies, and a background cameo from a Cadillac Eldorado Biarritz. But it's a 1957 Chevrolet Bel Air convertible in which Bond is chauffeured to Government House, in reality the Governor General's mansion King's House, that becomes the unwitting star of

Left: An archive contact sheet from the chase sequence as Bond heads to Miss Taro's house. Above: Sean Connery sends Bond stuntman Bob Simmons flying.

the first Bond car chase. When 007 queries his driver's speed, the cutaway to the speedometer is to a different car entirely – a Ford Fairlane by common consent, presumably because it's easier to read – and when he instructs him to 'take the next turning on the right', it's a move that could have ended a promising career in espionage there and then (the Bel Air's hefty steel ladder frame chassis did not lend itself to a last-gasp escape).

When he eventually arrives at Government House, Bond parks up outside and asks the policeman to keep an eye on his – now deceased – passenger. It's an early example of the deadpan one-liners that would become one of the franchise's signatures; they were usually improvised, and *Dr No*'s director, the urbane Terence Young, encouraged Sean Connery to deliver them.

But arguably the most significant car in the entire film is the Sunbeam Alpine. This has the distinct honour of being the first proper Bond car, although it's a hire car – no.5 in the parking lot – and not a gadget-laden Q branch special that he uses for his assignation with the mercurial and not altogether trustworthy Miss Taro (Zena Marshall). His journey will take him to the fictitious Magenta Drive, the location of which was the Grand Lido Sans Souci Hotel in the foothills of Jamaica's Blue Mountains. A Mercedes 180 saloon and a Renault Dauphine are glimpsed as he makes his way along the road, before heading up a gravel track.

Sunbeam is another one of those marques whose star waxed and waned in parallel with the fluctuating industrial fortunes of the UK. Originally registered in 1888 for bicycle manufacture in a suburb of Wolverhampton, the first Sunbeam car appeared in 1901. It was swiftly established as a leading player in these pioneering days of the automobile, with notable exploits in world land speed records and Grand Prix racing, and the company developed and also supplied aero engines during the First World War. Various ownership changes and market travails saw Sunbeam end up in the hands of the Rootes Group, whose sprawling portfolio eventually seeded the idea of the brand as a maker of affordable sports cars akin to MG.

The Alpine roadster was launched in 1959, decorously designed in a pseudo-American fashion under the aegis of Loewy Studios (that name again), hence the tail-fins and an aesthetic that was more west coast California than Weston-super-Mare.

Elizabeth Taylor drove an Alpine Series I in *BUtterfield 8* – she would win her first Academy Award for her portrayal of the impetuous call girl Gloria Wandrous – and the great Carroll Shelby would later transform it into the much more aggressive Tiger by installing a Ford V8. (Side note: Rootes had originally approached no less than Ferrari to rework the standard four-cylinder engine, to no avail.)

Bond's car was a Series II, an updated version with a firmer suspension set-up and more potent, twin-carburettor, 80bhp 1.6-litre engine and, although not a bargain by 1962 standards at £1,110, it certainly sent a more egalitarian and accessible message than the more celebrated Bond cars that would follow.

The film car was borrowed from a local resident, one Jennifer Jackson; on the call sheet, the tone is decorous, asking the producers to 'please pay this lady £10 per day for the two days we have used the car'. It was finished in Lake Blue paintwork with matching interior upholstery, and was fitted with optional wire-spoke wheels and white-wall tyres. In the film, the LaSalle hearse reappears and gives chase, and, while much of the action was done as pick-up shots at Pinewood against a back-projection, there was more than enough verisimilitude to amplify the film's robust physicality.

When the crew arrived to find an enormous Warner-Swasey excavator blocking the road, Terence Young decided to work with it. This is how stuntman Bob Simmons – who was the figure in the pre-credits gun barrel sequence in *Dr No*, *From Russia With Love* and *Goldfinger* – remembered it. 'Unperturbed, [Terence] walked over to the driver of the excavator and chatted briefly. Then he measured the distance between the open top of the sports car and the underneath of the massive machine. "Bob, your head will just go under," he said triumphantly.

'I sat at the wheel of the car as it swept along the road towards this earthmover. At 45mph the little sports job started to bounce as the tyres bit into the gravel on the road surface and the steering began to judder in my hands. Could I make it?

'Terence told me afterwards that he saw the car start to bounce only split seconds before I went under. And there was near-panic among the crew as it dawned on them what might happen to me if I didn't make it... once I was safely through I had a difficult time trying to bring the car to a controlled stop. After that, driving the hearse off the road and jumping clear before it exploded in the ravine seemed run-of-the-mill by comparison.'

In a significant continuity mis-step, the LaSalle morphs into a Humber Super Snipe Mk II as it veers off the road and ignites. The first but certainly not the last vehicle to meet that sort of fiery fate in a Bond film. It also prompts one of 007's finest quips; there would be plenty more where that came from.

Right: A production memorandum outlines vehicle requirements, including limousines, cars and canoes.

The owner was paid £10 per day. Little did she know what status her car would acquire

MEMORANDUM

TO: Stanley Sopel   DATE: January 23, 1962
FROM: L. C. Rudkin

Locals - Kingston

Please note the following car payments:

(1) Airport limousine owned by Geoffrey Taylor, 5 Sandhurst Terrace. Please pay him three days at £5 per day. We also owe him £40 for damage, £20 of which we would like to pay immediately and £20 on completion of his further two day's work for us.

(2) **Bond's Albine** owned by Jennifer Jackson, 53 Lady Musgrave Road. Please pay this lady £10 per day for the two days we have used the car and we are likely to use it several times more.

(3) We hired a Cadillac for BP plates but later changed this to a Chevrolet which has not yet been delivered. The Cadillac is owned by Mr. Keith Roberts, c/o Federal Motors, Cross Roads. We owe him £10 for one day and this car will not be used again.

CANOES

We have used a various assortment of canoes which I will verify with Clive Reed and Christopher Blackwell. Roughly speaking the canoes are £3 a day and there is a smaller "Honey's" canoe which is less. In addition, Mr. Prawl has supplied night watchmen at £3 per night for four nights. He will be at Morgan's Harbour tomorrow and perhaps you will give him a time when he may expect to receive payment.

L. C. Rudkin

hrn

This US one sheet from April 1964
was conceived by United Artists'
marketing chief, David Chasman.

CHAPTER 02

FROM RUSSIA WITH LOVE

1963

STARRING Sean Connery as James Bond

Bond interrupts lunch with Sylvia Trench to answer a call – in his 1935 Bentley 3.5-litre Drophead Coupé.

On 2 March 1962, the Bond film crew gathered to film what would become one of the most memorable scenes in cinema history. We don't see much of him at first, just a well-tailored shoulder, as the camera lingers initially on a casino card table, before settling on Sylvia Trench (Eunice Gayson). 'I admire your courage, Miss…?' our man notes off-camera, in an inimitable (though that wouldn't stop countless people from trying) Scottish burr. 'Trench, Sylvia Trench,' she replies, her tone suddenly laced with prurient curiosity as she sees him. 'I admire your luck, Mr…?' There's a close-up of hands on a cigarette case, and then *the* cinematic mic-drop moment to end them all.

'Bond. James Bond.'

Exactly one month later, the Bond production company's parent Danjaq took up the option to make a follow-up. A wise move. The fifth of Ian Fleming's original 12-strong series of novels (there were two collections of short stories), *From Russia, with Love*, was selected for the second big-screen adaptation. In terms of 007's travel itinerary, this was a story dominated not by cars but trains, one in particular and perhaps the most famous of all: the Orient Express. Bond's battle – and relationship – with SPECTRE assassin Donald 'Red' Grant (Robert Shaw) is one of the film's defining attributes, reaching its denouement as the locomotive powers relentlessly through Eastern Europe, Bond having won over Tatiana Romanov (Daniela Bianchi). It's a sequence that encompasses much of what made Bond so special, especially as the character was still finding his footing in the cinema: the impossible glamour of continental travel, the unusual physicality of the fight scenes, and the ruthlessness that underpins not just the film's antagonist, but also the hero. Bond, we quickly learn, has absolutely no problem getting down and dirty.

The car fan is surprisingly well-served by *From Russia With Love*.

EON PRODUCTIONS, LIMITED.   No: 77. (Loc.)

"FROM RUSSIA WITH LOVE"
T/Eon/52.

Director: TERENCE YOUNG.   DATE: Friday, 26th July, 1963.

LOCATIONS: As below.   UNIT CALL: 7.30 a.m. (Unit to
                                             rendezvous at Pinewood
                                             Studios, where a decision
                                             will be made regard to
                                             shooting).

Artiste:	Dressing Room:	Character:	Time req. at Studio:	Leave Studios:	On Loc:
EXT. RIVER AND HIGHWAY.. Sc.Nos: 51,52,52a,53,54,56,57a,58-Day:					
SEAN CONNERY.	90.	James Bond.	7.45	8.15	9.00
EUNICE GAYSON.	104.	Sylvia.	7.00	8.15	9.00
ELIZABETH COUNSELL.	100.	Young Girl.	7.00	8.15	9.00
MICHAEL CULVER.	103.	Young Man.	7.45	8.15	9.00
ALTERNATIVE WEATHER CALL:					
1. INT. BENTLEY.. Sc.No: 58a-Day. (Back Projection).. "C" Stage.					
SEAN CONNERY.	90.	James Bond.	From above.		
EUNICE GAYSON.	104.	Sylvia.	From above.		
2. EXT. TRAIN.. Sc.No: 308 Pt-Night:					
SEAN CONNERY.	90.	James Bond.	From above.		
3. EXT. UNDERNEATH TRAIN - Sc.No: 308 Pt-Night:					
SEAN CONNERY.	90.	James Bond.	From above.		
DANIELA BIANCHI.	88.	Tatiana.	S-by till 1.00 p.m.		
4. INT. RHODA'S TRUCK: Sc.Nos: 321-336 Part-Day. (Back Projection).					
SEAN CONNERY.	90.	James Bond.	From above.		
PETER BRAYHAM.	99.	Rhoda.	S-by till 1.00 p.m.		
5. INT. VENICE HOTEL SUITE (Sp/FX Stage).. Sc.No: 410,411 Comp.-Day:					
SEAN CONNERY.	90.	James Bond.	From above.		
Stand-Ins:		For:			
Bill Baskiville.	G.Block.	Mr. Connery.	7.00	7.30	
A.N. Other.	"	Miss Gayson.	7.00	7.30	
Phyllis Cornel.	"	Miss Bianchi.	8.00	8.30	

PROPS: As per script and breakdown, to include: Picnic basket, ice
                bucket, champagne, transistor pocket radio, chicken leg and
                repeats, Lektor, attache case, rifle, shoulder holster,
                Walther, flowers for Truck.
ACTION PROPS: Punts for artistes and set dressing.
                Bentley - to be on location.
BACK PROJECTION: Charles Staffel and crew to stand by in case of bad weather
                and unit have to shoot on "C" Stage.
PLUMBERS: To stand by for steam effect, please.

(continued)

Producer Cubby Broccoli beside Sean Connery, on location in Istanbul, May 1963.

Left: The call sheet for the scene with the Bentley (and others to be shot at Pinewood), Friday 26 July 1963.

Bond is enjoying lunch with Miss Trench when an early version of a pager summons him to his car which, it transpires, is fitted with a portable phone. This would have been an innovation of unimaginable exoticism in 1963. Nor was the vehicle it's affixed to idly cast by the film's producers. It's a 1935 Bentley 3.5-litre Drophead Coupé, with bodywork by Park Ward. Anyone who knows anything about Ian Fleming's creation will know that 007 was a Bentley man in the novels: he drives one in *Casino Royale*, *Moonraker*, *From Russia, with Love*, *Thunderball*, *On Her Majesty's Secret Service* and *The Living Daylights*. Fleming loved cars, and he understood their potency as character signifiers. That he favoured a battleship grey 1930 'Blower' Bentley 4.5-litre in the first book is another testament to Bond's thoroughgoing masculinity, as mighty a machine as it was almost comically conspicuous for a character who was never very good at flying under the radar.

There was also an important personal connection here: Fleming was friends with Charles Amherst Villiers, an automotive and aeronautical engineer and polymath whose supercharger did the blowing on those ferocious Bentleys. He was also an accomplished portrait artist who painted Fleming in 1962, and also supplied him with the first illustration of Chitty-Chitty-Bang-Bang.

In *Moonraker*, Bond wrecks his Bentley chasing Hugo Drax but replaces it with a Mark VI. In *Thunderball*, he's behind the wheel of possibly the best-looking Bentley in the company's 100-year history: the Mark II Continental. 'The most selfish car in England', Fleming writes, Bond's is a crashed car he commissions Mulliner to re-body. (In an example of life imitating art, Fleming himself, having owned several

Left: The call sheet for Friday 10 May 1963, for location filming in Istanbul. Right: A rarely seen contact sheet showing Bond's arrival at the MI6 HQ in the city, and his meeting with station head, Ali Kerim Bey. The Rolls-Royce is a late 1950s Silver Wraith.

Ford Thunderbirds, hired world-famous automotive couturier Henri Chapron to create a bespoke Bentley for him using unusual American design cues.)

Bond's big-screen incarnation, as we know, is far better known for his affiliation with a rival British sports car-maker. All of which makes the '35 Drophead Coupé a significant if fleeting presence in *From Russia With Love*. By this point, Bentley had been bought by and subsumed within Rolls-Royce, and the cars from this interwar period are known as Derby Bentleys because they were manufactured in the Rolls-Royce factory in the city. These were much less sporting vehicles than the ones made by WO Bentley, and majored on grace and comfort to such an extent that the marketing line was 'the silent sports car'. As was the fashion at the time, rolling chassis would be clothed by the many artisanal coachbuilders that existed – no fewer than 40 companies flexed their creative muscles, including blue-chip names such as Figoni et Falaschi and Saoutchik – but only 2,242 cars were made in total. Bond's Park Ward version was the most common, though still fearfully expensive in period. No mere civil servant, he. The car-phone is presumably a Q innovation, but he never appears on screen to explain it.

Although the title suggests some chilly Cold War-era goings-on, *From Russia With Love* is a much sultrier affair. Bond is despatched to Istanbul, whose rich history, Eurasian status and unique position astride the Bosporus makes it a proto-typical Bond setting. It is also a car-lover's paradise, as so many of the major locations in these early films would prove to be. The background teems with unusual or long-forgotten European and American cars: amongst others in *From Russia With Love*'s street scenes, you'll see a 1951 Plymouth Cranbrook, a '55 DeSoto Fireflite, a '57 Chevrolet One-Fifty, a '57 Plymouth Belevdere, a '57 Plymouth Savoy, a 1958 Fiat 1100 T Pulmino, and a 1962 Opel Rekord. (No name was too pompous or self-aggrandising for America's car-makers in the 1950s and 1960s, it would appear.)

Opposite: Sean Connery and co-star Pedro Armendáriz pictured between takes on a deleted scene. Left: The climactic helicopter assault was set near the Dalmatian coast but filmed in the Scottish Highlands.

The arrival of 007 at an airport always yields something interesting – whether it's upfront, in the background or both. On this occasion, he's met by an embassy Rolls-Royce Silver Wraith, clothed – like the Bentley he's left behind – in a body by Park Ward. In production from 1946 until 1958, this is a late model, so it was probably powered by a 4.9-litre, 175bhp version of the F-head in-line six-cylinder engine, running a four-speed automatic transmission, with independent front suspension and a live rear axle. Power steering and factory-fitted air conditioning were desirable extras that would certainly have been useful in Istanbul.

The Silver Wraith was popular with heads of state in Brazil, Denmark, Greece, the Netherlands and Ireland – but more pertinently its rather haughty demeanour and cartoonish 'posh car' appearance have made it a go-to vehicle for movie production designers. In addition to its appearance in *From Russia With Love*, Dudley Moore's feckless billionaire is wafted around Manhattan aboard one in 1981's box-office smash *Arthur*. Bruce Wayne is chauffeur-driven in a Hooper-bodied Silver Wraith in Tim Burton's 1989 *Batman*, while in 1992's *Batman Returns* he uses a Mulliner-bodied car. In Bruce Robinson's magnificent 1987 classic *Withnail and I*, the odious Uncle Monty finds his perfect automotive foil in the flamboyant shape of a Hooper-bodied '53 Silver Wraith, originally commissioned by the studiedly eccentric oil magnate Nubar Gulbenkian. And, of course, it's a Silver Wraith that carves through the desert to collect Bond and Dr Madeleine Swann for their appointment with Blofeld in *Spectre* – a subtle callback for Bond aficionados with petrol in their veins.

Back in Istanbul airport, we see a cream Dodge Coronet as Bond gets into the Rolls, with a rather lovely Opel Kapitan visible behind, but more significant is the Citroën Traction Avant 11 BL that follows him, containing a pair of Bulgarian agents. 'I suppose it's customary to have people tail you in these parts,' Bond notes drily to his driver. 'Oh yes, sir. Today it's Citroën H 31854… they follow us, we follow them, it's a sort of understanding we have.' 'That's very friendly.' Less so is 'Red' Grant, who in turn is tailing the Bulgarians…

In production from 1934 until 1957, the importance of the Traction Avant can hardly be overstated. In short, it pioneered front-wheel drive in mass production, used a monocoque chassis (as opposed to a separate frame), and featured independent suspension all-round. It was also safe – by the standards of the time, anyway – its first crash test consisting of it being pushed off a cliff. It was designed by Flamino Bertoni, who would also create its equally fabulous

A rarely seen contact sheet shows Sean Connery with Daniela Bianchi, while actor Robert Shaw is pictured alongside a DeSoto Fireflite.

successor the DS, and engineered by André Lefèbvre. Bertoni had connections with the Italian futurist movement, and was an artist and sculptor. Lefèbvre had worked for another French company, the aviation-influenced Voisin (celebrated architect Le Corbusier owned one). No wonder the Traction Avant was such a singular achievement.

It's also another car with a significant showbiz and cultural career: at the last count, sources suggest it has racked up around 1,300 film and television appearances. It was used both by Gestapo agents in occupied France during the Second World War and, more significantly, by the French Resistance, its distinctive snout and double chevron logo rendering it at once a friendly yet forbidding-looking thing – especially when glimpsed in a rear-view mirror, as is the case here.

One of the key characters in *From Russia With Love* is Bond's point man in Istanbul, MI6 station head Ali Kerim Bey (Pedro Armendáriz). We see him chomping a cigar and climbing into a 1955 Mercury Custom Station Wagon (79B) but, with the official Rolls out of the picture, more prominently featured is a then mundane but now rare and collectable 1960 Ford Ranch Wagon. Bey and Bond use it variously in the film including a visit to a gypsy encampment (actually filmed on the Pinewood back-lot because the Turkish authorities wouldn't grant permission).

Long before the dawn of the mini-van or SUV, the Station Wagon was a staple of American suburban life, as unthreatening and uncool as anything on four wheels. Ford is credited with starting this sub-genre, way back in the 1937 model year, and, though early cars used wood in their construction, by the 1950s the wood appliqué was an increasingly desperate affectation.

So was the Country Squire name, though the car used by Bey and his sons is a non-woody and less preposterous Ranch Wagon. The car could seat six passengers, had a massive tailgate, and a luggage capacity of 97 cubic feet. Armendáriz became ill during filming, and was subsequently diagnosed with cancer. The producers rearranged the filming schedule so he could complete his scenes, but – like his friend Ernest Hemingway – he shot himself, in the UCLA medical centre in LA. 'It was tragic, of course, but to many of us it was also brave and typical of the man,' producer Cubby Broccoli graciously noted.

Back on the Orient Express, Bond and Romanov are travelling under the aliases of Mr and Mrs David Somerset, returning to their home in Derbyshire. They end up fleeing in a stolen Chevrolet C30 Apache loaded with flowers, another regular background sight in movies at the time (though not always bearing flowers). The C30 was a one-tonne vehicle, and this early 1960s example was most likely powered by a 348 W-series big block V8, with a four-barrel carburettor. The script on the doors – *Rukotvorine Pikva* – is Croatian for 'artisanal', which would fit with the truck's cargo, while *Pikva* is probably a typo of the Slovenian town Pivka, which was close to the sequence's location on the northern Dalmatian coast.

Beset by weather problems, director Terence Young abandoned plans to shoot the film's climax on the Marmara Sea, south of Istanbul, and switched to the Scottish Highlands. That's why the scenes in which the Chevy truck is strafed by gunfire from a SPECTRE helicopter have an incongruously Celtic feel. (The action is brilliant, the exact location above a tiny settlement called Leckuary near Kilmichael Glen.)

The boat chase, meanwhile, was filmed in Crinan harbour soon after. Sealing his status as something of a real-life James Bond, Terence Young was on board a camera helicopter that ascended to about 40ft before plunging into the chilly waters. According to Daniela Bianchi, he said brightly as he emerged largely unscathed, 'At least my cigarettes aren't wet!'

They were filming again 35 minutes later.

This Japanese half sheet is actually
an early 1970s reissue, complete
with DB5 and Mustang.

CHAPTER 03
GOLDFINGER

1964

STARRING Sean Connery as James Bond

'This is gold, Mr Bond. All my life I've been in love with its colour, its brilliance, its divine heaviness.'
AURIC GOLDFINGER

Bond SFX wizard John Stears was truly unflappable, one of the heroes of the first eight Bond films and a pioneer of cinema. He would win a best visual effects Academy Award in 1966 for his work on *Thunderball*, and shared another Oscar 12 years later for his contribution to *Star Wars* (if R2-D2 had a father, then here he was). According to Professor Norman Klein, of the California Institute of Arts, '[John Stears] continued the spark that started the technological wizardry that gave birth to cinema itself.'

But in 1964 he also – unwittingly, it must be said – co-created what's widely regarded as 'the most famous car in the world': the *Goldfinger* Aston Martin DB5.

With pre-production on the third Bond film under way, now was evidently the time to cast the first definitive 'Bond car'. Ian Fleming's decision to put 007 in a DB Mark III (often referred to as DB3) in the *Goldfinger* novel pointed everyone in the same direction.

In 1947, Aston Martin's latest patron was machine tools and tractor manufacturer David Brown. The DB cars that followed were the archetypal post-war British sports cars, equal parts rakish and aristocratic. Ian Fleming would have appreciated their brutish sporting aspirations; he would definitely have respected Aston Martin's one-two finish in the 1959 Le Mans 24 Hours race, firmly eclipsing the Ferrari effort. (In fact, Aston's victory interrupted a seven-year winning streak for the Italians.)

But it was an Italian company to which Aston Martin turned to clothe its new generation of cars: Touring of Milan. This was and remains one of the great names in *carrozzeria*, not just creator of some of the most dazzlingly beautiful cars in history (the 1935–38 Alfa Romeo 8C 2900B and '52 Disco Volante, 1951's Ferrari 166 MM Barchetta, 1964's Lamborghini 350 GT), but also pioneer of a body-fabricating process that majored on lightness and flexibility, called *Superleggera*. The DB4 arrived in 1958, and was replaced by the visually similar but even prettier DB5 in September 1963. The big news was that its engine, a 4.0-litre in-line six-cylinder, now had the power to match its looks (282bhp was healthy enough in 1963). The DB5 coupé is a vanishingly rare car; only 899 were ever made, of which 13 were refashioned into elegant Shooting Brake form by English coach-builder Radford.

Its route into cinema immortality was more complicated than you might imagine. Despite the huge success of the first two Bond films, and Cubby Broccoli and Harry Saltzman's gimlet commercial eye, things unfolded in a way not untypical of the British car industry at the time: Aston's people initially failed to spot a copper-bottomed PR opportunity even as it stood on their doorstep.

'I did a sketch of the car, and then discussed that with John Stears,' Ken Adam recalled. 'I had a Jaguar, which was continuously being damaged by people parking badly. Having guns at the back of the Aston Martin and the over-riders becoming like boxing gloves and so on, became part of me releasing my frustrations… I'm a sports car freak myself, you see, so all the ideas for the gimmickry and gadgets were no problem. They were just my own dreams! I got rid of a lot of my inhibitions when it came to designing the Aston Martin.'

Stears and Adam visited Aston's HQ in Feltham, a few miles south of Heathrow airport, in November 1963. Aston's perennially fragile finances might have made the firm's management risk-averse; they were also in the process of relocating 60 miles north up the new M1 motorway to Newport Pagnell. Whatever the reason, they remained impassive and unimpressed.

Fast food, fast cars, two American icons… KFC meets 1964 Ford Thunderbird. Three icons, if we include Felix Leiter.

A Lincoln Continental prepares to meet its maker. What's left of it is transported in the Ford Falcon Ranchero.

John Stears never forgot what happened next. 'Ken and I went to Aston Martin Lagonda to try and make a deal with them. We saw this beautiful red DB4, which was the prototype DB5. I fell in love with this car. [They] were sort of half interested until Ken and I told them what we were going to do to it with all the gadgets. Then they just laughed at us and said, "Get out of here, you'll never do it. This car is packed with everything, there's no space to put anything."'

We shouldn't be too harsh on Aston; remember, at this point the 1960s weren't swinging so much as beginning to sway gently, and the company mentality was still a little haughty. As Steve Waddingham, Aston Martin's Senior Product Specialist and heritage expert, notes, 'Goldfinger was a massive turning point for Aston, because we were still a little bit stuffy in those days. The management was adjusting to the fact that some of our clients might actually now be wearing jeans. The original Britpop boom also changed things. Paul McCartney owned a DB5 and DB6, Mick Jagger bought a DB6 in summer 1966. Things were on the move, and Aston became less hard-nosed in response.'

The production needed two identical cars *gratis*, one for the action sequences, the other a 'hero' car for close-ups and interior shots. The publicity benefits that would accrue were persuasively explained. In the end, David Brown urged his general manager Steve Heggie to do what 'he felt was right', and Aston agreed to loan the production two cars, on condition that they be returned. One of them was actually that same prototype DB5 Stears had seen – chassis number DP/216/1, registration BMT 216A and originally painted Dubonnet red. Aston's engineering wizard Tadek Marek was tasked with helping John Stears to evaluate the car's gadget-friendliness.

Nor was there was any time to spare. Michael Lamont, brother of Bond stalwart Peter Lamont, drafted a series of beautiful full-scale working drawings envisioning Ken Adam's ideas. (The schedule was so tight he even did some work on Christmas Eve.) The car was delivered to Pinewood Studios in January 1964, whereupon John Stears and his team – Jimmy Ackland-Snow, Frank George, and Bert Luxford – could begin the seemingly impossible task of realising Adam's ideas via Lamont's drawings. 'There were no standbys,' Stears noted. 'This all had to go in the one car. It

Goldfinger's 1937 Rolls-Royce Phantom III is denuded of its coachbuilt bodywork.

was terrifying, because if that car had broken down, we'd have been in deep trouble. But it was a beautiful car, and it didn't give us any problems at all.

'The first thing I was gonna do was to make the hole for the ejector seat. I marked it out, and taped off the roof of the car. I looked at it, went away and had a cup of coffee, came back and got the drill, and drilled the hole. And that was it. We started.'

The DB5 isn't a big car so, although installing the various gadgets wasn't too difficult, the team had little space for the mechanical hardware – pneumatics, hydraulics, and acetylene and oxygen tanks – that would enable them all to function. The Aston's slim-line boot was soon full of wires, cables, and compressed air, nitrogen and oil cylinders. Luxford remembered that 'The rear lights that dropped down and the oil slick that came out of it was done for real with a big container in the back of the car. But we also had this lifting bulletproof shield. To get the tank in there, the bulletproof shield had to be taken out then put back after that shot for the bullet effects. So we were always on the go on that car. Never a dull moment.'

There must have been times all involved wished that someone would hurry up and invent CGI, although the timeless joy in John Stears' effects was that they were so authentic. (It's also why fans treasure *Star Wars* above the excessively CGI-ed *Phantom Menace*: you believed it.) The engineering that went into reimagining the DB5 was ingenious, using Bowden cables, tiny gear sets, electromagnetic valves, compressed air cylinders and much more. Although the pocket-sized prop man squeezed into the Aston's boot who was responsible for triggering the smoke screen may not have agreed. 'When I first mentioned to the lads my intentions, well, their language was rather choice to say the least. Let's just say they thought I was off my rocker,' Stears recalled.

The other gadgets? Well, everyone knows what they are: hydraulic rams on the bumpers, a Browning .30-calibre machine gun behind the front indicators, tyre slashers secreted in the wheel hubs, an oil slick dispenser, revolving licence plates ('my contribution,' the film's director Guy Hamilton noted, 'because I was getting a lot of parking tickets at the time…'), caltrops (spiked weapons, similar to the samurai's *makibishi*), and of course, the ejector seat, whose design adhered to the principles of the aviation industry standard Martin-Baker. This, along with the tyre-slashers, was only installed when

'When I first mentioned my intentions, the lads thought I was off my rocker'

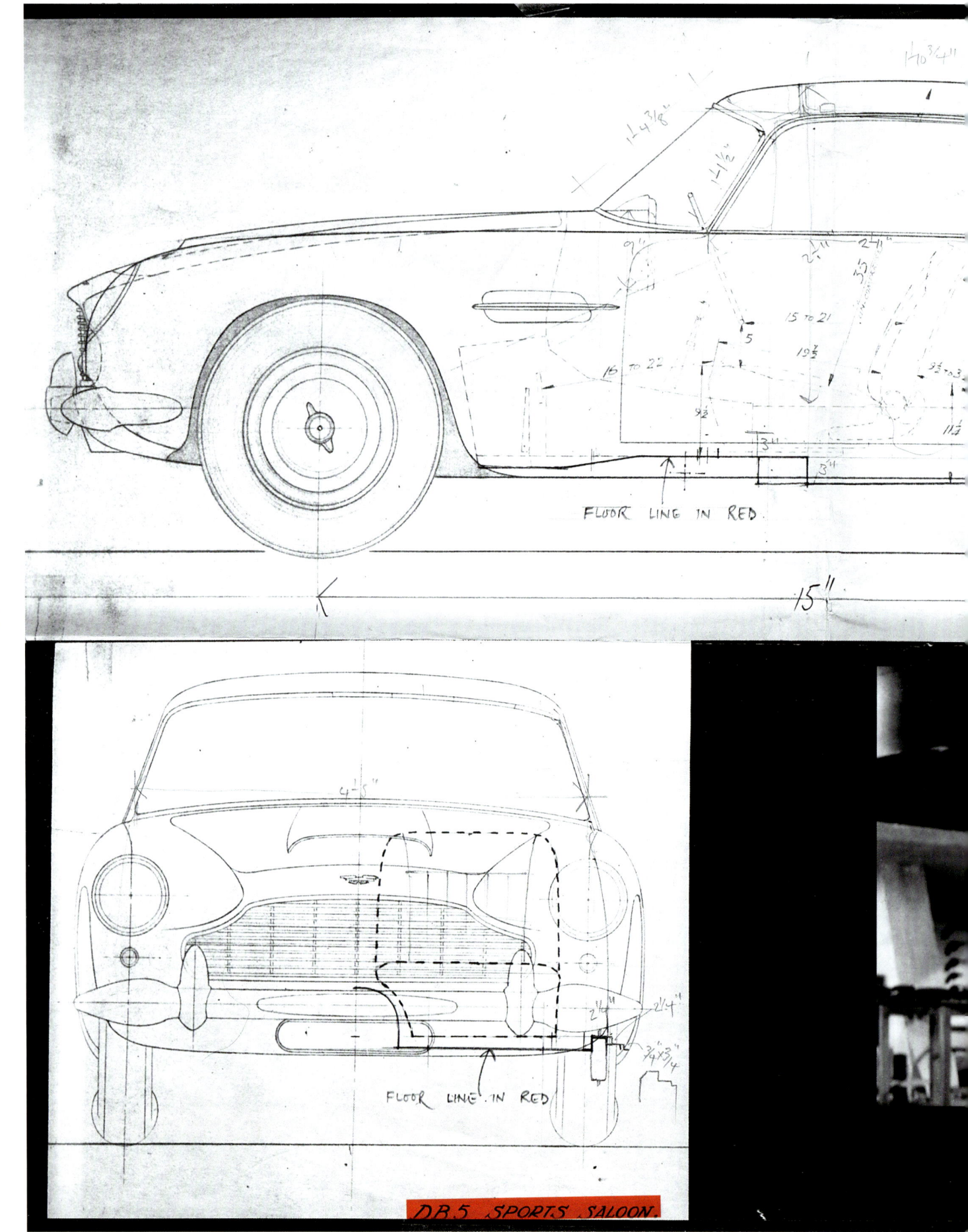

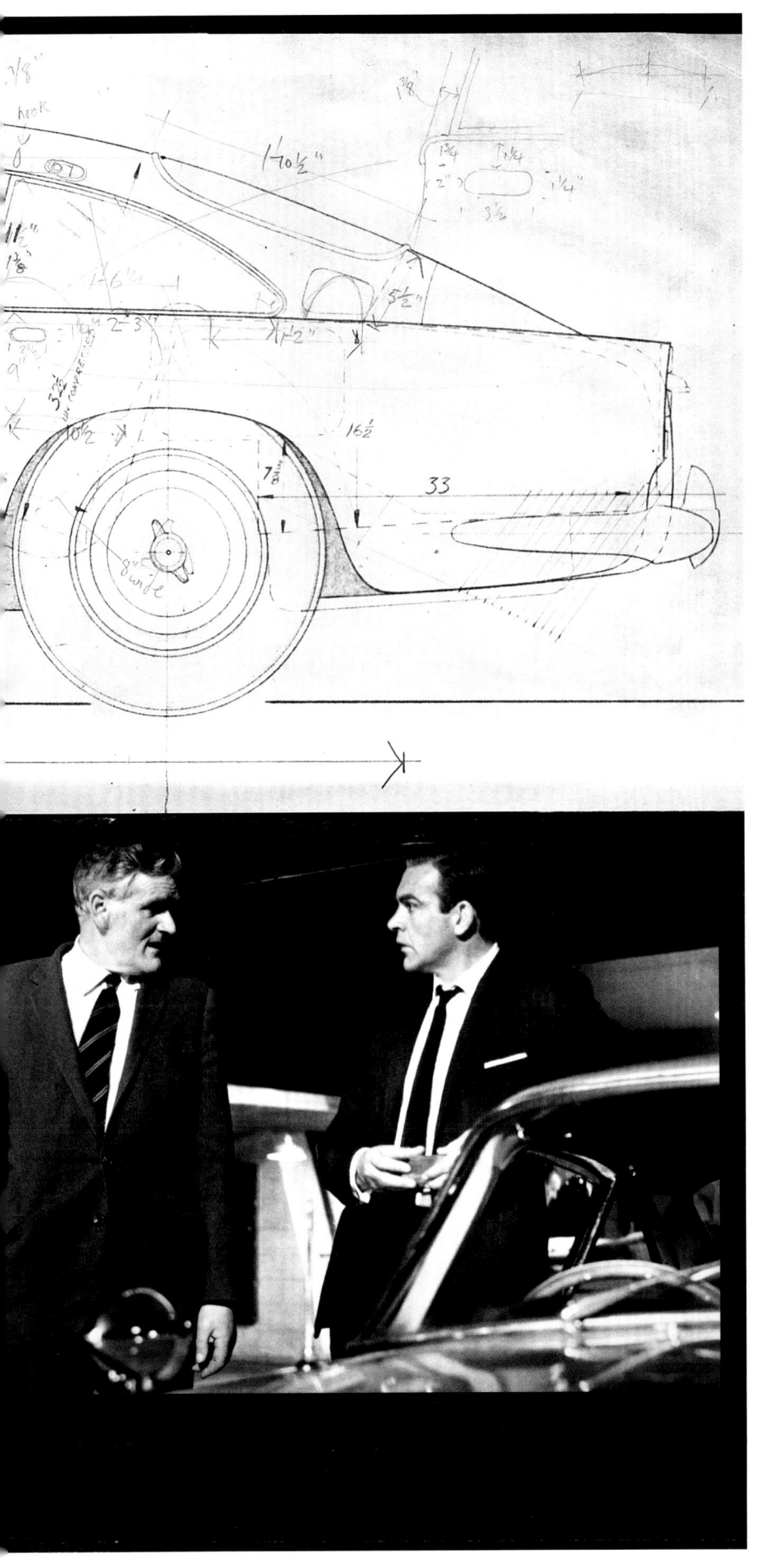

The original technical drawings for Bond's Aston Martin DB5, in the process of becoming the world's most famous car. Inset: Q and Bond, setting the template for the famous handover scenes, Friday 22 May 1964.

the script called for them, rather than being permanent fixtures. Frank George is credited with creating the ejector button, cannily concealed within the nub of the Aston's slender little gear-lever.

There was also a telephone in the driver's door, and a centre console mounted between the seats contained the controls for the various gadgets. The radar tracking system was hidden behind the radio grille; a weapons tray was stashed under the driver's seat, and housed a Mauser automatic with a separate silencer, a Magnum .357 revolver, a hand grenade, and a knife.

There were no cup-holders.

Some of Adam's ideas were shelved: two grille-mounted spotlights would have concealed flamethrowers, while plans for the DB5 to fire three-pronged nails from its tail-lights in order to puncture a pursuer's tyres were abandoned when the powers-that-be fretted about real-life copycats getting the wrong idea.

When Steve Heggie visited Pinewood in February 1964, he was startled to say the least. 'At first I couldn't believe the car in front of me was ours. There were panels everywhere, cables and pipes protruding from all angles, it looked a right bloody mess. I thought to myself, "Here's four and a half thousand pounds' worth of car all in pieces. I pray they know how to put it back together again."'

If only he had known the impact this incredible machine was about to have. In all, Stears and his crew completed work on the car in around six weeks, and it was returned to Aston to be resprayed in the now celebrated Silver Birch. Interestingly, the scene in *Goldfinger* in which the permanently harassed Q (the wonderful Desmond Llewelyn) introduces Bond to his new car contains a pointed back reference to his beloved Bentley – a car that only briefly appeared in the previous film.

'Where's my Bentley?' Bond asks, sounding a little miffed.

'Oh, it's had its day, I'm afraid,' Q replies tartly.

'It's never let me down...'

'M's orders, 007. You will be using this Aston Martin DB5. With modifications. Now pay attention please...' (Llewelyn also later confirmed that his famous riposte when Bond, aghast, says, 'Ejector seat? You're joking...' was added for a re-shoot the day after they shot the DB5 handover scene. 'I never joke about my work, 007' – it almost never happened...)

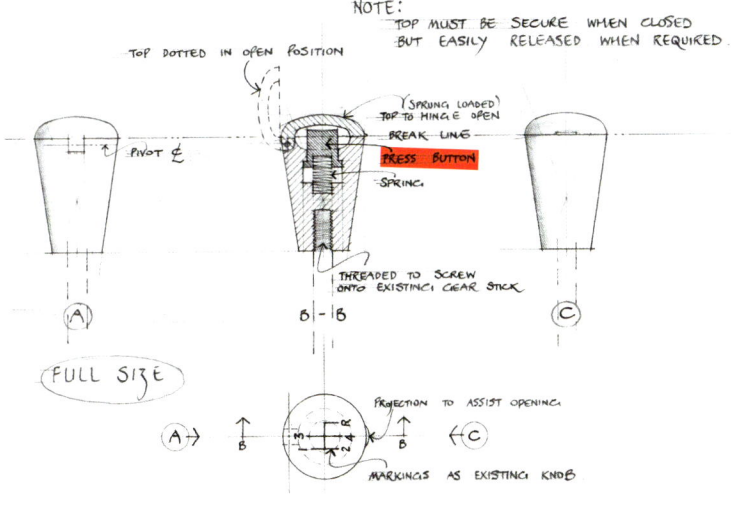

Opposite: Filming at Southend Airport as Bond prepares to track the nefarious Goldfinger across Europe.
Above: The DB5's transformation was overseen by special effects wizard John Stears, whose small team of craftsmen and engineers did the job in a matter of weeks – including that famous ejector seat.

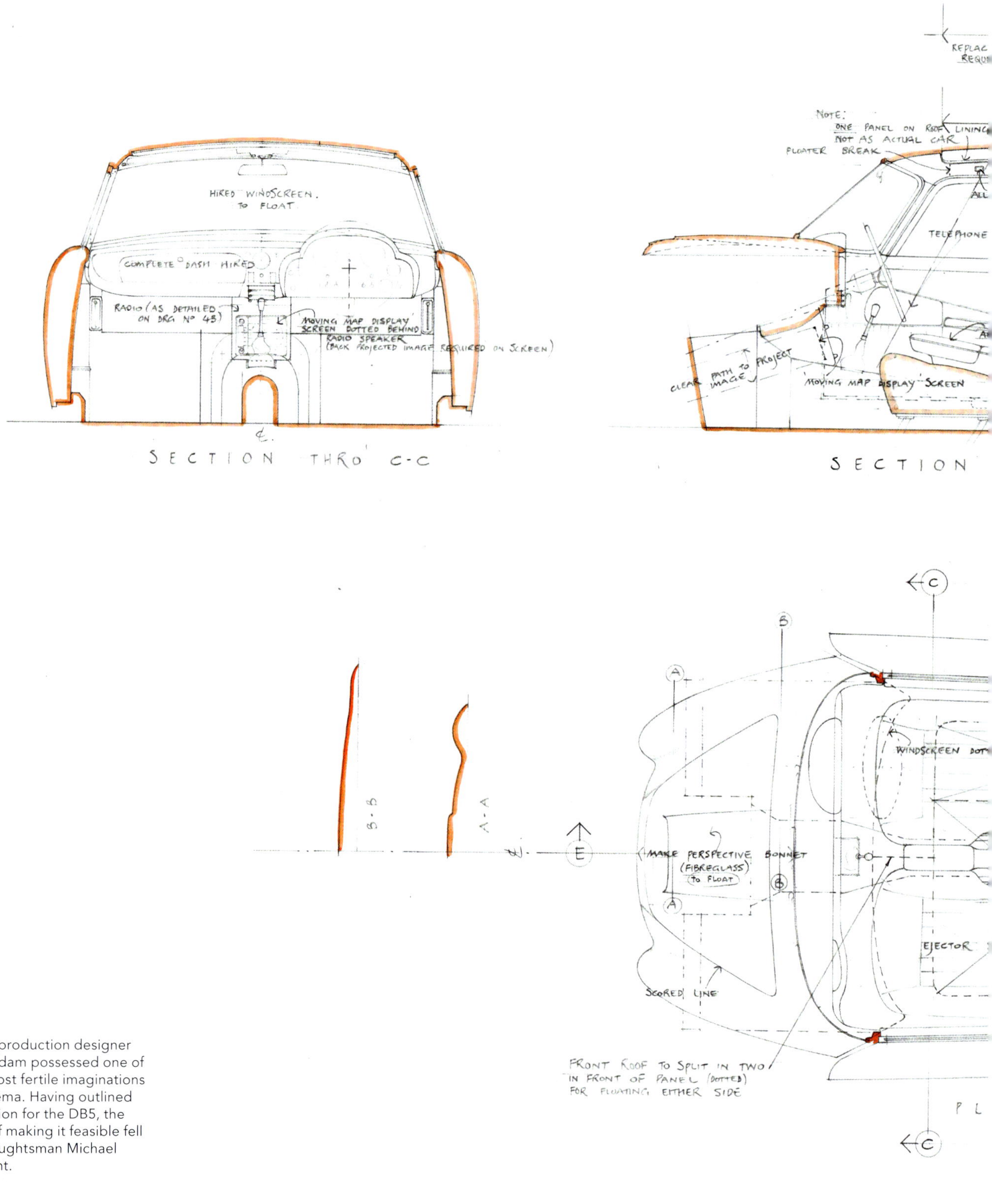

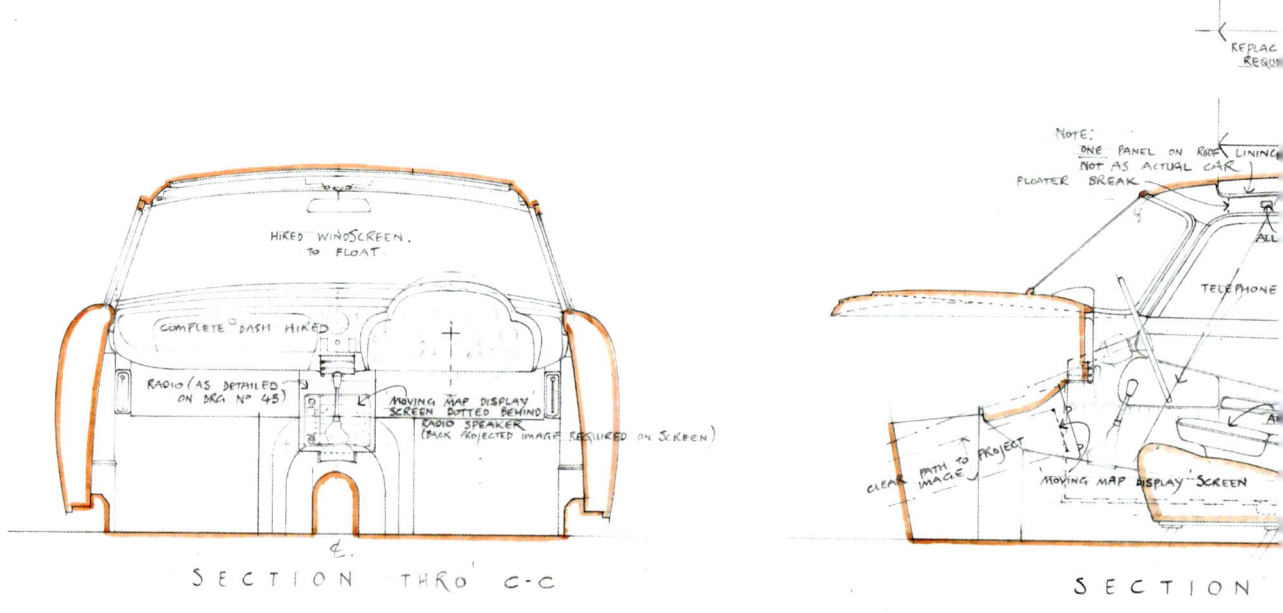

Bond production designer Ken Adam possessed one of the most fertile imaginations in cinema. Having outlined his vision for the DB5, the task of making it feasible fell to draughtsman Michael Lamont.

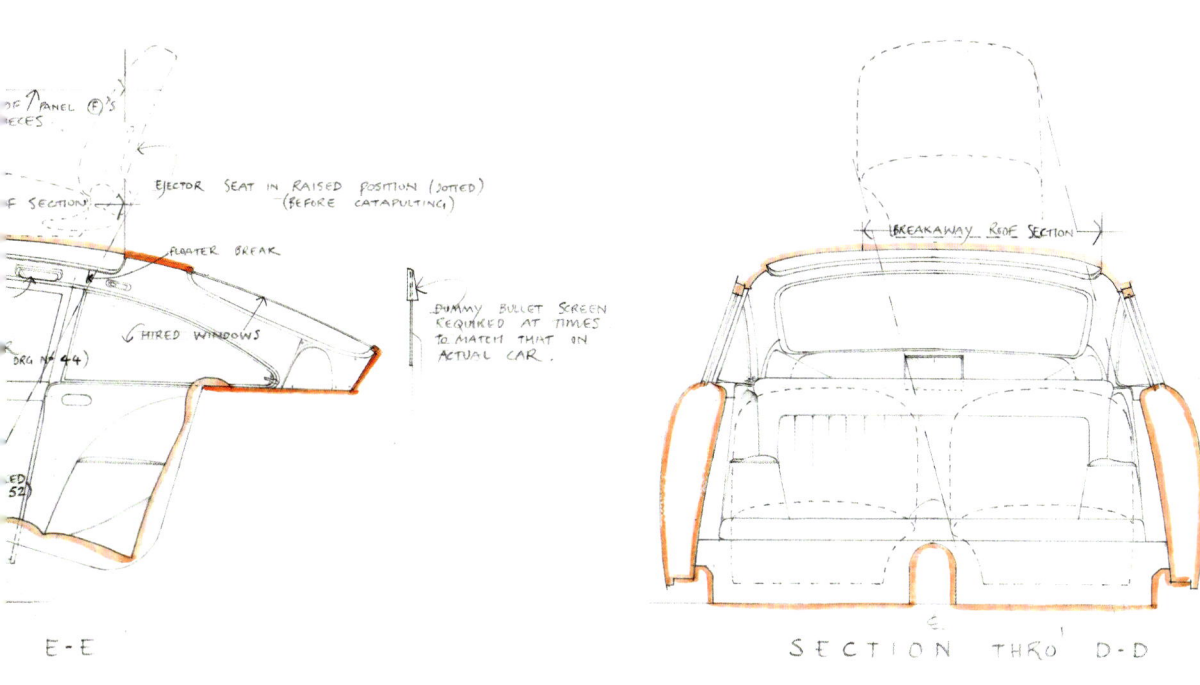
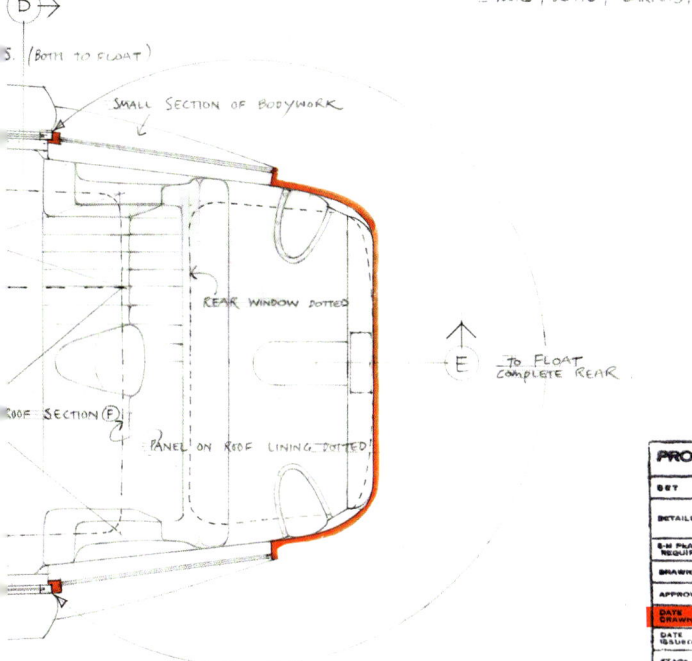

Tilly Masterson (Tania Mallet) prepares for a close-up in the newly unveiled Ford Mustang.

Given the effort that its creators had gone to, a back-up DB5 was definitely required, and Aston obliged. Originally registered as FMP 7B, chassis no: DB5/1486/R was swiftly turned into a facsimile of the car referred to on the call-sheet as 'Trick Aston Martin', and dubbed 'Road Car'. Some small detail differences remained – the number plate surrounds don't match – but in continuity terms these were minor transgressions. It also featured a new five-speed ZF transmission, which was much nicer to use than the four-speed gearbox in the Trick car. If not yet fully proven…

Filming on the DB5's night-time chase scenes began on 9 March 1964, with Black Park, a 500-acre wood adjacent to Pinewood, doubling for the hinterland around Auric Goldfinger's Swiss HQ. With Sean Connery still to wrap on Alfred Hitchcock's *Marnie*, stunt double Bob Simmons was behind the wheel as Bond is pursued by Goldfinger's Mercedes-driving henchmen (there were two 180 saloons and a 220 S). It's during this sequence that the ejector seat is famously deployed; Stears and co removed the passenger seat, and replaced it with an ultra-lightweight version, complete with a hollow tube into which they could fit a cylinder of compressed air. It worked, and cinematographer Ted Moore expertly captured a flailing dummy being fired 30 feet into the air above the Pinewood back-lot. And with that, an entire generation was captivated forever.

The DB5 may tower over the other automotive cast members, but Goldfinger's black and yellow Rolls-Royce, if not as lissom as the Aston, is certainly well-cast and plot-critical. A 1937 Phantom III Sedanca de Ville with bodywork by London-based coachbuilder Barker, the movie car was originally commissioned for Huttleston Broughton, the first Lord Fairhaven of Anglesey Abbey. Its registration – AU 1 – references the chemical symbol for gold on the periodic table.

As an early automotive pioneer, and the most high-profile occupier of what would later be known as the 'luxury space', Rolls-Royces were the preserve of royalty, industrialists, and turn-of-the-century movers and shakers. Before the company designed its own cars, Barker was its couturier of choice; indeed it was responsible for the so-called 'Roi des Belges' open-topped touring body fitted to the 1907 40/50hp, registration AX 201 and better known as Silver Ghost (the nickname given to it by Rolls' MD Claude Johnson). This

EON PRODUCTIONS LTD

CALL SHEET No.83

PRODUCTION: "GOLDFINGER" PROD.NO: T/EON/62
CALL: 7.30 a.m. leave hotels DATE: Saturday, 11th July '64
 7.45 a.m. on location

SETS: EXT. CRASH SEQUENCE... APPROACH ROAD TO FURKA PASS
 EXT. GARAGE... GARAGE FELIX CHRISTEN (B.P.GARAGE) ANDERMATT
 S/By EXT. MOUNTAIN ROADS... SUSTEN PASS

ARTISTES	ROOM	CHARACTER	Time reqd. in M/U	Leave	Time reqd. on loc.
SEAN CONNERY	21	JAMES BOND	7.15	7.30	7.45
TANIA MALLETT	28	TILLY	6.00	7.30	7.45
HAROLD SAKATA	Own hotel	ODDJOB	8.30	8.45	9.00
Doubles:					
Bill Baskiville	"	For Mr. Connery	7.15	7.30	7.45
Phyllis Cornell	22	For Miss Mallett	7.15	7.30	7.45
John Stears	-	For Goldfinger	As required.		
Crowd:					
John Meadows	-	Garage Proprietor	As required.		
Jackie Saltzman	-	Pump Attendant	As required.		
5 Children	-	Flower Sellers	8.30	8.30	9.00

PROPS: As per Script and Breakdown to include Tilly's suitcase and guncase, flower stall, plums.

SPECIAL EFFECTS: To be on location for crash sequence.

CATERING: Lunch and tea breaks as arranged with Bergidyll Hotel.

ACTION VEHICLES: Bond's Aston Martin, Tilly's Mustang, Goldfinger's Rolls Royce - to be on location at 7.45 a.m.

ROLLS ROYCE TRACKING CAR: To be on location 7.45 a.m.

FIRST AID/INTERPRETER: Dr. Stabler to be at Bergidyll at 7.30 a.m.

TRANSPORT: As per to-day.

POLICE: 2 Policemen to be at Bergidyll at 7.30 a.m.

MILITARY PERSONNEL: 1 Military Representative to be at Bergidyll 7.30 a.m.

ROUTE TO SUSTEN PASS FROM ANDERMATT: From Andermatt descend mountain pass (Zurich direction) for 10 Kms. to the town of Wassen. In centre of town, clearly marked, is the signpost pointing LEFT marked "Susten". Continue up this road where Richard Jenkins will be waiting to direct vehicles. If in doubt rendezvous in the village of "Meien-Dorfli" which is approximately 7 Kms. from Wassen and await directions.

SCENE NUMBERS: 153,154 DAY. 158,159,161,162 DAY - to complete.
 148A DAY.

FRANK ERNST
ASSISTANT DIRECTOR

The call sheet for Saturday 11 July 1964, filming in Andermatt. Note that special effects boss John Stears is also doubling as Goldfinger.

was the car that really put Rolls on the map, and is arguably the second most famous car in the world – after a certain Aston Martin.

Bond meets the car for the first time when he engages Goldfinger in a round of golf, at Stoke Park (also near Pinewood). The plot pivot here is revealed when Bond tracks Goldfinger to Switzerland, and discovers that he smuggles gold by 'hiding' it in the car's bodywork, later dismantling the car and melting the parts down. If an Aston Martin fitted with an ejector seat isn't already having its wicked way with the audience's credulity, then just imagine how heavy a Rolls-Royce that weighed 3,100kg *before* its larcenous make-over must have been.

That said, the Phantom III was the first Rolls to be powered by a V12 engine, in this instance an all-aluminium 7.3-litre monster with some notable advancements for the time. By this point, Rolls was competing with the multi-cylindered likes of Cadillac and Hispano-Suiza, so its turn of speed was respectable.

Ken Adam's love of cars helped the automotive production values of the Bond films enormously. He called his beloved 1959 Rolls-Royce Silver Cloud I convertible his 'das ding', and still owned it until not long before he passed away in 2016, having racked up an impressive 250,000 miles. (It was auctioned by RM Sotheby's the year before for an impressive £218,400.) 'I've always loved cars,' he told *Frieze* magazine. 'I've had E-type Jaguars and a Mercedes-Benz 540K. The Mercedes was supercharged, which was fantastic even though it guzzled so much fuel, which was a problem after World War Two because of fuel rationing. I guess a Rolls-Royce convertible is something like their sports car version; or as close to a sports car as a Rolls can get.'

His empathy for, and love of, well-engineered machinery probably accounts for his response to the scene in *Goldfinger* in which Oddjob (Harold Sakata) disposes of Mr Solo (Martin Benson), the gangster who unwisely decides not to participate in Goldfinger's audacious Operation Grand Slam, by driving to a scrapyard and crushing him in the Lincoln Continental. As Adam recalled, 'I'll never forget that we were completely speechless to see this beautiful new Lincoln, minus its engine, being squashed and ending up as a cube. We were all feeling, for want of a better word, castrated.' In general, Oddjob is notably friskier with his steel-rimmed bowler hat than he is behind the wheel of his boss's cars, especially on those Swiss passes.

A nod, also, to Goldfinger's other cars: a Ford Falcon Ranchero (the rear deck of which would carry the crushed remnants of the Lincoln), and a rather lovely Ford Country Squire. The latter is an intriguing example: the scenes at Goldfinger's stud farm were all filmed in the UK, and it's thought that this particular car might have been an export car due to its unusual Rangoon red paint, smaller hubcaps and the worrying absence of any exterior mirrors (Ford was the king of the options list in the 1960s, but yet to become overly safety conscious). It's likely to have been owned by Pinewood studios, and it's almost certainly the same car that appeared in

Movie tracking vehicles have become rather more advanced since these scenes were filmed in 1964.

1967's *Billion Dollar Brain*, the third in the film series that sees Michael Caine as the anti-Bond Harry Palmer (though 007 alumni Harry Saltzman, Ken Adam, Peter Hunt and John Barry all worked on the first instalment, *The Ipcress File*).

Felix Leiter and his wingman Johnny also scored a great set of wheels in *Goldfinger*: a 1964 Ford Thunderbird convertible, a fourth-generation car (of 11, in all) and one of the pillars of America's automotive love affair. This '64 car was a reskin of the platform that had done service in the previous two generations, although its rear deck was longer and the rear bumper

housed rectangular tail lamps rather than round ones. Leiter's Wimbledon white example was also mercifully free of the side trim and door edge protectors that were beginning to blight US cars in this period (more optional extras for the dealers to up-sell). And it's worth noting that Bond's DB5 wasn't the only car fitted with a tracking device: this CIA T-bird also features one, which the duo use to track Oddjob's Lincoln. Once they've finished their KFC.

With a tough shooting schedule to adhere to, director Guy Hamilton still had to factor in an important location recce. 'During the course of the picture I had to sneak off and do the whole of Switzerland in one weekend, to find just two things: a wiggly road where Bond is tailing Auric Goldfinger in his Rolls-Royce, and I found that so we could do a triple zoom; and suitable roads for the Mustang and the girl and Bond and the Aston. We found all those around Andermatt.'

There were a few off-camera tribulations as the crew prepared to film the Swiss sequence, during July 1964. First, the DB5 hero car was damaged crossing the English Channel, necessitating more long shots than Guy Hamilton or Ted Moore would have originally intended (look closely and you'll see a crease in the off-side front wing). Still, the spectacular scenery in that part of the Alps – the vertiginous Susten Pass, and of course the famous Furka Pass – was certainly a helpful distraction. Then the DB5's shiny new five-speed gearbox began to malfunction, and producer Harry Saltzman asked John Stears to have the Trick car swiftly flown to the location.

Behind-the-scenes on one of the most iconic images in cinema – Sean Connery as James Bond, with the Aston Martin DB5 on the Furka Pass, Switzerland.

On *No Time To Die*, there were eight rigorously fettled DB5s on location in Matera for the film's opening sequence. But it's the irreplaceable gadget DB5 that's being thrown around by the stunt driver in the *Goldfinger* sequence where Bond assails Tilly Masterson's Ford Mustang – most likely the only one in Europe at the time, given that the Mustang had made its world debut at the New York World Fair a scant three months earlier. Some more Stears jiggery-pokery ensured that the scene unfolded with the expected verisimilitude; the DB5's rear arch and panel was a dummy fibreglass one, as was the side of the Ford. The scythe slicing into the Mustang was shot in close-up, and used an electrically operated 24in steel rod, that motors out of the DB5's hubcap. The Ford was mounted on a moving platform, and the finished scene was projected against back plates of the Alpine location.

A day after shooting the Swiss footage, the first unit was back in Pinewood and resumed the DB5 chase sequence. If some of it looks a little odd, it's because Ted Moore 'undercranked' the camera – shooting at a slower frame rate to heighten an impression of speed when played normally. Bob Simmons' assistant George Leech was doubling for Connery in the scene in which the Aston buries itself in a (polystyrene) wall. Once again, the priceless gadget Aston found itself replacing the 'hero' car. One of the Mercedes crashes into a tree; the other meets its maker when the DB5's oil slick sends it slithering off a cliff and into one of Goldfinger's buildings. This was shot at Harefield Quarry, the car being returned to Pinewood for the final fiery death throes. The last scene Sean Connery filmed was Tilly Masterson's death, in Black Park, on 21 July.

The last scenes filmed for *Goldfinger* were pick-ups done on 12 August, the very day that Ian Fleming passed away. He wouldn't live to see his creation achieve his greatest box office success yet, but this was the film that truly sent Bond into the stratosphere – and made life easier for the films' creative team. It had its Royal premiere at the Odeon in London's Leicester Square on 17 September 1964. A quick turnaround for Guy Hamilton, the editor Peter Hunt, and the rest of the team.

'With the success of *Goldfinger*, sales of Aston Martins went up by 60 per cent. We never had any more problems getting cars from manufacturers,' Ken Adam observed. 'I thought it was an elegant-looking car,' Sean Connery said many years later. 'I remember driving it in Switzerland and it impressed a lot of people. But I think it's telling that its setting in the story and the film gave it a more unique quality than the car actually possessed.'

Maybe so. But you could also argue that it was the combination of the car and the movie star that really did the trick.

POSTSCRIPT: There has been some confusion over exactly how many Bond DB5s were made, and where they are now. Following the release of *Goldfinger*, Bondmania ensued, with the Aston Martin almost as popular as its Scottish leading co-star. EON elected to capitalise on this for *Thunderball*'s release by ordering two more DB5s – in Silver Birch – and they were subsequently pressed into worldwide media duty. Both were adapted to include as many of Ken Adam's 13 original modifications as was practical. The Bond production company Danjaq sold the two promotional cars in 1969 to British collector Anthony Bamford (now Lord Bamford, owner of JCB). He sold one – chassis no: DB5/2008/R – in 1970 to a US buyer, who kept it until 2006, when RM Sotheby's auctioned it. 'I went to Pinewood and met [associate producer] Stanley Sopel,' Lord Bamford told me in 2010. 'They were in the backlot, wonderful film props. And a while later I swapped one of them for my Ferrari 250 GTO, the '64 car that I still have…' It's difficult to imagine a more glamorous car deal than this – the world's most famous movie car and the most valuable Ferrari in a once-in-a-lifetime trade (the GTO's current market value is approximately £50m). In August 2019, RM Sotheby's sold the DB5 again, for $6.38m. Of the original quartet of cars – the two *Goldfinger* film cars and the two EON promotional cars – only three survive. The first John Stears-modified car made its last screen appearance in 1981 caper *The Cannonball Run*, having had its gadgets removed then badly reinstalled at an owner's behest (Aston Martin refused to do it, but other specialists obliged). It was later kept in storage in an aircraft hangar in Florida when it was apparently seized, put on a plane and disappeared into the night never to be seen again. 'Some say it was dropped in the ocean,' Steve Waddingham avers, 'but I prefer to imagine that it's ended up on an island somewhere, being tended to and appreciated by some Blofeld-style megalomaniac car collector.' Meanwhile, in 2018 Aston Martin announced that it would be manufacturing 25 'new' continuation *Goldfinger* DB5s, complete with the original gadgets, and overseen by long-standing Bond effects boss Chris Corbould. Deliveries are now well under way.

'The Aston Martin has always been a favourite of ours, from *Goldfinger* on.'
CUBBY BROCCOLI

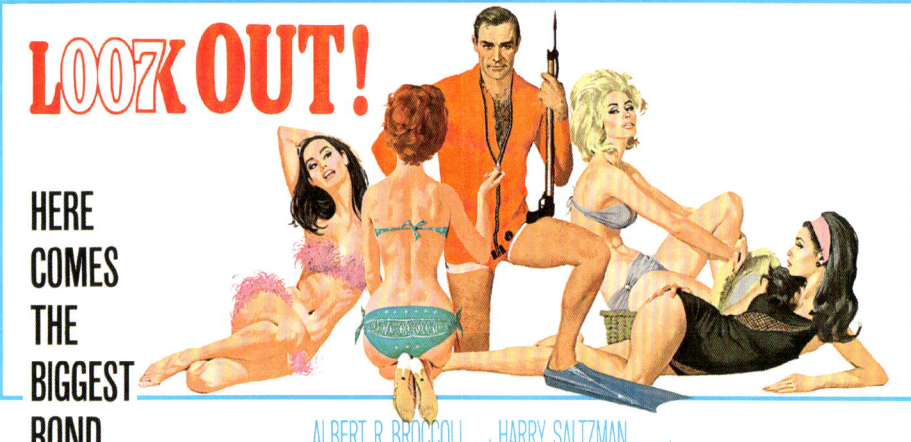

A US one sheet from December 1965, with artwork by Robert McGinnis and Frank McCarthy.

CHAPTER 04
THUNDERBALL

1965

STARRING Sean Connery as James Bond

"**L**ook up! Look out! Look down! James Bond does it everywhere!' the promotional posters for *Thunderball* proclaimed, but the marketing team could easily have added, 'Look behind the wheel!' because 007 was still doing plenty there, too.

Filming on this fourth Bond movie began on 16 February 1965 at the Château d'Anet, a 90-minute drive west of Paris, where the first scenes shot were the first scenes of the film (the shooting schedule on any film rarely follows the chronology of the movie itself). After attending his own funeral service, SPECTRE agent Jacques Bouvar leaves the chapel and gets into a black Lincoln Continental stretch limo to be chauffeuered to the chateau. Bond stunt legend Bob Simmons found himself playing Bouvar disguised as a woman in order to effect his escape.

Perhaps it was Ken Adam, upset by its brutalisation in *Goldfinger*, who insisted that the Lincoln stage a comeback in *Thunderball*. It features twice, which is only appropriate for one of the great modernist masterpieces of mid-century American design. In the post-war era, Ford designer Franklin Hershey proposed the idea of a 'personal' car, which manifested itself in the first-generation Thunderbird, a sports car with an immense feel-good factor, yet crucially still mass-produced. Lincoln was Ford's upscale brand, and thus the Continental became its 'personal luxury car'. Frank Sinatra was an early adopter, for whom the second-gen Conti was the four-wheeled incarnation of Twin Palms, the 'Desert Modern' house he commissioned architect E Stewart Williams to build for him in 1947 in the Movie Colony neighbourhood of Palm Springs

(just three bedrooms, but the piano-shaped swimming pool was a nice touch).

Its 1961 successor made a far bigger dent on the collective conscious. Creativity in car design in the US at this point was at an all-time high: post-war prosperity, the dawn of rock 'n' roll and the influence of the Jet Age all fed into the design offices in Detroit and beyond. The fourth-generation Continental was originally a proposal for a Thunderbird update, and Ford CEO Robert McNamara suggested adding two doors and back seats and turning it into a Lincoln. Chief stylist Elwood Engel, one of the great talents of the time, assembled his best guys and said,

The Sixties Lincoln Continental is a real go-to car for movie production designers

'I want a clean car – no garbage.' The '61 Continental was awarded the Bronze medal by the Industrial Design Institute, and it was the first production car to feature curved glass, which helped its volumes and proportion. Its rear-hinged 'suicide' doors meant the occupants could get in more easily, and the seats riffed on Mies van der Rohe's famous Barcelona chair. Under the bonnet sat a 7.0-litre, 430 cu in V8, the biggest engine ever used in a mainstream Ford.

This was also a car with huge cinematic star power. As well as high-profile appearances in the Bond films – 007 himself drove a pale blue convertible in the Bahamas scenes in *Thunderball*, in addition to the Lehmann and Peterson stretched version used in the pre-credits, and the crushed *Goldfinger* vehicle – the car's timeless looks and imposing presence have made the 1961–69 Continental a regular go-to for movie production designers. Amongst hundreds of appearances, it has featured in *Animal House*, *Mad Men*, *Marnie*, the *Matrix* trilogy, and even survived 500 years as a relic of better times in Kevin Costner's post-apocalyptic *Waterworld*. But its iconography was set forever by its key role in the events that occurred on Main Street, Dallas, 22 November 1963; John F Kennedy was travelling in an open-top Continental – codenamed SS-100-X by the US Secret Service – when he was assassinated. (Somewhat surprisingly, the car continued in presidential service for another eight years, having received titanium plating and bulletproof glass.)

Thunderball assuredly did look up and down. A quarter of the film's screen time is submerged, those scenes handled with aplomb by Ricou Browning (who also had the unusual distinction of playing the Gill-man in the celebrated B-movie *Creature from the Black Lagoon*). When Ken Adam arrived in the office ahead of filming, production designer Peter Lamont remembers, he said, 'Children, we're going to the Bahamas to do *Thunderball*, so you lot better learn to swim underwater.'

The Lincoln Continental reappears in *Thunderball*, the car below used by Bond in Nassau. Opposite: A rarely seen contact sheet from the carnival scene.

Above and below right: The Aston Martin DB5 received a few modifications in *Thunderball*. Opposite: Emilio Largo flouts Parisian parking regulations outside SPECTRE's HQ, 35 Avenue d'Eylau, in his Ford Thunderbird.

But they looked up, too, and had an interesting new approach to flight. The producers had upped the ante once again. Having dealt with Bouvar, Bond flees to the waiting Aston Martin DB5 using a jet-pack. Called the Rocket Belt, a company called Bell Textron had been developing it for the US air force. It had been created by a Bell Aerospace engineer called Wendell Moore, who had worked on the Bell X-1 (as flown by the legendary Chuck Yeager, and documented by Tom Wolfe in *The Right Stuff*). They sent their most experienced pilot, Bill Suitor, to fly it. Suitor would rack up 1,200 flights in it, but on that sub-zero day in France he flatly refused John Stears' requests to do so without a helmet. 'It was developed under an army contract with the idea that foot soldiers would be flying around with these Buck Rogers devices,' Suitor recalled. 'It was so incredibly controllable you could do just about anything with the darn thing.' The Rocket Belt was powered by two tanks of hydrogen peroxide and nitrogen, mixed with a catalyst to produce a high-pressure steam fired through two nozzles, for an average flight time of 21 seconds. Long enough to upstage the Aston Martin waiting on the ground, newly rigged with fire hoses to send jets of freezing water at Bond's assailants. Suitor did six flights during filming on *Thunderball*. 'During one of my flights I bounced four feet in the air and almost went over backwards. The scene I get a kick out of is when [Bond] takes it off and throws it in the trunk, like no well-dressed man would be without one.'

Back in the French capital, meanwhile, the film's primary villain, Emilio Largo (Adolfo Celli), has to double park in a Parisian boulevard to avoid being any later than he already is for a meeting of SPECTRE operatives. Like so many master criminals, he also

February 1965, Château d'Anet, near Paris, and Bond's Aston Martin DB5 does its best not to be upstaged by the Rocket Belt jet-pack.

On 21 June 1965, the Bond production crew gathered at Silverstone Circuit in England to shoot another memorable chase sequence. SPECTRE agent Count Lippe is being pursued by Fiona Volpe, who destroys his Ford Fairlane 500 Skyliner with a missile. But the real hero that day was legendary Bond stuntman Bob Simmons, who was driving the Ford. Note the unusual tracking car.

A Japanese one sheet from December 1965. Note the DB5 and exploding Ford. The tagline translates as, 'With the deep blue sea stained a crimson red, the fourth instalment of the series brings with it double the tension, three times the action and amazing new weapons. It's the most interesting episode yet!'

appears to be hiding in plain sight; his 1965 Ford Thunderbird certainly stands out alongside the Citroën DS, Ford Consul Corvair, Peugeots 403 and 404, and Simca Aronde P60 Elyseé that are visible. (Simcas pop up in various Bond films, a reminder that this now long-gone French brand was still very popular in the 1960s.) Largo's Thunderbird is almost identical to the car driven by Felix Leiter in *Goldfinger*; amongst other detail differences, the '64 car has the Thunderbird name on the leading edge of the bonnet, where the later car has a winged logo…

There's a bigger role for another Ford in *Thunderball*. SPECTRE's number four, Count Lippe, has been deemed expendable by Blofeld. (Lippe has backed the wrong guy to hijack a Vulcan jet bomber that's armed with atomic bombs – the plot's 'inciting incident'.) Lippe is tracking 007 – he in a Ford Fairlane 500 Skyliner, Bond in the DB5 – but, unbeknownst to Lippe, he has a SPECTRE assassin tracking *him*. In fact, it turns out to be Largo's right-hand woman Fiona Volpe (Luciana Paluzzi), whose BSA Lightning motorbike happens to be armed with missiles of its own. Lippe and that rather startled-looking Ford are duly blown to smithereens.

The sequence was shot at Silverstone Circuit on 21 June 1965 – three weeks before that year's British Grand Prix – and it features another outstanding performance from Bond stunt supervisor Bob Simmons. As John Stears recalled: 'I prepped two Ford Fairlane Skyliners to blow up, then rehearsed the action with Bob. He was sitting low down on a board in the doorway. We fixed the steering mechanism for him, and being a left-hand drive car we put a dummy of Count Lippe driving the car.

'I told the stunt rider Johnny Walker when to fire the rockets, and Bob when to explode the car. It was all worked out in great detail because these vehicles were

A rarely seen contact sheet of Sean Connery and Luciana Paluzzi, as her character Fiona Volpe prepares to unnerve Bond with some spirited driving in a Ford Mustang.

going really fast. The bike was doing over 100mph, the cars 70mph-plus.

'It all happened perfectly: the car exploded, went off the track, down the ditch, and then we cut. We raced up the track with the ambulances and a fire engine. Bob wasn't there. We thought, "God, where is he, has he gone under the car?" Everybody was really panicking, then a voice behind Terence [Young, the director] said, "How was that, guv?" He'd crawled out, and come round the back of us…'

Young was sitting on a converted Rolls-Royce tracking vehicle: 'I didn't see Bob leave the car, which he should have done. We're very cold-blooded, us directors, and I let the thing run on until I'd got the shot. Then I raced down the hill and couldn't find Bob. But he was alive. He was a very nice man, and I'd used him on other pictures. He was one of the people I insisted on having in this film.'

The Fairlane Skyliner wasn't a particularly pretty car, but it certainly delivered on the 'surprise and delight' that Detroit's marketing wonks were using to

'We raced up the track with ambulances and a fire engine, but Bob wasn't there…'

woo baby boomers in the late 1950s. Namely, its retractable hard-top roof (even if Peugeot had pioneered such a thing 23 years earlier in the 1934 601). Ford's head of advanced design, Gil Spear, built a scale model showcasing the 'Roof-O-Matic' concept, and Ford bosses ponied up $2m to make it production-ready. It needed that level of investment: the car used 185.9m of wiring, seven reversible electric motors, four lift jacks, umpteen relays, solenoids and locking mechanisms and, while it measured a lengthy 5.3m, most of that was taken up by a trunk big enough to accommodate the roof. Either way, that's a lot of a car to blow up, which meant a lot of explosives for John Stears.

It also makes more of a statement than the Morris Minor convertible Bond gets a lift to his hotel in – one of the more incongruous sights in any Bond film – or the Triumph Herald soft-top that one of Largo's minions uses on his way back to his boss's Villa Palmyra lair. British cars were popular in the Bahamas in the mid-1960s, especially as rentals for tourists, because they were easy to drive and easier to park than their vast American equivalents.

Having left her BSA Lightning in England, Fiona Volpe still manages to ruffle Bond's feathers with her determined driving in a Ford Mustang convertible, although the pace she demonstrates is a bit optimistic for the 289-cubic-inch version we see the pair in. Nevertheless, this was one of the world's hottest cars in 1965. Indeed, it remains one of the most significant cars in automotive history. Industry legend and then Ford vice president Lee Iacocca wanted something that would appeal to a younger audience, in particular to more women, and would also encourage buyers to spend more on desirable options. Nevertheless, by utilising chassis, suspension and drive-train components already in production and used elsewhere in the Ford range, the price was kept down to an eye-catching $2,734 (about $22,000 in today's money, and two-thirds of the price of a Chevrolet Corvette back in the day.)

Which probably explains why the Mustang shattered Ford's sales projections, shifting 100,000 units in three months, and hitting the million mark in just 18 months. It also kick-started the American muscle car phenomenon; by the late 1960s this formerly female-friendly sports car had been doused in testosterone, and grown horns. In fact, as driven through San Francisco by Steve McQueen in *Bullitt*, the '68 Mustang GT Fastback in Highland Green might be one of the few cars that could rival James Bond's Aston Martin DB5 for global fame.

A 1967 Australian 'daybill' using
artwork by Robert McGinnis
and Frank McCarthy.

CHAPTER 05

YOU ONLY
LIVE TWICE

1967

STARRING Sean Connery as James Bond

Helicopters are a regular presence in Bond movies, but rarely like this... next stop, Tokyo Bay.

'**I** remember script conferences where the idea was to think of as many outrageous suggestions as you could. I remember, for example, a suggestion where a big magnet gets hold of a car, and lifts it. The producers and the director and everybody would say, "That's a great idea. Let's see how we can develop that." And it built from that. What's going to happen? Dump it in the middle of Tokyo Bay. It was an exhilarating time because, if you came up with those ideas, it would work itself into the script, and we'd then work the story backwards and forwards to achieve that.'

William Cartlidge was a young assistant director on the fifth Bond film, *You Only Live Twice*. His account encapsulates the larger-than-life, can-do attitude that prevailed in the Bond camp in 1966 as work began. Remember, this is the Bond movie written by celebrated children's author Roald Dahl (he'd never tackled a screenplay before), that opens with Bond faking his own death, and the one in which Blofeld is fully unmasked for the first time (originally played by Jan Werich, who was deemed too avuncular and quickly replaced by Donald Pleasence). And the magnet picking up the car? That was Dana – wife of producer Cubby – Broccoli's idea…

Following the Fleming source material to set the action in Japan would also give the film a dramatic new aesthetic. The director Lewis Gilbert, hot from instant classic *Alfie*, production designer Ken Adam and the producers spent a month traversing the country in search of quasi-mythical locations. Japan was – and still is – that sort of place. Ian Fleming was certainly entranced.

'We covered about two-thirds [of the country] in about three weeks, flying seven hours every day,' Adam noted. 'We found this unbelievable volcanic area in Kyushu, the southern island of Japan… there were about eight volcanoes all next to each other.'

The villain, it was decided, would live in an extinct volcanic crater (rather than a Japanese castle surrounded by a 'garden of death', as in the novel), and Adam was able to propose a set on a scale he could only have dreamt of a few years earlier. When Cubby Broccoli queried the likely cost, Adam said £1m. 'If you can do it for a million, go ahead…' was the no-nonsense reply.

You Only Live Twice is that sort of film, exotic in the now expected Bond manner, yet shot through with a look and feel quite unlike any of its predecessors. From an automotive point of view, it's a stone-cold classic, but not if it's traditional crowd-pleasers you're after. There is no Aston Martin DB5 here, and the four-wheeled co-stars are upstaged by a portable autogyro nicknamed Little Nellie (actual

UNITED ARTISTS
A Transamerica Company

25, rue d'Astorg   75 - PARIS - 8ᵉ *(FRANCE)*

TÉLÉPHONE :
265-48-35 à 38
265-45-90 à 93
265-71-36 à 38
Cables Address :
UNARTISCO - PARIS

April 2, 1968

Mr. Stanley Sopel
"Chitty Chitty Bang Bang"
Iver Heath - Pinewood Studios
Bucks

<u>YOU ONLY LIVE TWICE</u>

Dear Stanley:

Regarding the Toyota car, I have turned over this matter to our Distribution Publicity Department and you will be hearing directly from Jean Nachbaur.

My understanding is that the car is currently not in our possession, but with a Toyota dealer in Copenhagen.

All best wishes.

Sincerely,

Saul Cooper

cc: Mr. Guenter Schack
      Mr. Jean Nachbaur
      Mme. Ines Auerbach

      Mr. Fran Winikus

Above: Bond is rescued by Aki (Akiko Wakabayashi) in the specially made Toyota 2000GT convertible. Even with the roof chopped off, Sean Connery still struggled to fit in.

Left: Our archive research suggests that the Toyota 2000GT used in the film took some time to return to Europe once filming was complete.

name: Wallis WA-116 Agile). However, because we're in Japan in the mid-1960s, the background detail is endlessly fascinating – whether it's the architecture, the furniture or the cars. Yep, this is one for the detail fetishists, and indeed the cultural historians.

With its self-image in tatters, Japan initially struggled to reassert its identity post-war, and the electronics revolution was still some years away. It's also worth noting that, during Japan's reconstruction, Toyota resisted the licensing deals and manufacturing collaborations with Western car-makers that other Japanese companies embarked on, in favour of going it alone. So the car that we see dangling from that magnet is more significant than you might first think. It's a Toyopet Crown, whose predecessor played a pivotal role in establishing Toyota – now the world's number one car manufacturer – in the rapidly expanding post-war American market.

In fact, the original Toyopet Crown has the honour of being the first Japanese car to be sold in the USA, via a dealership set up in Hollywood, of all places, in October 1957. It wasn't a success – just 287 cars sold by the end of 1958 – thanks to its pitiful lack of power, a name that was firmly lost in translation, and some lingering anti-Japanese prejudice. But from this rather ornate-looking acorn the mightiest automotive oak tree would soon flourish.

The second-gen Crown that's seen in *You Only Live Twice* was a vast improvement, even if its upgraded 2.0-litre, 105bhp six-cylinder engine was still easy meat for the helicopter and magnet. It's an elegant-looking car, bigger and more luxurious than its rather dainty forebear. It was the first production car in Japan to be sold with a torque converter automatic, and a later twin carb 'S' derivative cranked the power up to 125bhp. It was also the first Toyopet Crown to make it to Europe, in 1963, thanks to a forward-thinking Danish importer, Walther Krohn of Erla Auto; Dutch company Louwman & Parqui B.V would follow suit a year later. (As an aside, the Louwman Museum in The Hague is home to one of the world's greatest car collections – including one of the original EON-commissioned Aston Martin DB5s, modified for publicity purposes to include all the gadgets.)

You Only Live Twice is, however, much better known for another Toyota. The 2000GT is a somewhat mysterious masterpiece with a complicated genealogy, but it's usually described as Japan's answer to the Jaguar E-type. It's much rarer, though: as Jay Leno says, 'It's considered to be the most collectable Japanese car of all time.' Its design is often credited to Albrecht von Goertz, a German expat living in America, whose encounters first with the fabled industrial designer Raymond Loewy and then with Max Hoffman – a critical figure in establishing BMW and Mercedes in the USA in the 1950s – set him on a unique career path. (He was responsible for the lovely BMW 507, a rare and special coupé owned by the likes of Elvis Presley, who bought one while he was doing military service in the US army, in Germany.)

As for the 2000GT, it actually began life as a Nissan co-production with Yamaha; Goertz was contracted to Nissan from 1963 until 1965, and worked on the sports car programme. When Nissan bailed, Yamaha offered it to Toyota, whose image as a purveyor of worthy but dowdy mass-market cars needed a shot in the arm. At this point, Toyota tasked one of its designers, Satoru Nozaki, to rework the car. Its form language is clearly influenced by the best work coming out of Europe at the time – the body's 'fuselage' and flowing front and rear wings have an Italianate flair – but there are plenty of local flourishes.

Alongside the debut of the Shinkansen bullet train and the Tokyo Olympics, the 2000GT certainly gave notice that Japan was rapidly becoming a force to be reckoned with. Its pop-up headlights, its wraparound visor-like side windows and windscreen, its aero mirrors and wing-mounted service panel are all suggestive of an automotive superpower-in-waiting. The engine was Toyota's 2.0-litre, in-line six-cylinder, fed by triple carburettors, with a cylinder head engineered by Yamaha. By modern standards, 148bhp is supermini stuff, but the 2000GT looked dynamite, and a five-speed manual box and disc brakes helped. It went well enough for none other than Carroll Shelby – creator of the AC Cobra and the man who helped turn Ford's GT40 into a multiple Le Mans 24 Hours winner – to enter it into the production car category of the 1968 SCCA race series. Indeed, Toyota invested almost $500k in the programme, so they weren't messing around; the cars looked fantastic – white with a blue bonnet and classic racing graphics – they were stiff, and they handled well. But the lack of power hampered the effort, and the drivers finished third and fourth overall (not high enough for Toyota, who pulled the programme at the end of 1968).

It was also a more compact and delicate car in the flesh than it looks in images. This accounts for the anomalous version that appears in *You Only Live Twice*: two of the 2000GT's extremely small production run of 351 cars were transformed into convertibles because Sean Connery couldn't fit into the coupé without folding his limbs into a position that simply wouldn't look right on camera. The work was done in just two weeks, the rough edges hidden by a tonneau cover. In the film, Bond's escape from Mr Osato's headquarters is aided by the arrival of Aki (Akiko Wakabayashi) in the Toyota; the newly completed Hotel New Otani in

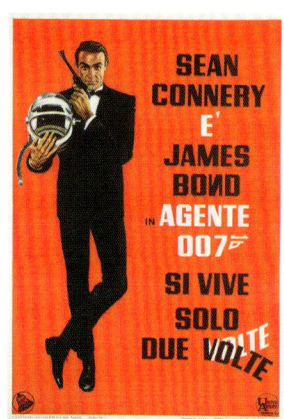

Right: An Italian one sheet from August 1967. Note that Bond has been flipped and is left-handed. Below: Concept art for the garage where Little Nellie is assembled.

Tokyo doubles as Osato's HQ, and was also home to most of the film crew while they were in the city. (The hotel was named after Yonetaro Otani, a former sumo wrestler who owned the land on which it was constructed.)

Tellingly, 007 doesn't drive the Toyota much in the film – maybe Connery just couldn't fit behind the wheel – but it's a Bond car with eternal star power for many, including the current 007 Daniel Craig, who revealed in a *Top Gear* '50 Years of Bond Cars' television special, 'I love that car a lot. That's one of my favourites.'

We'd agree, and recommend you keep your eyes peeled the next time you're watching *You Only Live Twice*. The supporting cast includes rarely seen examples of period flotsam and jetsam, so step forward the Datsun Sunny van, Dodge Polara, Mazda B360 van, a '64 Mitsubishi Colt, Morris 1100, Nissan Cedric, Prince Gloria, Prince Skyline, an adorable Subaru 360, a Subaru Sambar, and a Toyota Publica van. A Pontiac Parisienne convertible is also lurking in the garage as Little Nellie turns up to steal the entire film.

That's assuming, of course, that you don't award that accolade to the Mini Moke that helps prop up Blofeld's bid for global domination and is seen inside his volcano lair. Mini creator Alec Issigonis had originally intended this spin-off to be a military vehicle, light enough to be parachuted into battle, and sufficiently simple and robust in construction to survive. But it didn't have the necessary ground clearance, and its 848cc engine was barely powerful enough to get out of its own way, never mind propel the armed forces out of trouble. Still, it has enjoyed a notable afterlife and is now a leading exponent of vogueish Riviera chic amongst 2020's billionaires. Or minion transport, if you happen to be a homicidal megalomaniac…

This page: Scenes from *You Only Live Twice*. Inside Blofeld's volcanic lair, where stolen space rockets sit cheek-by-jowl with yellow Mini Mokes. Bond makes contact with agent Aki at a sumo fight – the password is 'I love you'. Bond and the Toyota 2000GT, before fleeing from Osato's HQ. This film fully demonstrated the imagination of production designer, Ken Adam, down to the pods used by Blofeld's henchmen to shuttle round his lair.

A hand-tinted Japanese one sheet from
December 1969. The title is translated
as 'The Queen's 007'.

CHAPTER 06

ON HER MAJESTY'S SECRET SERVICE

1969

STARRING George Lazenby as James Bond

ON HER MAJESTY'S SECRET SERVICE

1. Dangerous bend Loc. Portugal..

2. Bond nearly forced off road...

3. He follows white car leisurely..

We do not see in this sh...

6. Bond's P.O.V.

7. Bond's car comes to a halt...sound off...

8. P.O.V.

9. Int. Bond's car

11. Tracy walks into sea.. Double..

12. Bond starts off....

13. Tracy in rough sea double.

14.

16. Bond arrives at edge of sea...

17. Double? Bond into rough sea..

18. Camera crane? or raft.

19. Bond lays T... down on beach

Note. At no time do we see the new Bond clearly until he saves Tracy and lays her on beach. sc. 20-21

5 Bond starts off after white car..

10 Bond uses telescopic sight...

15 Bond turns onto beach..

20 Tracy.. Dialogue..

21. My name is BOND...
JAMES BOND..
This is the first time we see new Bond....

Syd Cain
Prod: Designer

O*n Her Majesty's Secret Service*'s standing in the Bond canon has grown hugely in the past 50 years. No wonder: it was meta in a way no big film would have dared at the time ('This never happened to the other fellow,' 007 says at the end of the pre-credits), it has some of the best cinematography of any Bond film, and its ending has a Bergman-esque bleakness that catches your breath. History now records Lazenby, in his first acting role, as the underdog Bond, and who doesn't love one of those?

'For me there's no question that cinematically *On Her Majesty's Secret Service* is the best Bond film,' Oscar-winning director Steven Soderbergh noted in a 2015 blog. 'The anamorphic compositions are relentlessly arresting and the editing patterns of the action sequences are totally bananas. It's like Peter Hunt took all the ideas of the French new wave and blended them with Eisenstein in a Cuisinart to create a grammar that still tops today's "how fast can you cut" aesthetic. There are as many big set pieces in *OHMSS* as any Bond film made.'

Rewatching it now also serves as a reminder that *On Her Majesty's Secret Service* has elements of reboot: Maurice Binder's credits sequence is a montage of scenes from the previous five films, while John Barry's brooding Moog synthesizer-driven title theme rings the changes by being instrumental. Diana Rigg's kick-ass portrayal of Tracy di Vincenzo is another stand-out. A desire to move on is clearly telegraphed – while still keeping the faithful happy.

The same could be said of the star car. There's no DB5 here, and no gadgetry. But there is an Aston Martin, and this one represented a similarly concerted effort by its creators to forge a new path. The late 1960s was the apotheosis of a certain kind of louche GT; it stands for Gran Turismo, of course, a romantic notion embraced by Europe's wealthy jet-trash when they didn't need the jet and fancied driving from St Moritz to St Tropez instead. Ferrari, Lamborghini and Maserati all had new cars on the market, styled in spectacular fashion by Italy's *carrozzeria*, while rivals like Jensen's magnificently named Interceptor – surely the Bond car that never was – and outliers like Gordon-Keeble and Swiss mavericks Monteverdi were all chasing the same fashionably well-heeled customer.

Aston Martin's owner, David Brown, figured a replacement for the now ageing DB6 was critical to keep pace. Long-standing Aston creative partner Touring of Milan was hired to design a replacement. Two concept cars, later dubbed DBSC, were duly shown at the Paris,

Right: The Aston Martin DBS and Mercury Cougar on Guincho beach, Portugal, May 1969. Opposite: A rarely seen contact sheet from filming for the pre-credits sequence.

London and Turin motor shows in 1966, in right- and left-hand drive forms. A slimmer iteration of the famous Aston grille is evident; the C-pillar and bodywork slats owe a debt to Ferrari's 275 GTB.

In fact, the car that sat alongside the DB6 Volante on Aston's stand at the Earls Court motor show in '66 was wearing the number plate 'DB S', probably a reference to its high speed potential and likely extremely limited production. More limited than anyone would have anticipated: troubled Touring went bankrupt by the year's end, and the project was abandoned. But the DBS name stuck.

Aston hired a former Rootes Group and Rover designer, William Towns, to work up the new car, which he did in double-quick time. Aston had planned to introduce a new V8 engine in the car, but its development was behind schedule and the DBS duly debuted at the suitably aristocratic – and future Bond location – Blenheim Palace in September 1967, toting the same 282bhp, 4.0-litre straight-six as the DB6. But it sat further back in the chassis, and independent suspension all-round substantially improved its handling prowess. A Vantage version was also available, its triple Weber carburettors (made in Bologna, so there was some Italian input) lifting the power output to 325bhp.

Towns was something of an iconoclast, and drew on a wide variety of influences, many of which would have displeased Aston's hardcore clientele. (If they had a problem with the DBS, 1975's Lagonda – also a Towns creation – would frazzle their minds. It remains one of the most outrageous-looking production cars of all time.) *Autocar* magazine was impressed: 'Without the aid of an Italian stylist, the Newport Pagnell team came up with something as modern, handsome and Italianate as anything from the Turin coachbuilders at that time.'

Six inches wider than the DB6 – which continued in production alongside the new car – the DBS's size and expanse of bonnet definitely saw Aston getting its head around the new GT car paradigm, quad headlamp set-up and all. The bonnet duct, 'knock-off' wire wheels and front wing air vents were among the signature design elements. In 1969, the Tadek Marek-designed fuel-injected 5.3-litre V8 was finally ready, and its installation in the DBS briefly made it the world's fastest four-seater. Although the DBS ceased

The film's ice race took weeks to film. Diana Rigg did a lot of the driving herself.

production in May 1972, it morphed into the visually almost identical but now single headlamped V8, which enjoyed various modifications to remain in production until 1989. (The 'Oscar India' refers to October Introduction, an arcane example of internal nomenclature. This iteration arrived in 1978, and later starred in *The Living Daylights*. And we'll see it again in *No Time To Die*...)

Following the Aston-free zone that was *You Only Live Twice*, the Bond production team was keen to return to the company for the new film. But while *On Her Majesty's Secret Service* has practically psychedelic overtones – witness the sequence in which Telly Savalas's fabulous Blofeld hypnotises his Angels of Death in his Piz Gloria lair – Peter Hunt wanted a more realistic character for his directorial debut. That meant no gadgets. 'I didn't want to put tricks and gimmicks in the film,' he noted some years later. 'It didn't need it, it was all there in the story.'

Special effects supervisor and Bond staple John Stears, perhaps with some relief, had a different mission on this one. 'We wanted to go away from the gadgets, and go more into the personality of the actors.' There was one optional extra in the car: an Armalite AR-7 rifle, with a silencer and scope that lives in the car's glovebox.

The DBS debuts in the film before the main titles, and we meet it before we get acquainted with the new Bond. The sequence in which 007 tracks Tracy's Mercury Cougar was actually shot at the end of *OHMSS*'s principal photography, on the Estoril coast in Portugal in the Cascais municipality. The production had two DBSs at its disposal. The hero car wears registration GKX 8G, distinguishable by the GB badge it wore on its rear (the other car didn't have it). The second car was originally registered FBH 207G, and was used primarily for interior shots, and some tracking shots. The rear window and boot-lid were removed to house a cameraman when the shot required it. The cars were painted Olive Green (ICI paint code PO31-TW-21900 – so now you know), and had a Connolly black leather interior with a grey headlining.

Bond's wheels had to play second fiddle to Tracy's Paris-registered Mercury Cougar in terms of screen time, though. Following the outrageous success of the Mustang, Ford was hell-bent on surfing the 'Pony car' wave for all it was worth. Launched in 1967, the first-generation Cougar was both pretty and striking, smartly surfaced, well-proportioned in the emerging muscle car idiom, and had some imaginative flourishes: the vertical slatted grille and concealed headlamps broke the mould. US car-makers were geniuses at stoking demand, and by 1969 the grille slats were horizontal, the Cougar was newly available as a convertible, and in XR-7 guise it didn't hang about. Tracy's car was fitted with a 390-cubic-inch (6.4-litre) four-barrel V8, known by fans as the 428CJ (Cobra Jet), with Ram Air induction. The producers used three in the film, though given what they put them through it's a surprise they didn't need more. Tracy is

Filming for *OHMSS*'s ice racing sequence began at the end of January 1969, on a flooded playing field. It kept thawing out, which gave the crew endless problems.

Another example of an improvised tracking car (below), but as with the rest of the film, the racing sequence was thrillingly executed.

Diana Rigg receives coaching from Austrian racing driver, Erich Glavitza.

never less than committed behind the wheel, not least when her efforts to shake off Blofeld's goons – piloting the obligatory black Mercedes 220 saloons (W110 model) – see her and Bond gatecrash a motor race. On ice. Anthony Squire is prominently acknowledged in the film's opening credits (for the 'stock car sequence') and the whole set-up is one of the most inspired in the Bond series. It also took serious preparation. A playing field in Lauterbrunnen was flooded with water and took two weeks to freeze to a satisfactory level. On 26 January 1969, Austrian racing driver Erich Glavitza (who would work on the Steve McQueen project *Le Mans* the following year) and his team of stunt drivers got to work. As well as marshalling the cars, Squire had 1,000 extras on set and was running four cameras. During the day, the sun would melt the ice, and the crew had to wait for it to re-freeze. Stuntman Dickie Graydon recalled: 'We had steel studs in the tyres to give us grip, but we couldn't skid with them so they were taken off. Which meant we were virtually out of control most of the time.'

The second unit was filming for three weeks before Lazenby, Rigg and Peter Hunt arrived to do the close-ups. Rigg, by all accounts, happily got stuck in, revelling in the ability to trade paint with the stunt drivers with – relative – impunity. Rigg had driving tuition from Glavitza in an Escort ahead of filming, but George Lazenby was possibly less enamoured, and managed to overturn a car. 'It's hard to drive on ice, I found out...' 'Once you get in that car it doesn't matter how much you damage it,' Hunt reflected. 'You're going to skid and

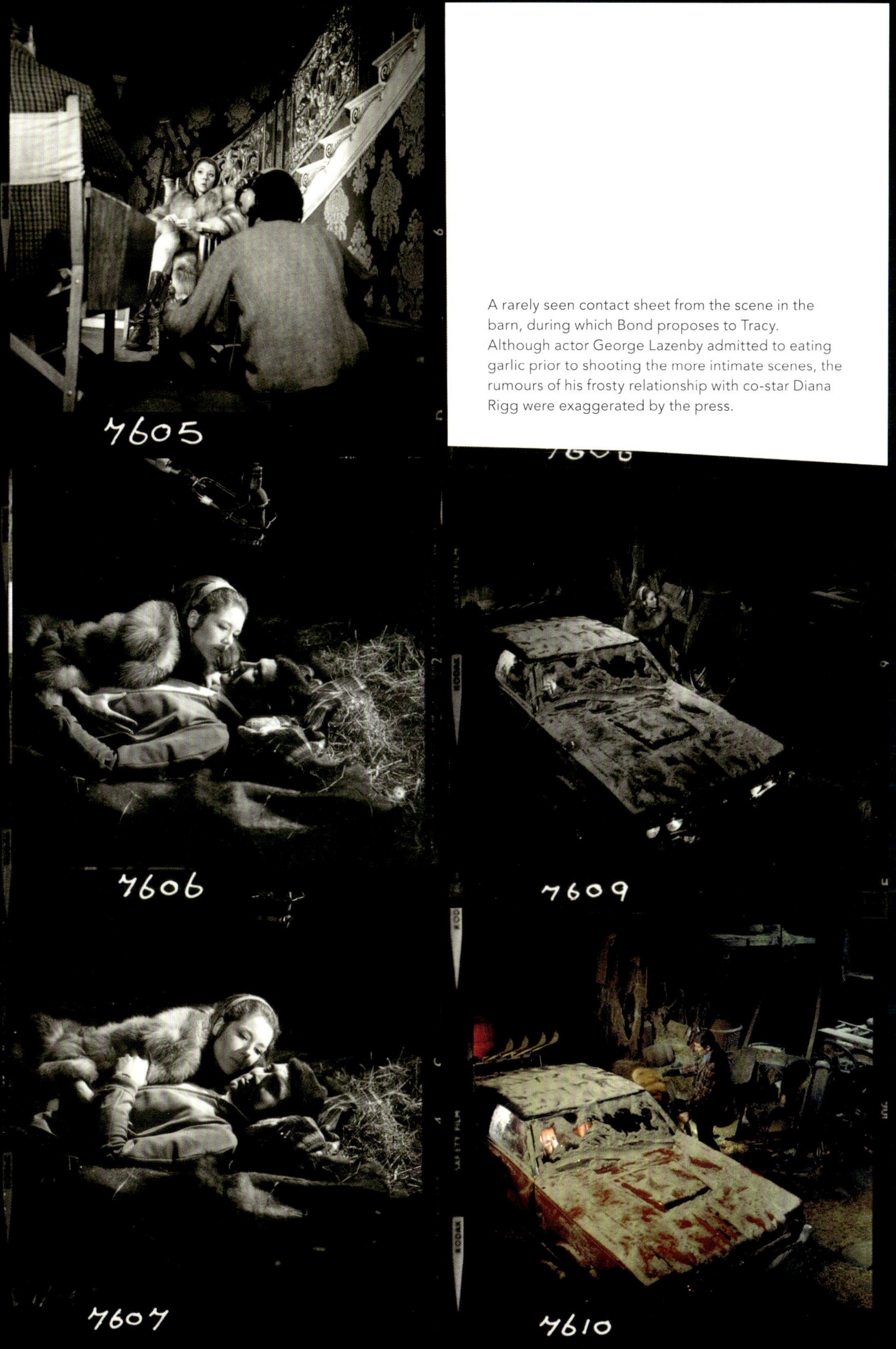

A rarely seen contact sheet from the scene in the barn, during which Bond proposes to Tracy. Although actor George Lazenby admitted to eating garlic prior to shooting the more intimate scenes, the rumours of his frosty relationship with co-star Diana Rigg were exaggerated by the press.

Left: Filming in Draco's Rolls-Royce Silver Shadow Drophead and, below, following Bond's marriage to Tracy. Director Peter Hunt is holding the megaphone; note the second Aston Martin DBS in shot behind.

Bond and Tracy apparently have all the time in the world

fly all over the place. You enjoy it. Diana Rigg said it felt so good not having to worry that you're skidding into somebody or banging someone. It's a bit like dodgems at a fair.'

It's difficult to imagine a film director being quite so laissez-faire these days, but the sequence certainly has a thrilling kineticism. The Cougar's co-stars include an Austin Mini and various Ford Escort Mk Is – seven were used in the film – one of which ends up on its roof. Although we see it happen, one of the shots used in this sequence is the movie equivalent of poetic licence – second unit director (and *OHMSS*'s editor) John Glen inverted a close-up shot of the driver. 'It was just a simple editing trick but it got a good laugh in the cinema,' he recalled. And the rest of the action up to the barn – in which Bond proposes to Tracy as a storm rages outside – is equally well choreographed.

As befits its glamorous location at the tail end of the 1960s, *OHMSS* features a host of cameos from some intriguing cars. Outside Tracy and Bond's Portuguese hotel, the Palácio Estoril, there's a Chevrolet Chevelle Malibu, a Jaguar Mk X, and a long wheelbase version of a Mercedes 220D (W115 model); also just visible is an Austin 1100 and Ford Cortina Mk 1. Tracy's father, Marc-Ange Draco, is head of the SPECTRE-rivalling crime syndicate Union Corse, and uses a glorious Rolls-Royce Silver Shadow Drophead with coachwork by Mulliner Park Ward, one of 505 made between 1967 and 1971 (at which point it was renamed Corniche, and continued in production with cosmetic changes right up until 1995). An Alfa Romeo Giulia Super trails them over a bridge, and an Opel Rekord is seen outside as Bond prepares to break into Gumbold's office in Bern (it's now the Schweizerhof Hotel, and this scene also debuts the ingenious safe-cracker/photocopier). Various Fords can be seen throughout: a 1968 Taunus 17M Turnier (P7), a '61 Taunus 17M (a P3, nicknamed 'Badewanne' or bathtub at its launch), and a '64 Consul Corvair. The VW Beetle is a semi-permanent presence; its rear-engined layout gave it impressive traction in snowy conditions.

More committed car nerds will enjoy the fleeting glimpses afforded a Lancia Flavia, and award yourself maximum points if you clock the DKW F12 roadster as Bond's train pulls into Murren (Blofeld's lair, Piz Gloria on the peak of Schilthorn Mountain, is nearby). DKW was one of the four companies that composed the famous German combine Auto Union, and was later owned by Daimler-Benz, and sold to Volkswagen in 1964. It favoured quirky little two-stroke engines,

proving unexpectedly hardy in European rallying, until the marque was quietly absorbed into Audi in 1965.

And so to that shocking ending. Bond and Tracy are newly married and apparently have all the time in the world, when destiny arrives at high speed round a mountain hairpin. If you know your cars, you'll know immediately that the sight of a Mercedes 600 Grosse is unlikely to be a harbinger of glad tidings. This is a vehicle loaded with symbolism. In its day – and for many years after its 1964 introduction – the 600's combination of elegantly impassive styling, bank vault build quality and groundbreaking engineering made it the default choice for many of the world's wealthiest and most famous people, good and bad: George Harrison bought his off fellow Beatle John Lennon, while Coco Chanel, David Bowie, Elizabeth Taylor and Jack Nicholson all owned a 600 at one time or another. But then so did 'Papa Doc' Duvalier, Idi Amin, Nicolae Ceausescu, Pablo Escobar and Saddam Hussein. Blofeld, we can safely assume, fits into the latter category, and is actually pictured at the wheel of his gunmetal grey 600 – with neck brace, following his nasty toboggan run experience – as Irma Bunt (Ilse Steppat) opens fire on the Aston Martin. Many of the 600's amenities, electric windows included, were hydraulically driven, an extremely complex solution to the car's remarkable specification.

James Bond wouldn't be the only institution returning in *Diamonds Are Forever*. The Mercedes 600 – inextricably linked in the Bond universe with a moment of profound emotion – would also reappear, alongside its nefarious owner.

A US one sheet from December 1971 with artwork by series regular Robert McGinnis.

CHAPTER 07
DIAMONDS ARE FOREVER

1971

STARRING Sean Connery as James Bond

WALT TAYLOR
PRODUCT PROMOTIONS

EQUITABLE BUILDING, SUITE 2426
3435 WILSHIRE BOULEVARD
LOS ANGELES, CALIFORNIA 90010
TELEPHONE (213) 385-3265

August 13, 1971

Mr. Stanley Sopel
Eon Productions Ltd.
1, Tilney Street
London W1, England

Dear Mr. Sopel:

  As you know, the automobiles supplied by Ford Marketing Corporation to Eon Productions for use in the filming of "Diamonds Are Forever" were recently returned to us after completion of shooting in Nevada and California.

  Of the vehicles returned, twelve were so severely damaged as to preclude their being repaired for service and had to be sold as wrecks for parts salvage. These twelve wrecked units were sold for a total of $ 6,450 whereas the wholesale value of comparable cars on the current used car market is $ 28,525, a net difference of $ 22,075.

  Making an allowance of $ 2,075 below wholesale to adjust for any minor damage or wear, we are requesting payment in the amount of $ 20,000 to reimburse Ford Marketing Corporation for the loss sustained in the sale of these vehicles.

  For your information, attached is a list of the specific cars involved showing the wholesale value and the price received for each vehicle.

         Sincerely yours,

         Walter E. Taylor

WET:wp

Enclosure

On screen and off, everything about the sixth Bond film was bigger and blingier. Including, of course, the cars and the car chases. A big chunk of the action is set in Las Vegas so, a decade on from *Dr No*'s rather restrained palette, this film shimmers with as much subtlety as the titular stones. *Diamonds Are Forever* is the Bond film that still gets heavy rotation on television, so the big chase sequence has an enjoyably familiar feel: 53 cars falling over each other in the Fremont Street area of Vegas, cops being made fools of, culminating in a deceptively simple but brilliantly executed eight-car, semi-aerial manoeuvre out of a parking lot. Not to mention a desert escape in a lunar rover. Plus, a return for the man who was at the time – and remains to this day – the embodiment of Bond in many people's eyes.

Needing to replace George Lazenby, producers Cubby Broccoli and Harry Saltzman considered a range of actors (including a certain Timothy Dalton, who felt he was too young) before casting John Gavin, who had appeared in *Psycho* and *Spartacus*. They had signed a deal with Gavin by the time they learned that David Picker, Head of United Artists, had already signed up Sean Connery to return. Connery had brokered a mega deal for this unexpected comeback, plus an agreement in which United Artists back two further films of his choosing, which he could star in or direct.

Diamonds Are Forever is a film with an unusual mix of flavours. Britain in the early 1970s is typified by the Triumph Stag which Bond purloins from diamond smuggler Peter Franks at Dover – ambitious but a bit rubbish. Its glamorous styling was the work of Italian designer Michelotti but, as Triumph was now subsumed within British Leyland, its 3.0-litre V8 was poorly – and rather cheaply – engineered. This own goal was compounded by the fact that Triumph could have used the 3.5-litre V8 that was available elsewhere in the group and by now well-proven. The Stag stole defeat from the jaws of victory via warped cylinder heads, defective timing chains, truculent main bearings, and useless water pumps. But apart from that it was great.

The car used in *Diamonds Are Forever* was a pre-production unit and would certainly have done time as a press demonstrator. The registration plate RVC 435H confirms this status, because a little detective work proves that other Triumphs with this prefix appeared in *Straw Dogs* (as Dustin Hoffman's transport) and in episodes of such quintessentially Seventies British television fare as *The Sweeney* and *The Professionals*. Few cars are quite so redolent of the era.

It's also worth noting that the Franks / 007 Stag sounds like another car altogether, and doesn't emit the expected V8 rumble. Alongside the background cars that feature around it – variously a Commer van, an Austin 1300 Countryman, and a Wolseley 6/110, as well as the Renaults 10 and 16 plus a beautiful Fiat 124 coupé that's just visible – the Triumph Stag still cut a distinctly rakish dash when it first appeared

Opposite: A rarely seen letter to associate producer Stanley Sopel from the man who brokered the loan of Ford vehicles to the film. It seems he's not entirely happy… Below: Bond and Miss Moneypenny as 007 prepares to travel to Amsterdam; Tiffany Case in her Ford Mustang Mach 1; Bond attempts to avoid his own funeral.

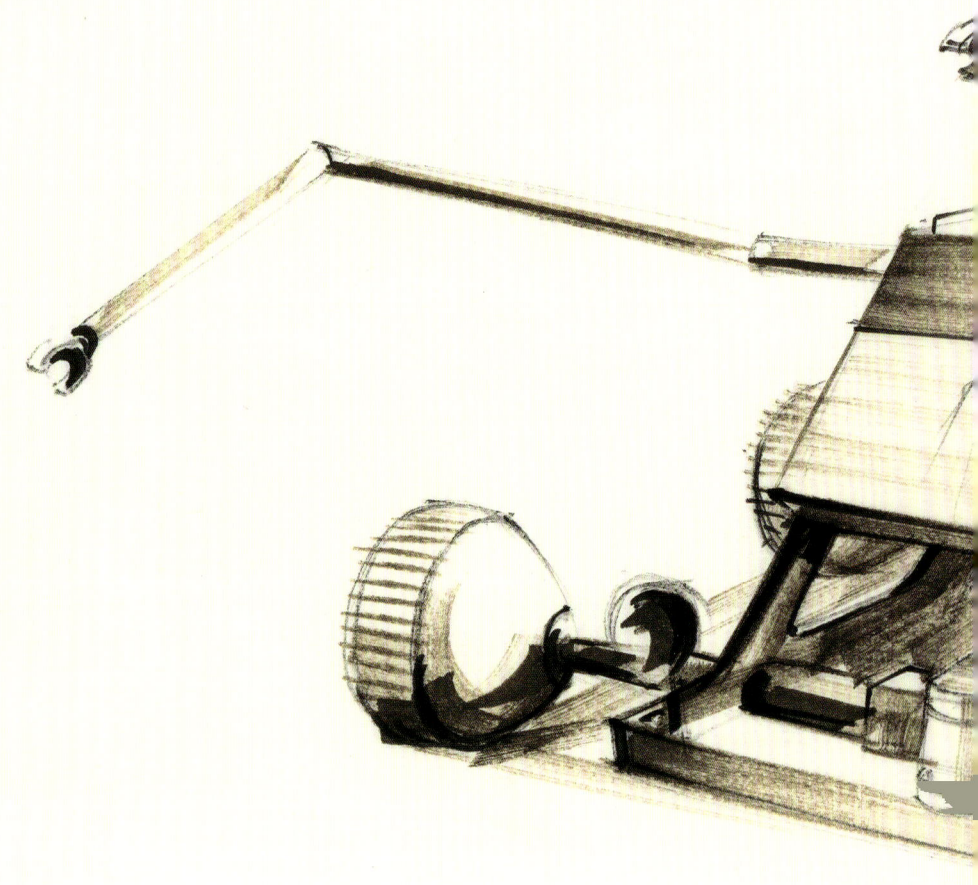

DIAMONDS FOR EVER "LUNAR VEHICLE"

The original concept art for the moon buggy – 'lunar vehicle' – as envisaged by Bond production designer Ken Adam.

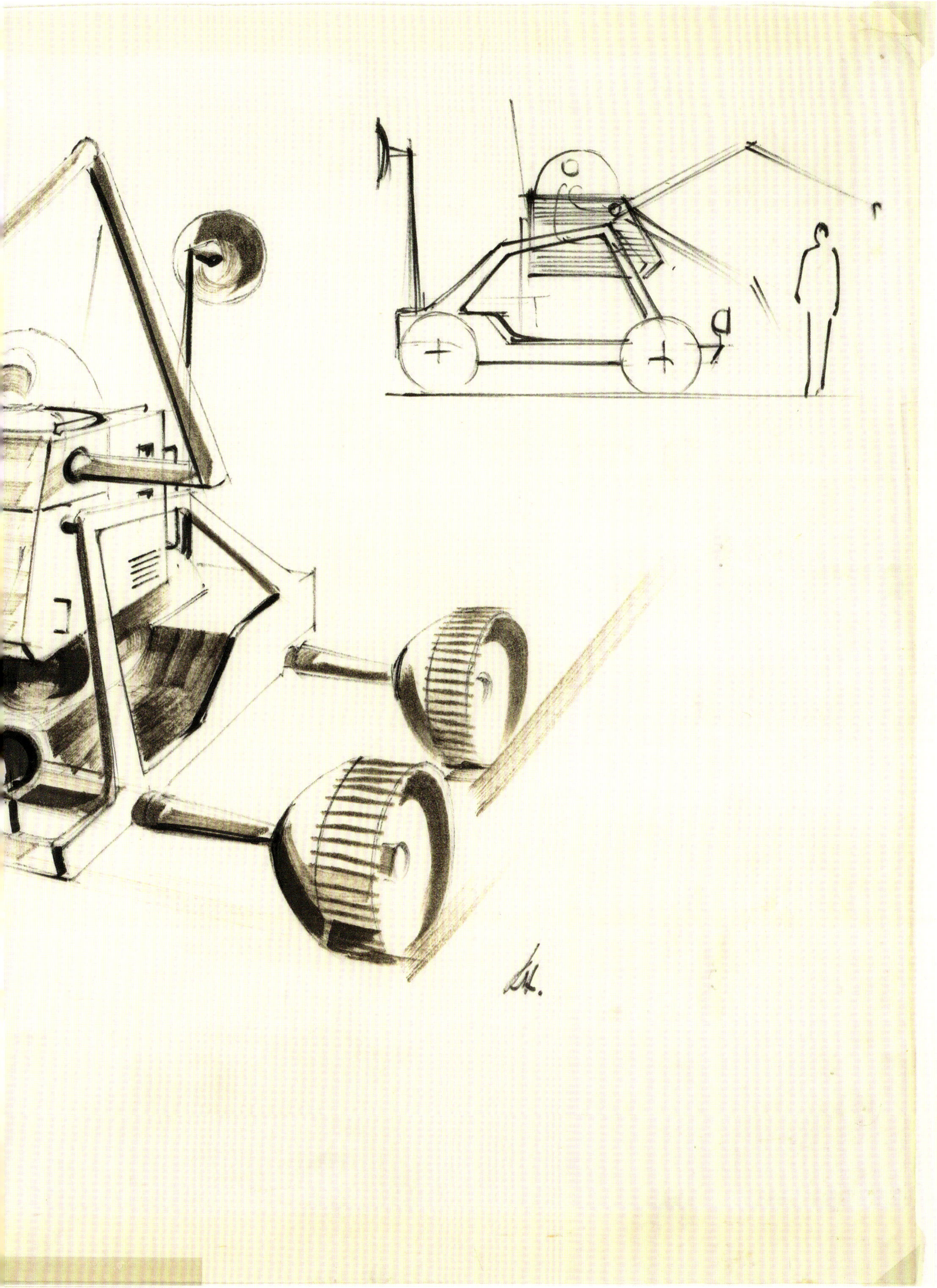

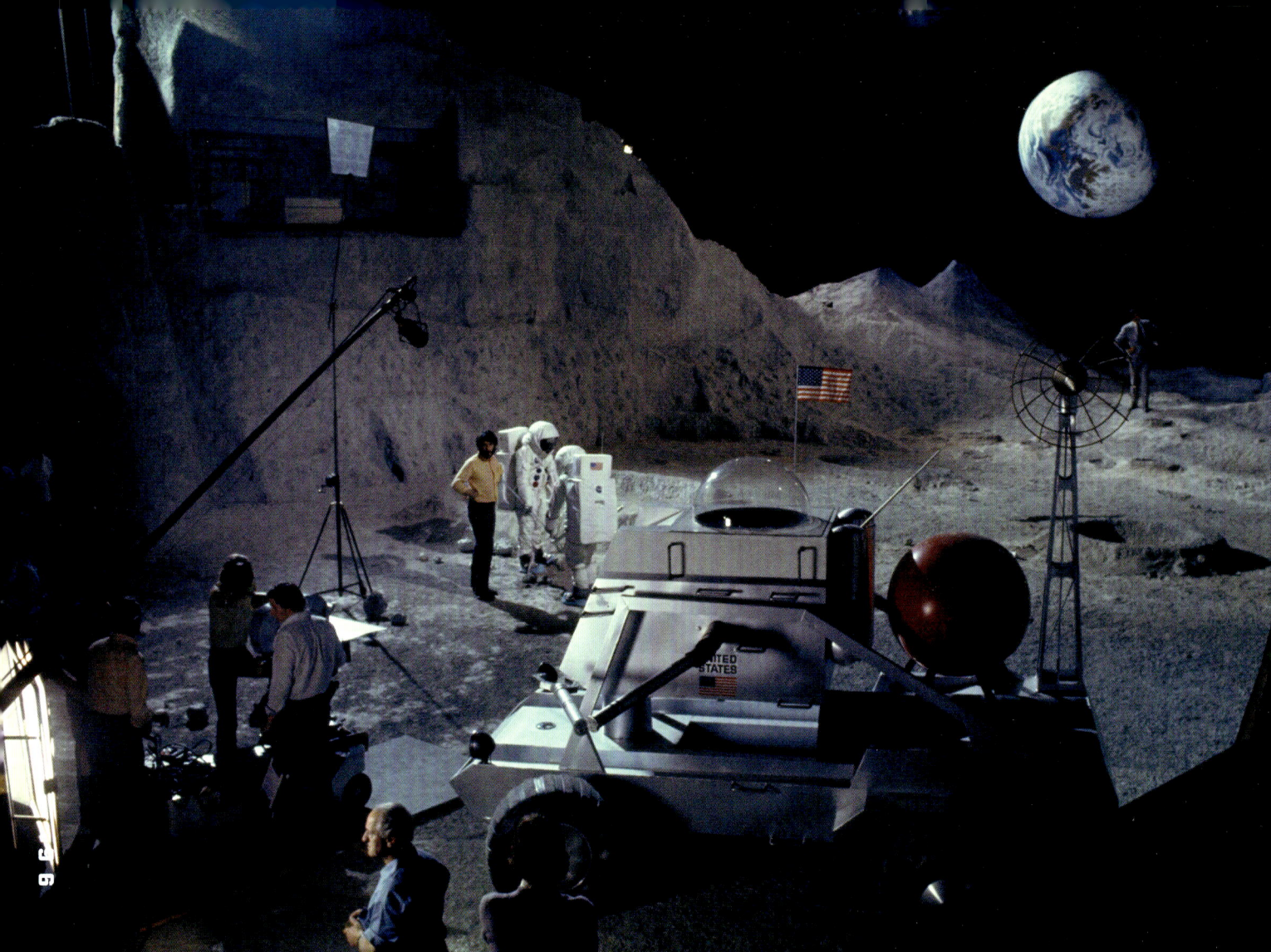

Above: On set during filming. The moon buggy's escape was shot in early May 1971.

in 1970, and it's easy to see why. Vegas, via Amsterdam, or bust.

Cubby Broccoli had dreamt of Howard Hughes one night, a nocturnal inspiration that fed into *Diamonds Are Forever*'s Willard Whyte character. But Broccoli also knew Hughes personally, a connection that worked wonders when it came to shooting the film in Vegas. 'We got VIP treatment,' Ken Adam recalled. 'We never had to pay a hotel bill, and when it became difficult to get permission to shoot somewhere, Cubby used to phone Howard's associate at the penthouse, and we got permission within seconds.'

Ford had a long association with EON, but in *Diamonds Are Forever* its cars enjoyed a higher-than-ever profile. The red Ford Mustang Mach 1 owned by Tiffany Case (Jill St. John) is right up there in the pantheon of Bond cars, and was probably responsible for more kids power-sliding their model cars into skirting boards worldwide than anything else for years. Had any of us ever seen a car on two wheels before? Guy Hamilton, back in the director's chair, recalled watching French driving wizard Rémy Julienne on a BBC programme. 'I saw Rémy pop a car up on two wheels and drive around an airfield. I thought, "That's sensational. That's got to be for Bond."'

The identity of the actual cars used is somewhat hazy: the 'hero' car was a Mach 1 fitted with the juiciest engine, the 429 cu in 7.0-litre V8, with several other smaller 351 cu in (5.8-litre V8) cars used for the stunt scenes. The driving was done by an American outfit called Tournament of Thrills, led by a gentleman called Buzz Bundy. They reworked some of their signature moves – the 'dive bomber crash', reverse J-turns, the ramp to ramp jump, and the 'Hi-Skis' (on two wheels) – into the Bond scene.

Of course, the two-wheeled alleyway sequence will live on unto eternity not just because it's so cool, but also because it features an

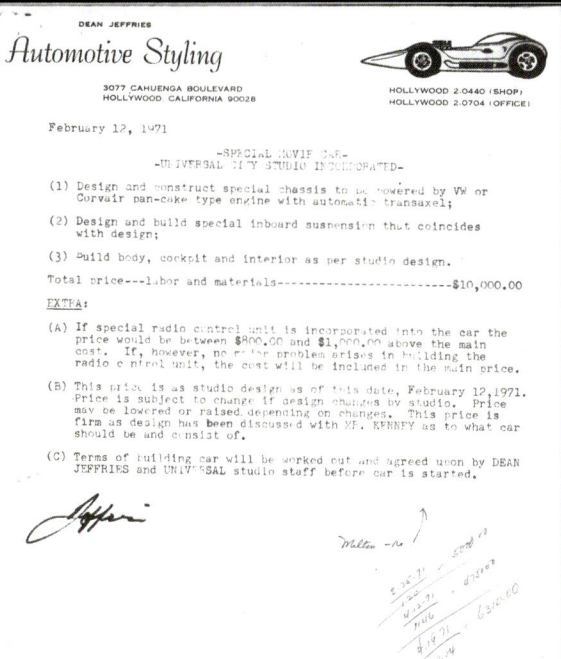

almighty continuity blooper. In Vegas, Hamilton was unhappy with the alleyway exit, and the scenes were re-done as pick-up shots in Universal City studios' backlot from 9 June onwards. It's partly because the car looked a little wobbly, but also because a crowd of onlookers had gathered in the background (indeed, a crowd is visible in Fremont Street, too). Julienne and his crew completed the sequence – exiting on the opposite two wheels to the ones on which the car entered. That alleyway must have been bigger than we thought.

Other Fords in the film include Bert Saxby's Club Wagon (wearing two different front registration plates), a variety of Ford Custom 500 sedans that have neither the robustness nor ground clearance to pursue Bond during his moon buggy getaway (although Bond is seen

Rarely seen correspondence (top left) documenting the moon buggy's specification, and the agreement with Dean Jeffries, a well-known car customiser in Hollywood; (top right) its status as a vehicle versus prop is the subject of considerable debate with the British authorities. Above: Bert Saxby's Ford Club Wagon.

earlier in the film in a Custom 500 rental), a Galaxie 500, a '61 Thunderbird, a Pinto, a Falcon Ranchero and a vast, pillowy soft Thunderbird Landau as used by the assassins Mr Kidd and Mr Wint (Putter Smith and Bruce Glover: Smith was a jazz musician who'd played in Thelonious Monk's band,

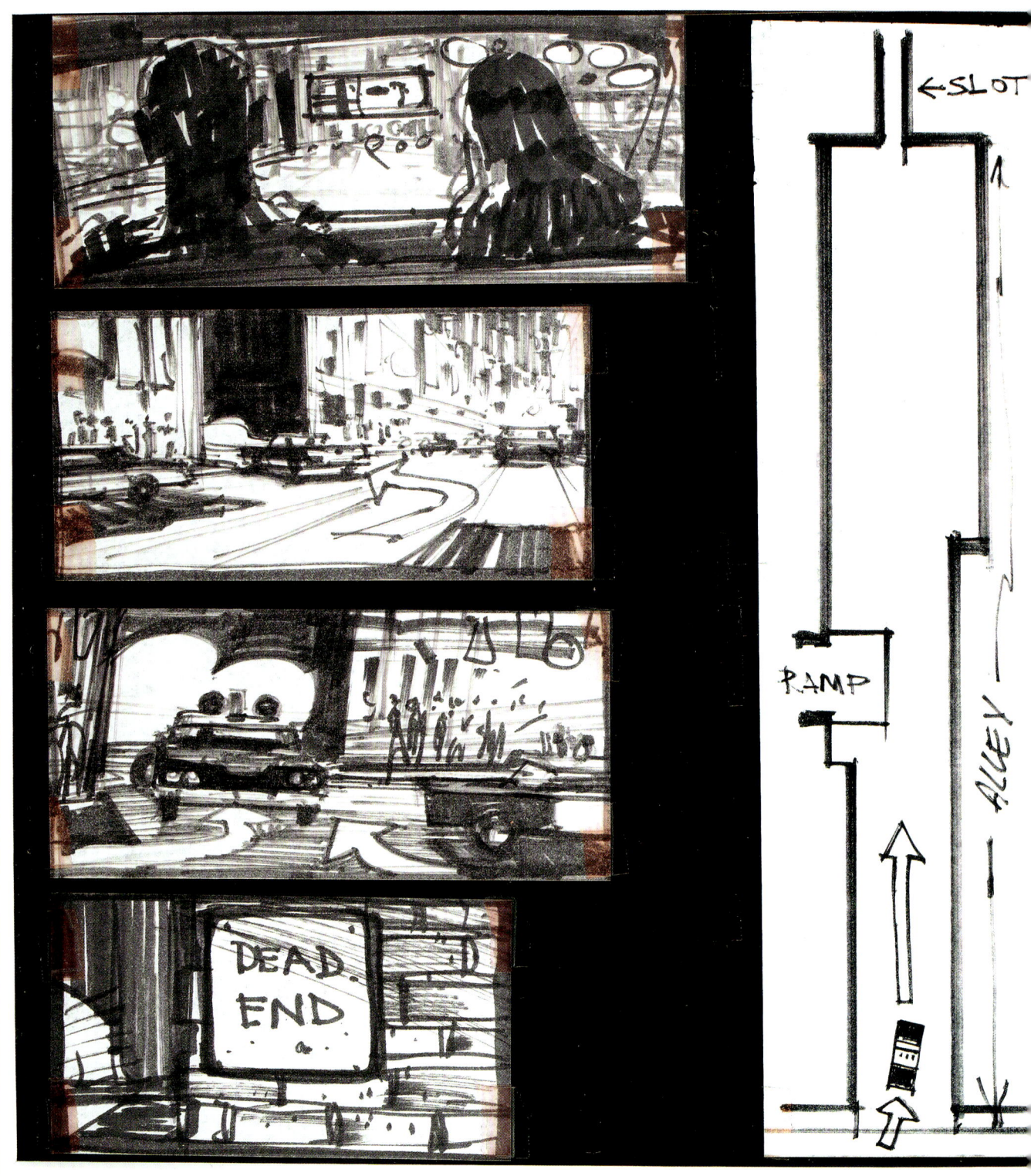

The original storyboard for one of the most celebrated car chases in movie history. James Bond, Las Vegas and Ford Mustang Mach 1.

while Glover's son, Crispin, would play George McFly in 1985's *Back to the Future*). By this point, the T-bird had rather lost its way, as often happened when Ford executives grappled with evolving their product range. 'One gets the impression that the T-bird is about to move off in a new direction,' *Motor Trend* magazine drily observed, 'and hasn't yet made up its mind as to the intended path.' It also noted the car's 'Cave of Love cockpit, with button-tufted brocade cloth upholstery', well-matched to the film's flamboyant hitmen.

The 1970s would not be kind to the US car industry – the 1973 energy crisis was ruinous to its gas-guzzling land yachts – and the Thunderbird Landau was proof that, when trouble struck, Detroit would be inadequately prepared to deal with it. As was Ford when it came to the machinations of movie-making. Elsewhere in this chapter is a reprint of a letter sent by the company's retained product promotion man, Walt Taylor, to Bond's associate producer, Stanley Sopel. If nothing else, it demonstrates what a difference half a century makes when it comes to deal-making. Having noted that the producers had returned the cars loaned, Taylor continues: 'Twelve [of the vehicles] were so severely damaged as to preclude their being repaired for service and had to be sold as wrecks for parts salvage … we are requesting payment in the amount of $20,000 to reimburse Ford Marketing Corporation for the loss sustained in the sale of these vehicles.'

Riffing off the notion that the moon landings were faked – seven years before the conspiracy thriller *Capricorn One* did the same, only with Mars – Bond inexplicably stumbles on a movie set inside Whyte's Techtronics Space Centre. He escapes by stealing a moon buggy, originally envisioned by Ken Adam who was keen to anthropomorphise it by adding flailing arms. Its structure used a welded tubular steel frame with aluminum panels, and it had a working cockpit covered with a Plexiglas dome.

Although not up there with the Aston Martin DB5 or submersible Lotus Esprit in the pantheon of Bond vehicles, the moon buggy is still much loved. It was created by Dean Jeffries Automotive Styling workshop; Jeffries was a sometime racing driver who drifted into the burgeoning Californian custom car scene. In particular, he was known for 'pinstriping' and had the honour of inscribing James Dean's nickname for his beloved Porsche 550 Spyder – Little Bastard – on the rear of the car. He also created the Monkeemobile and fabricated the Green Hornet's Chrysler Imperial (Black Beauty), before being commissioned to make the *Diamonds Are Forever* moon buggy.

The sequence was shot at Johns Manville Gypsum Plant between 1 and 4 May 1971, and the buggy was originally meant to have broken out and driven off up a service road. Instead, Guy Hamilton decided to take it off-roading. It was never designed for that, and wheels kept breaking (one can even be seen bouncing back into shot); fitting it with balloon tyres helped. Following star billing in a worldwide promotional tour, the buggy fell into disrepair, was discovered in a field in Kent, and restored by a private collector. In December 2004, Planet Hollywood's owner Robert Earl paid £23,000 for it in a Christie's auction; in September 2019's *The Icons & Legends of Hollywood* auction – whose other lots included the coat worn by Orson Welles as Charles Foster Kane in *Citizen Kane*, Harry Potter's spectacles, and Tom Skerritt's Dallas space-suit from *Alien* – the buggy sold for $512,000.

At the time of writing, an original boxed Corgi toy version of the moon buggy is on eBay for £450. Clearly, it's not just diamonds that are forever.

The Vegas Mustang car chase was the work of an American outfit called Tournament of Thrills, later completed by Bond regular Rémy Julienne in the Universal City studios' backlot.

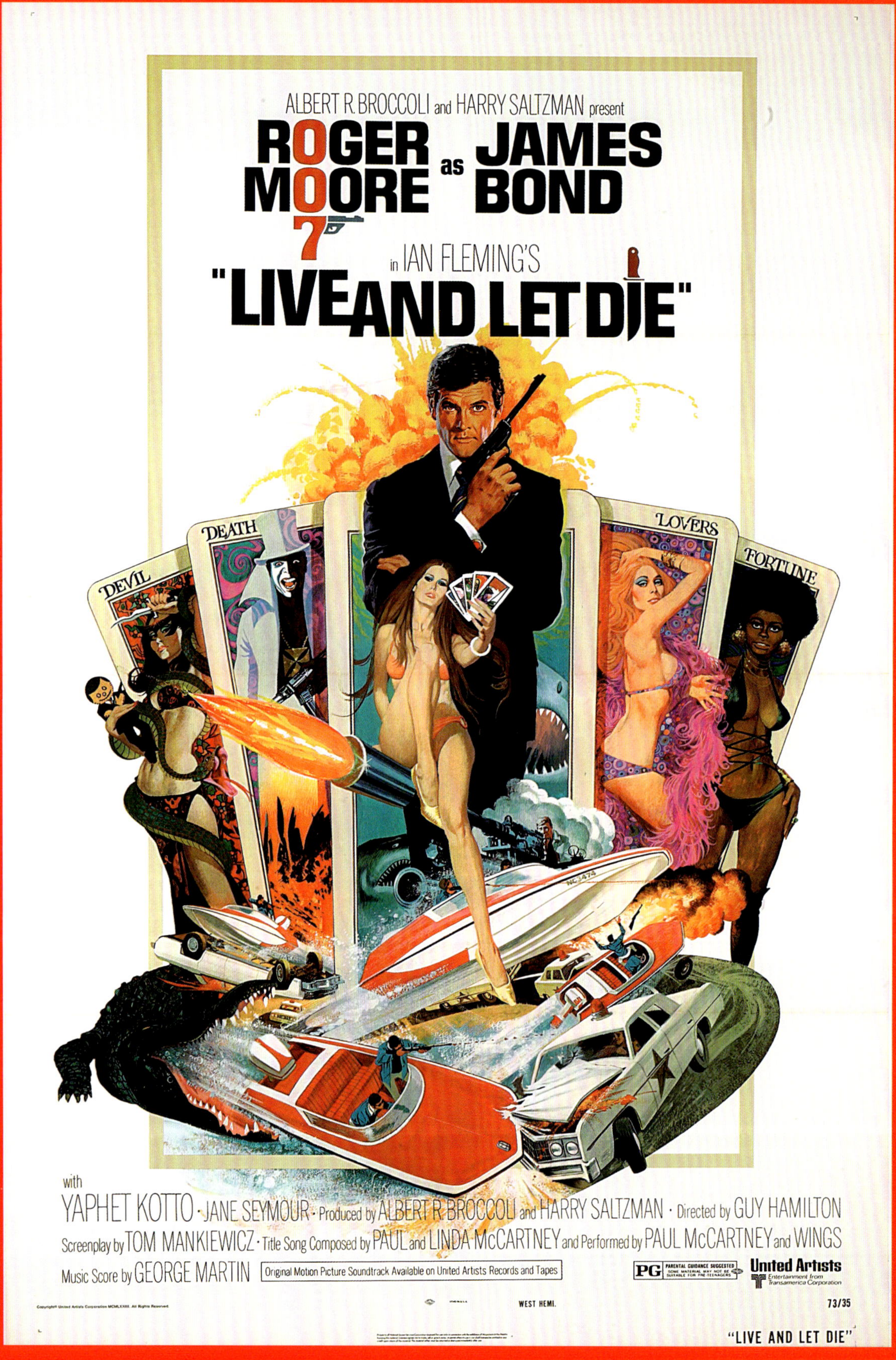

ALBERT R. BROCCOLI and HARRY SALTZMAN present
ROGER MOORE as JAMES BOND
007
in IAN FLEMING'S
"LIVE AND LET DIE"
DEVIL
DEATH
LOVERS
FORTUNE
with
YAPHET KOTTO · JANE SEYMOUR · Produced by ALBERT R. BROCCOLI and HARRY SALTZMAN · Directed by GUY HAMILTON
Screenplay by TOM MANKIEWICZ · Title Song Composed by PAUL and LINDA McCARTNEY and Performed by PAUL McCARTNEY and WINGS
Music Score by GEORGE MARTIN
Original Motion Picture Soundtrack Available on United Artists Records and Tapes
PG PARENTAL GUIDANCE SUGGESTED SOME MATERIAL MAY NOT BE SUITABLE FOR PRE-TEENAGERS
United Artists
Entertainment from Transamerica Corporation
WEST HEMI.
73/35
"LIVE AND LET DIE"

US one sheet from
June 1973, with artwork
by Robert McGinnis.

CHAPTER 08

LIVE AND LET DIE

1973

STARRING Roger Moore as James Bond

'What are you? Some kind of doomsday machine?'
SHERIFF JW PEPPER

How we view and appreciate a film changes over time, but even so this 1973 film is a compellingly leftfield outing for 007. Writer Tom Mankiewicz was drawn to Ian Fleming's second Bond novel, in which 007 is despatched first to New York and then to Florida on the trail of a French-Haitian SMERSH agent called Mr Big. He figured he could transpose some of its themes and characterisation to the early 1970s, finding a contemporary resonance in the Black Power movement. 'I thought it would be wonderful to have a Bond with black villains and in a black culture of some kind,' Mankiewicz explained. (He knew it meant walking a fine line, so added the idiot Southern sheriff for some balanced comic relief.)

Nonetheless, *Live And Let Die* became the Bond film which tapped into the Blaxploitation sub-genre, that struts and swaggers like John Shaft, and looks and feels unlike any of the previous films. Then it stirs in a swampy Bayou gumbo and trifles with voodoo for good measure. You could view it through a Tarantino-esque filter, and marvel at the sheer incongruity of a British secret agent in Harlem (a new Bond, at that, although Roger Moore's laconic wit and arched eyebrows add a welcome knowingness), or just enjoy it for what it is – an unexpectedly vibrant pop-cultural time capsule.

But there was serious intent here, too. As well as the likes of *Shaft*, *Superfly* and the groundbreaking *Across 110th Street* (which starred the terrific Yaphet Kotto, who would play corrupt politician / drug-smuggling kingpin Dr Kananga / Mr Big in the new Bond movie), films such as *The French Connection* and *Serpico* had a crunch and grit to them that threatened to render Bond superfluous. As daft as it sounds, for *Live And Let Die*, 007 had to get real.

Like *Diamonds Are Forever*, this is a mostly American odyssey. It's also a curious one for car fans, primarily because the film's action centrepiece chase uses speedboats rather than cars (to truly brilliant effect). There's also no hero vehicle, unless you count the Mini Moke Bond uses briefly or the AEC Regent bus that he decapitates. And a production deal with Chevrolet means there's an ocean of corpulent Yank tanks, none of which history has been kind to, although their presence reinforces the gritty Seventies milieu.

That's not to say there isn't a gadget car – it's just that Bond is on

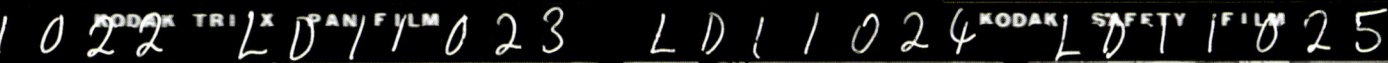

'Hey man, that's fly... not only is that fly, it's superfly!'

the receiving end this time. When his driver is slain as they head up the Westside Highway by a poison dart fired out of the door mirror of a passing car (they crash into a Ford Econoline van), identifying said vehicle isn't an especially tricky task: 'Get me a make on a white Pimpmobile!' Felix Leiter barks.

He's not wrong. The villains here don't go a bundle on subtlety. Mr Big's henchman, Whisper, drives a device called the Corvorado, a mainstay of a peculiar Seventies automotive subculture that took the idea of customisation in a crazy new direction. King of this scene was New Jersey-based Les Dunham, whose company Dunham Coach was pimping rides long before Xzibit's MTV show rocked up. Twenties-inspired Gatsby-esque flamboyance was married to the vast acreage of metal that characterised contemporary US luxury cars and suddenly found itself at the epicentre of early Seventies urban culture. Dunham was initially perplexed, as he recalled. 'Guys came in to my shop and said, "Hey man, that's fly... not only is that fly, it's superfly!" I says, "What the hell kind of terminology is this?"' He'd find out pretty quickly. When Gordon Parks, the director of the *Superfly* film, saw one of Dunham's creations – a 1971 Cadillac Eldorado – in New York, he persuaded its owner to rent it to the production (it's also prominent on the film poster). As so often happens, an underground fad swiftly went overground. *Superfly* grossed $30m off a budget of $500k, and the incomparable Curtis Mayfield scored two million-selling singles and a huge hit album with the soundtrack.

Whisper's Corvorado, Dunham noted, was 'a combo car. Not everyone wanted a big car, so I figured I'd build my own Eldorado, but I'll make a small one. So I cut down an Eldorado and dropped it on a Corvette [C3]. Corvorado!'

Marginally less eye-popping, though still scarcely flying under the radar, was Mr Big's Cadillac Fleetwood 60 Special Brougham – a tenth-generation car also given the light touch by Dunham Coach (Texas-registered, curiously). Cadillac is the American car brand that has surely notched up more appearances in films and television than any other: its post-war path delineates the rise of the baby boomer and the vaulting ambition

Left: Rarely seen contact sheet from the scene in Mr Big's Harlem garage. Bond finds refuge beside Whisper's Corvorado. Above right: An elaborate camera rig.

Right: Roger Moore looking relaxed in front of a typically offbeat example of 007 parking, Lakefront Airport, New Orleans. Opposite: A rarely seen storyboard for the double decker bus chase.

of America's car designers when they were high on jet-era inspiration (check out the fins), to peak during the *Mad Men* period. When Donald Draper buys a '62 Coupé de Ville in Season 2 of the television series, the salesman asks him what he's currently driving. 'A Dodge,' he replies. 'Those are wonderful if you want to get somewhere, this is for when you've already arrived'.

By the time *Live And Let Die* was released, Cadillac was still a major signifier of upward mobility (before anyone called it that), and thus perfect for pimps, hustlers and anyone else on the make who wanted everyone else to know they'd made it. Mr Big's car is pictured outside the Fillet of Soul restaurant (a modest front for the operation's money laundering), and has a baroque majesty perfect for this particular villain. Bond calls it a 'jukebox', which is an accurate enough description. By now, these behemoths were running 472 cu in (7.7-litre) or 500 cu in (8.2-litre) V8 engines, but hauling 2.3 tonnes of metal around meant that performance was still at a premium. The Brougham appellation added a certain formality in the form of a padded roof, the Dunham makeover running to whitewall tyres, fake motifs in the C-pillars, quasi-heraldic door handles, and chrome accents. Parked in front of it outside the restaurant is a Cadillac Fleetwood Eldorado, another Dunham Coach job.

The rest of *Live And Let Die*'s automotive cast is predominantly Chevrolet. Bond gets to enjoy the overly soft suspension in a Bel Air when he arrives in New York. His doomed driver, Charlie, was played by Joie Chitwood Jr, who set a world record for driving on two wheels (5.6 miles) as part of the Joie Chitwood Thrill Show. This was an outfit set up by his father, Joie Chitwood, a former racing driver (he entered the Indianapolis 500 seven times, scoring three top five finishes), which at its peak had up to five separate teams performing across the USA, and ran for 40-odd years.

The Chevrolet Impala makes a decent on-screen impact, on either side of the law. CIA agent Harold Strutter intercepts 007 – 'A white face in Harlem? Good thinking, Bond' – in a not inelegant 1973 Impala Sport Coupé, complete with a disguised radio receiver that gives rise to the immortal line, 'a genuine Felix "lighter"...' Mr Big's minion, Adam, outwits Sheriff JW Pepper in an Impala Custom Coupé. Pepper himself sees his Impala patrol car destroyed by a flying speedboat. Bond and Solitaire, meanwhile, use a lovely '64 Impala Convertible on the (fictional) Carribean island of San Monique (home to Mr Big's poppy fields). During the airport chase, Bond is assailed by a '73 Chevelle Malibu and a C-10 pick-up. And the clueless

Roger Moore finds an unusual vantage point during filming, Hampton Wharf Jetty, Falmouth, Jamaica, Sunday 10 December 1972.

Clifton James (right) played heroically hapless lawman Sheriff JW Pepper.

Above: During October 1972, the Bond crew created perfectly orchestrated mayhem in the Phoenix, Louisiana area.
Opposite: Rarely seen contact sheet with actors Julius W Harris, Tommy Lane, Roger Moore and Jane Seymour on set.

state police smash up a load of red and white Bel Air saloons (driving their Chevys to the levee, no less). There's also a smattering of Plymouth Furys, cops in Chevy Novas, a Nova Coupé (the bronze car that ends up parked on the wing of a light aircraft), a Lincoln Continental Mk IV (Dunham coached), a '62 Cadillac Sedan DeVille, a Chevy Caprice estate, a police Ford Galaxie, a Rambler Marlin, and blink-and-you-miss it cameos from a Datsun 411 and a Toyota Corolla.

And what of Bond's spell as a bus driver? This famous sequence was filmed on days 38, 39 and 40 of principal photography. Over to Roger Moore himself to pick up the story: 'I remember that day well: it was 7 December 1972, on location in Montego Bay, Jamaica, and I had to drive it under a low bridge, sheering off the top deck. Maurice Patchett from London Transport's Chiswick depot had spent three months preparing for the stunt, including taking me on a crash course on the Chiswick skid pad. The first time you do it, they feel as though they're going to tip over. But they don't tip over. Maurice took over the driving as the bus headed for the bridge; the top deck had been carefully removed and replaced only on rollers, to ensure a relatively clean detachment as it hit at precisely 30 mph.

'Maurice said that if the film game didn't work out for me, I'd make a good London bus man. That would have pleased my mum, who still lived in hope that I might one day get a proper job.'

A US one sheet dating from
December 1974, with artwork
by Robert McGinnis.

CHAPTER 09

THE MAN WITH THE GOLDEN GUN

1974

STARRING Roger Moore as James Bond

Significantly, *The Man With The Golden Gun* (1974) was the last Bond film to be jointly produced by Cubby Broccoli and Harry Saltzman. It sure has its moments. In fact, one of them could lay claim to being the single greatest stunt ever performed in the series, the peak of a car chase that had already pushed the envelope by taking place in rush-hour Bangkok. It culminated in a jump over the Khlong Rangsit canal that many people still believe to this day was somehow faked. Even those who watched it unfold with their own eyes.

But the 360-degree 'astro spiral' stunt was for real, and even benefited from an early form of computer modelling by way of preparation. That said, it was another example of a Bond car stunt whose roots lay in America's insatiable post-war hunger for an automotive carnival. Joie Chitwood, who'd played Charlie in *Live And Let Die* and was the scion of automotive stunt-driving royalty himself, tipped director Guy Hamilton off about a corkscrew jump he'd seen being performed by the American Thrill Show, staged by a company called JM Productions. (The stunt was first performed at the Houston Astrodome on 14 January 1972.)

'The exercise is quite complicated,' Hamilton noted, 'because the car has to be perfectly balanced, with the driver and the steering wheel in the middle. As it goes along, there's a curve on the ramp that causes the initial spin. The receiving end isn't flat either. The car must do exactly 40mph – there are two tachometers on board to check this – and you need a very long run-up.'

The JM of JM Productions was a gentleman called Jay Milligan. 'I was sitting in a hotel in Harrisburg, PA, with a competitor of mine who had also done stunt work for Bond,' he recalled, presumably alluding to Chitwood. 'I had a phone call, and the fellow on the other end of the line said, "This is Cubby Broccoli in London, are

Top left and right: Roger Moore faces off against Christopher Lee. Opposite: A rarely seen 'vehicle condition report' showing extreme damage to the right rear of the car.

JM PRODUCTIONS, INC.
VEHICLE CONDITION REPORT

Date July 2

Car no. 3 (three)   Serial no. A4C037N317301
Mileage 44   Model 7403-7   Color (original) D7
AMC invoice no. 1206   Copy attached: Yes X   No

GENERAL

Vehicle condition: Excellent_____ Fair_____ Poor ✓
Damages (if any): EXTREME DAMAGE R. REAR OF CAR
ANTENNAE + WHEEL RINGS IN TRUNK

SPECIFIC CONDITION DAMAGE REPORT (Indicate exact area)

Left side: O.K.

Right side: COMPLETE R.R. QUARTER PANEL

Rear: TRUNK - TAIL LITE ASSY - ROCK GAURD. LOWER TRUNK PANEL

Interior: O.K.

Suspension: O.K. ?? QUESTIONABLE R.R. AREA

Tires: O.K.

Drilled holes: NONE

Paint: O.K. EXCEPT R.R. AREA

Trim: "   "   "   "

Major damage (if any): Right REAR - Very Obvious

Items missing on acceptance: NONE

Present missing items: NONE

Key no._____ Ignition K842   Trunk L987

I agree this report describes the condition of the above vehicle. No
other damage is visible or evident.

JM PRODUCTIONS, INC.   EON PRODUCTIONS LTD.   KWANG THAI AMC DEALER

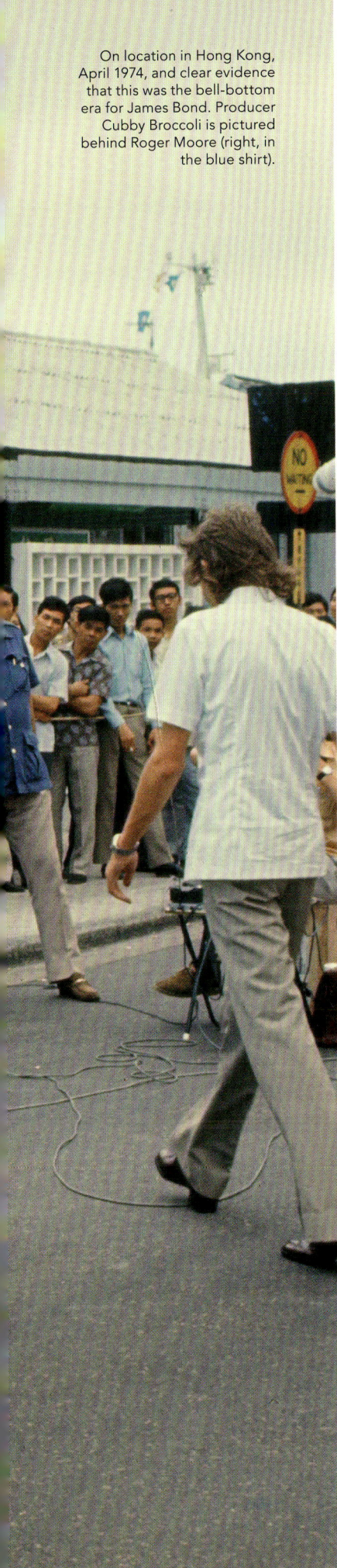

On location in Hong Kong, April 1974, and clear evidence that this was the bell-bottom era for James Bond. Producer Cubby Broccoli is pictured behind Roger Moore (right, in the blue shirt).

Top: Lieutenant Hip (Soon-Tek Oh) waits for Bond outside Hai Fat's estate. Above: A Datsun Cherry 100A in Bangkok, one of many cars that enlivened this memorable sequence in *The Man With The Golden Gun*.

you the chap who designed or did the car stunt in the Houston Astrodome?" My competitor said he was preparing to go to Singapore to do a Bond film, so I had to excuse myself from our breakfast meeting and get back to Cubby Broccoli...'

Says Bond producer Michael G. Wilson, 'We thought it was an interesting stunt, but we weren't quite sure how to use it in a film.'

They figured it out, using a combination of empirical measurement and gigantic chutzpah. Far from the nation's sports stadiums, researchers at Cornell University in upstate New York had been using computers to run simulations for the National Highway Safety Bureau, in particular to ascertain the manner in which a car reacted to irregularities in the road surface. An organisation called the Calspan Corporation, which had grown out of the R&D division of the Curtis-Wright Airplane company, was also involved.

'When a car goes over a bump at the same speed, it always reacts the same way,' Milligan remembered in a 2009 interview. 'Calspan… got federal money to investigate the repetition of cars rolling over,

and we hired them to use some of their mathematical equations.' In fact, one of Calspan's employees, Raymond McHenry, had filed a patent on the apparatus needed to perform a spiral jump, perhaps with an eye on the burgeoning early 1970s toy market, which was in thrall to Evel Knievel and Hot Wheels toy race tracks at the time. Little did he know where his thinking was going to lead.

JM Productions used an AMC Javelin SST in its performances, which is how the Bond producers ended up collaborating with the company; 007 borrows a Hornet from AMC's Bangkok dealer when it turns out that the kidnapped Mary Goodnight (Britt Ekland) has the keys to the Mercedes they've been using. AMC was a relative minnow compared to Detroit's Big Three, and was formed in 1954 when the Nash-Kelvinator Corporation and the Hudson Motor Car Company merged. (Packard and Studebaker were all subsumed within the group, and Jeep would later become part of it, too.)

The first Vice President was future governor of Michigan George Romney (father of 2012 White House hopeful Senator Mitt Romney), and well-regarded designer Dick Teague helped formulate a range of cars that at least served as an alternative – and also introduced the American consumer to the idea of a 'compact car' before the 1973 oil crisis made it a fait accompli: total car sales in the USA dropped from 9.7m in 1973 to less than 7.5m in 1974. (Indeed, the early 1970s energy crisis is one of the narrative hooks in *The Man With The Golden Gun*, along with less political riffs on the contemporary obsession with kung fu.)

All in all, then, the Hornet wasn't quite the joke car some made it out to be, even if the presence of Sheriff JW Pepper in the showroom during his Thai sojourn is a bit of a stretch. ('Who are you after this time boy – commies?') It was also heavily modified for filming duty. As the indefatigable Peter Lamont explained, 'The car was cut in half and widened by two inches, and everything was centralised. We found a stunt driver, Lauren "Bumps" Willert. I sat for many hours with Cubby and we discussed about what would happen if the car failed, if the take-off ramp broke...' As well as a wider front and rear track, the suspension was reinforced, the tyres were running 60psi, and there was a rollcage. The computer modelling prescribed a car weighing 1,460kg, with a 15.86m gap between the ramps, and a take-off speed of 64km/h.

Mary Goodnight is seen in Hong Kong driving an MGB, about which Bond is rather rude

Opposite: Roger Moore and Cubby Broccoli outside the AMC showroom in Bangkok, June 1974. Opposite below: Actor Hervé Villechaize, who played Scaramanga's sidekick, Nick Nack.

Christopher Lee played Bond's dark alter ego Francisco Scaramanga in the film. As well as being Ian Fleming's step-cousin, he'd also served in the wartime intelligence services himself. 'When people asked me if I'd done this, that or the other during the war, I'd say, "Can you keep a secret?" "Yes, yes!" "Well, so can I…"' Lee was among the many who watched the spiral jump being performed, with what sounds like a genuine degree of trepidation. 'I'd never seen such a mass of lifting equipment, and some very worried people, too. There were divers in the water with a cable; we could have had the car and driver out of the water quicker than just going after the driver. He was sitting in the middle, completely blacked out, with two dummies either side. Then we heard "Action!" and everyone was rather white-knuckled.'

'Roger Moore came up to the driver with tears in his eyes. "You fellas made me look good," he said'

The film's signature stunt was performed on 1 June 1974, day 35 of principal photography. With Guy Hamilton running up to eight cameras, the astro jump went entirely to plan. 'There was a roar of applause,' Christopher Lee remembered, 'and relief, I would think. It was done in one take. Unbelievable. I still have a great and vivid memory of Roger Moore coming up to the driver with tears in his eyes saying, "You fellas made me look good."'

Too good, perhaps. Guy Hamilton was contemplating another run, as film directors are wont to do. 'It looked too perfect, people were saying, "What were you worried about?"' Lee recalled. 'And I remember [Guy] saying, "I wonder if we should do it again…" And I remember the answer he got from Mr Willert. "We are certainly not doing it again, not with me, because that was the first time I'd done it." I mean, he could easily have been killed. Easily. That was probably the most remarkable thing in the entire film.'

Hy Smith, United Artists' marketing supremo, had invited members of the press to watch, which seems remarkable in retrospect. 'We took about 100 press from Europe in a rented 747 to Thailand. Despite the fact that they saw the car corkscrew 360 degrees from one side of the river to the other, when the picture came out many of them said it was the most wonderful special effect they'd ever seen. Whereas immediately afterwards we clamped wings on Scaramanga's Matador Coupé, then filmed a model taking off, and everybody thought that was for real.'

The bulk of the car chase was shot the next day, the action taking place in the Phra Nakhon district against a background that includes significant Bangkok landmarks such as the Democracy Monument and the Giant Swing. Jay Milligan recalls that the AMC showroom floor had been so thoroughly polished by the building's janitors that he couldn't get much traction as the Hornet smashed through the windows and onto the main road. The chase itself and its exotic location makes this a special experience for pause-button car nerds: it's odds-on that this is the only film in history where you'll see three 1974 Toyota Crown saloons trip over each other. It's a festival of arcane Japanese automobiles: you'll see various period Datsuns – a 2000, 200C, Bluebird, Cherry, and a Sunny – several Mazdas, a Nissan Cedric and Echo, a Toyota Carina, Corolla, Corona and Hiace, a Toyopet Crown (a Mk I and a Mk II), and the briefest of

One of the most famous automotive stunts in the Bond canon was performed on 1 June 1974, the astro jump across the Khlong Rangsit canal.

```
BROCFILM LDN
RCA0818/01
NARITEL BK2708
TELEX   24351
BROCFILM ENGLAND


FOR MIKE WILSON REG BARKSHIRE

SPIRAL JUMP COMPLETED SUCCESSFULLY FIRST TIME WITH FOUR
CAMERAS AT NOON TODAY JUNE 1ST.

CUBBY




NARITEL BK2708
BROCFILM LDN


.............

9
```

June 13,
6/3/74

MWGL
action-t

Opposite: The astro jump was performed by stuntman Lauren 'Bumps' Willert, and was completed in one take, as this rarely seen telex from Cubby Broccoli to Michael G. Wilson confirms. Above: Bumps and his crew celebrate.

cameos from a lovely Celica coupé as used by Scaramanga and his sidekick Nick Nack. Various Fords pop up, a few Simcas, a rare Holden Torana, and more incongruously a handful of lovely Italian cars, including an Alfa Romeo Giulia Super, a Fiat 1500 L, 125 Special and 850 Coupé, and a Lancia Fulvia Berlina (and we also see Bond in a Fiat 132 in Beirut). The local police drive AMC Matadors – unlikely to have been the case for real – and a BMW 2500 makes a brief appearance. A chrome-free Chevrolet 210 is driven by its distracted driver into a Plymouth. And of course several significant British automotive stalwarts feature in the film's Hong Kong sequence: Mary Goodnight's little MGB, and the Rolls-Royce Silver Shadows that make up the courtesy cars at the imperious Peninsula Hotel. (These days, the Peninsula chain is the world's biggest customer for the Rolls-Royce Phantom. Its owner is Sir Michael David Kadoorie, who himself is a leading car collector.)

Specials effects supremo John Stears helped the film's other AMC, Scaramanga's Matador Coupé (in a special edition version whose trim was designed by Hollywood couturier Oleg Cassini) to transcend its basic function. In considerable style: if Bond's Hornet briefly got airborne, this one took off and stayed in flight. Well, sort of. A flying car is a very James Bond conceit, but this example had its inspiration in the real world. As *The Man With The Golden Gun* was entering pre-production, California-based inventor and

The AMC Hornet used in the film was heavily modified for stunt duty and safety.

aeronautical engineer Henry Smolinksi had replaced the cockpit of a Cessna Skymaster light aircraft with an entire Ford Pinto. The idea was simple: drive to the airport, attach the airframe to the car using high-strength self-locking pins, take off, detach at the other end, and repeat...

Based in Van Nuys, near Los Angeles, Smolinski and his friend and pilot Harold Blake formed AVE (Advanced Vehicle Engineers) and worked with a former Lockheed engineer AM Kaplan to develop the programme. Named Mizar, the concept had a projected range of 750 miles, would take off at 65mph using the Pinto's 1.6-litre engine, had an air speed of 130mph courtesy of the Cessna's 210hp engine, a maximum altitude of 12,000ft, and could come to a halt on a runway after 525ft. The car was attached to the airframe, and had 40-plus modifications in order to make it airworthy. The steering wheel operated the ailerons, and moved backwards and forwards to control the elevation. Rudder pedals were added. The suspension was reinforced, and a panel was welded underneath to improve aerodynamics. Inside, flight instruments including air speed and rate of climb gauges, an altimeter and directional gyro were introduced. LA Ford dealer Galpin Motors recognised a

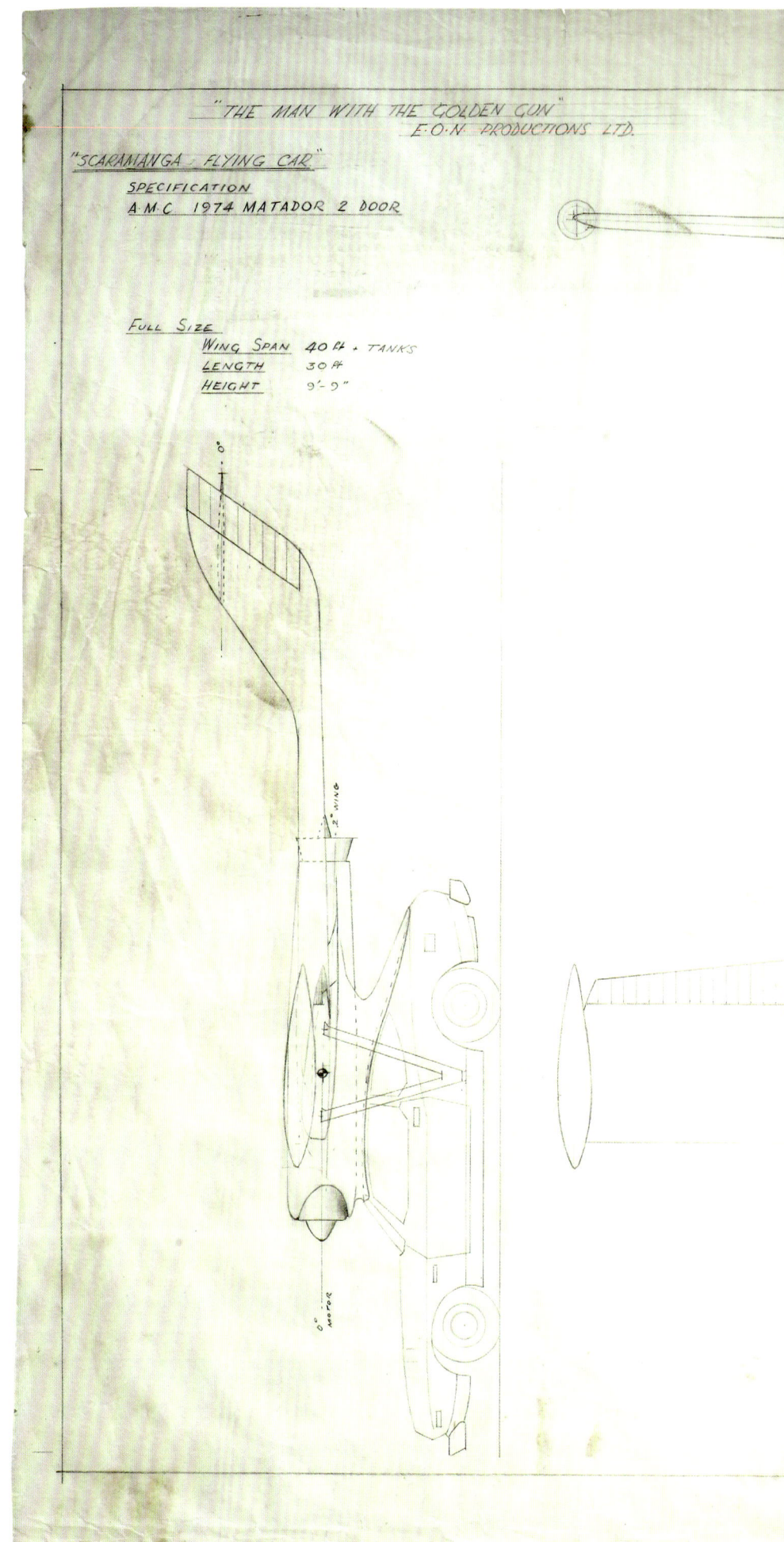

Rarely seen original technical drawings envisaging Scaramanga's flying car, based on an AMC Matador.

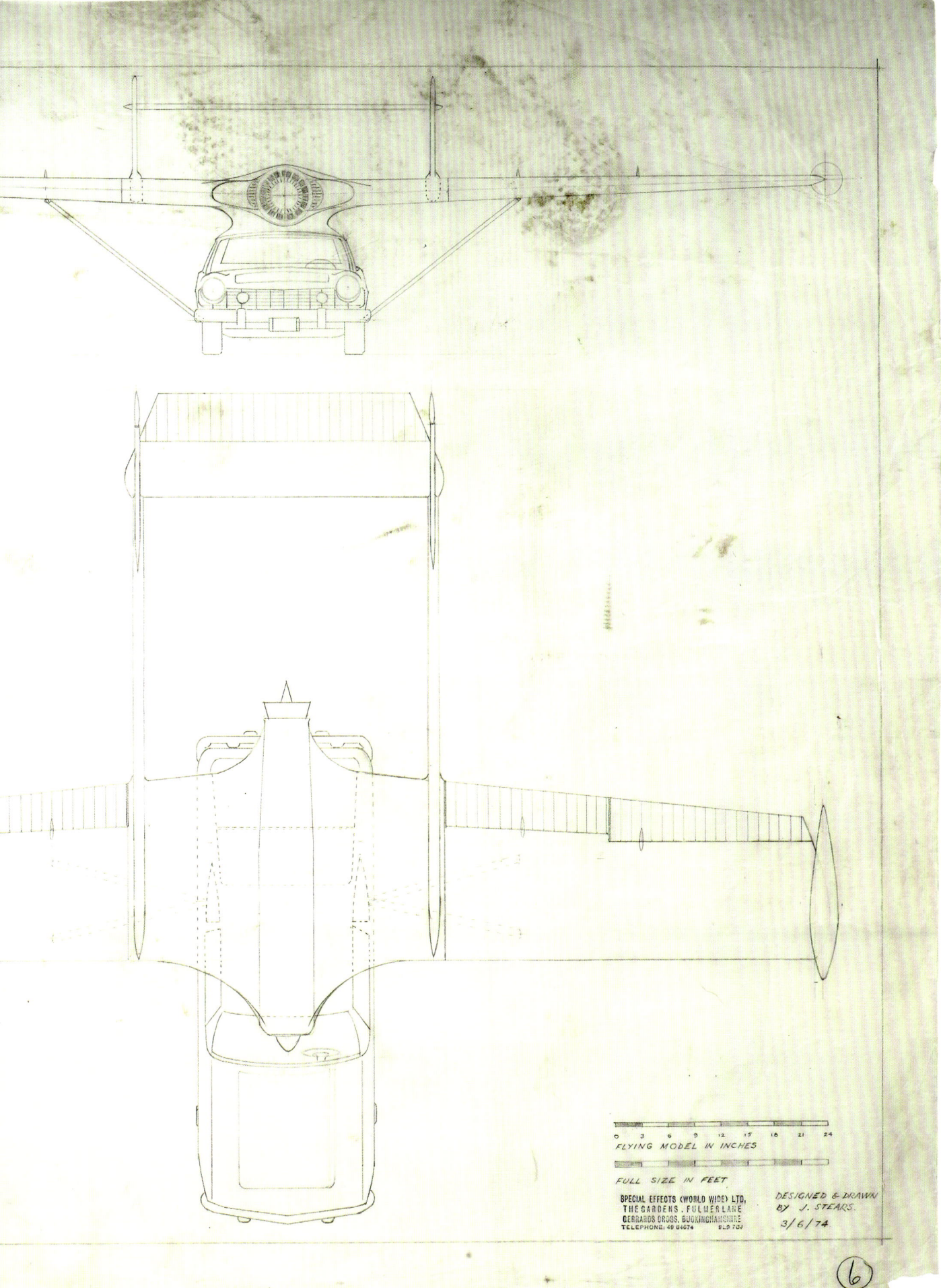

Bond special effects supremo John Stears was tasked with making the flying car into a reality. Although inspired by a real-life equivalent, the movie vehicle was a model.

If Bond's AMC briefly got airborne, Scaramanga's car took off and stayed in flight

commercial and PR opportunity when it saw one, CEO Bert Boeckmann noting: 'Commercially, I didn't know if it would ever take off, but I thought it would certainly generate a lot of publicity.'

This much was true but, after one promising but glitchy test flight, Smolenski and Blake were killed when the Mizar's wing strut failed and the thing fell apart in mid-air. It was a tragic end to a plan that had some engineering merit to it, and that had certainly made the special effects team on Bond think about the possibilities.

With no actual flying car, Stears made a full-size airframe for the close-ups shot at the Royal Turf Club, Phitsanulok Road, in Thailand, and a remote-control scale model for the flying sequences, which were filmed at the less balmy RAF Bovingdon airfield in Hertfordshire.

From flying cars to diving ones…

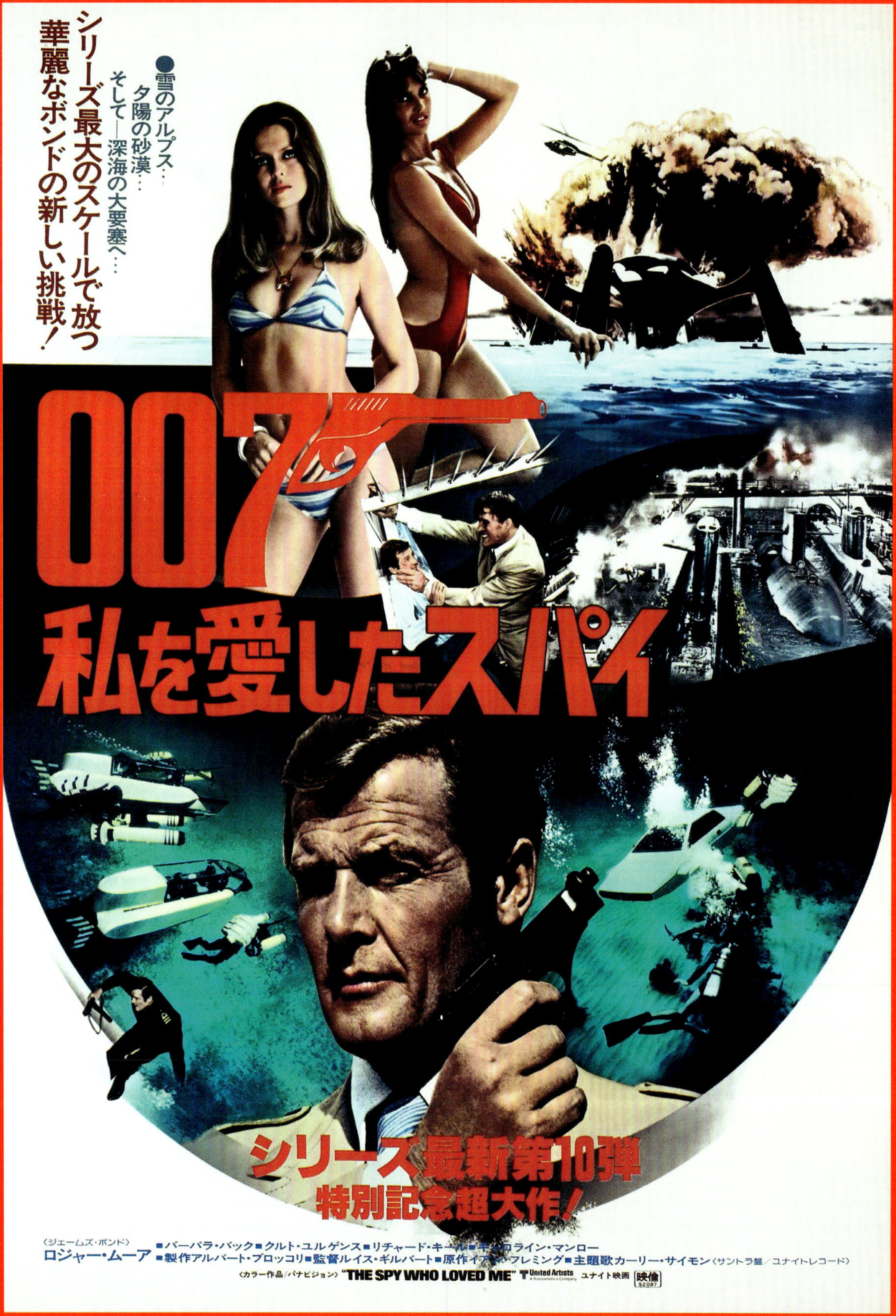

Japanese one sheet from December 1977.
'The only series on such a great scale
reveals Bond's magnificent new challenge.'

CHAPTER 10

THE SPY WHO LOVED ME

1977

STARRING Roger Moore as James Bond

THE SPY WHO LOVED ME

Produced by
ALBERT R. BROCCOLI

Roger Moore and producer Cubby Broccoli enjoy a little on-set distraction.

The stakes are always high in the James Bond universe, but as work began on the tenth film, *The Spy Who Loved Me*, there was even greater pressure than usual. Co-producer Harry Saltzman's financial travails finally forced him to relinquish his half of the Bond business, ceding full control to Cubby Broccoli. The relative under-performance, creatively and commercially, of *The Man With The Golden Gun* intensified matters, a situation not helped by Broccoli's dissatisfaction with the script treatments landing on his desk.

'The basic story was simple enough: an attempt to hijack nuclear submarines and use them to blackmail major powers. But somehow, developing the action for the kind of story I wanted defeated one writer after another,' Broccoli observed. 'We had 24 writers, all very clever men with established reputations. But in my view, they couldn't write Bond.'

This gives some idea of the alchemy involved. Happily, for all its tribulations, *The Spy Who Loved Me* would see Bond resurgent, securing Roger Moore as 007 in the eyes of a new generation, garnering Oscar nominations for its soundtrack, as well as the soaring title song, and for Ken Adam's production design.

Nobody does it better? On this film he surpassed even himself, the belly of Stromberg's supertanker so thoroughly realised that Cubby Broccoli paid for the construction of the famous 007 sound stage in order to accommodate it (an expensive but shrewd decision, because it's always in demand). Adam, who had worked with Stanley Kubrick on *Dr Strangelove* and *Barry Lyndon*, for which he

SWL 10109

SWL 10112

SWL 10110

SWL 10113

SWL 10111

SWL 10114

Opposite: A rarely seen contact sheet shows actor Richard Kiel, the gentle giant who played Jaws, demonstrating the space efficiency of a humble Ford Fiesta. Above: Actress Barbara Bach and Roger Moore abandon their Sherpa getaway van for a long walk through the Egyptian desert.

'Driving the Esprit every day was like going to work in a spacesuit'

won an Academy Award for best art direction, managed to persuade the fabled director to visit Pinewood to view the set, and solicited his opinion on how best to light this vast space. (He suggested floodlighting it, advice the film's director of photography, Claude Renoir – grandson of *the* Renoir – wisely decided to heed.)

There was also a car, for many *the* Bond car, the first and only to truly rival the Aston Martin DB5 then and now, the one that fired the imagination of the world's dreamers in ways we'll mostly never know. Elon Musk was such a fan he paid almost $1m for one of the prop cars at an auction in 2013: when asked in a 2019 Tesla shareholder's meeting whether he'd consider an aquatic car, he replied, 'Funny you should mention that… we do have a design for a submarine car like the one from *The Spy Who Loved Me*.'

Ladies and gentlemen, we give you: the Lotus Esprit.

Not only a titan of pop-culture, the Esprit also connects one of the automotive world's greatest innovators, Lotus founder Colin Chapman, with perhaps the most celebrated car designer of them all, Giorgetto Giugiaro. This Italian *maestro*, born in Piedmont in 1938, may once have described using a car such as the Lotus Esprit on a daily basis as 'like going to the office in a spacesuit', but by the mid-1970s it was apparel James Bond was happy to wear. Giugiaro, a practical thinker as well as an unparalleled visual stylist, was also responsible for the original Volkswagen Golf, Fiat Panda, and the Fiat Uno (credited to his company Italdesign, which he co-founded

Desmond Llewelyn, Roger Moore and Barbara Bach, on set in Sardinia, September 1976.

in 1968). He regarded himself as a problem-solver as much as he was an artist.

But he was also one of the initiators of the trend away from lissom curves towards dramatic wedges and impossibly raked windscreens. He'd rehearsed the moves on 1970's Porsche Tapiro and 1971's Maserati Boomerang concepts, but the concept car that appeared on the Italdesign stand at the 1972 Turin Motor Show inched the wildness ever closer to production reality. In fact, he'd already presented a 1:4 scale model to Colin Chapman, who'd been unhappy with the car's resultant aerodynamics and threatened to can the whole project.

Fortunately, Chapman was later assuaged, development work continued apace, and

The Lotus PR man parked an Esprit prototype outside the entrance of Pinewood studios

the Esprit duly appeared at the 1975 Paris salon, entering production in mid-'76. The body-side rubber strip disguised the point where the two fibreglass clamshells that made up its body were glued together, mounted on a steel backbone chassis. The Esprit was small and light, as per Chapman's 'simplify and add lightness' mantra, which was a good job because the first cars – designated S1 – were rather under-powered: the mid-mounted, 2.0-litre four-cylinder engine could only muster 160bhp. Nor was its build quality or Lotus's parts-bin parsimony (Morris Marina door-handles, Fiat X1/9 tail-lights) the stuff of dreams. Of course, none of this mattered then and it doesn't now, because this was the car that James Bond *drove into the sea*. Whereupon it transformed into a submarine, and fired missiles out of its engine bay. (Perhaps only *Back to the Future*'s time-travelling DeLorean can top that, and it too was designed by Giugiaro.)

How the Esprit ended up in *The Spy Who Loved Me* is a tale in itself, and a tribute to the fast thinking and persistence of Lotus's PR man, Donovan McLauchlan. He'd supplied a Lotus Europa to diamond heist thriller *11 Harrowhouse* (a 1974 curio stuffed with big-shot British acting talent like James Mason, Trevor Howard and John Gielgud), and had been working to nail a supply deal with Pinewood, specifically for the television series *The New Avengers*. British Leyland got there first: Patrick Macnee's character drove a highly desirable road-going copy of the muscle-bound Seventies Jaguar XJ12 Coupé racing car.

'Another contact I'd met on *11 Harrowhouse* came up during lunch at Pinewood and slid a bit of paper on my plate which said, "See me – Bond". So I said goodbye to the *New Avengers* people and went to see him,' McLauchlan recalled in a 2003 interview. 'He ran a company that did placements, and he told me roughly what they were doing.'

The next part of the plan was ballsy to say the least. Don borrowed an Esprit prototype from the company's Norfolk HQ and drove it to Pinewood, having taped over the Lotus logo wherever it appeared on the car. 'I parked it early in the morning outside the main door of Pinewood where all the directors and bigwigs have to go to their offices. Everyone had to walk round it to get into the building. Then I moved it during the day to several other blocks. There were three or four people gathered around it when I returned, so I said, "Excuse me, excuse me please," and just got in and drove off.' It piqued the right people's interest. McLauchlan was duly approached by Bond SFX boss Derek Meddings and found himself

in a meeting with him, Cubby Broccoli, the film's director Lewis Gilbert, DoP Claude Renoir and then art director Peter Lamont. 'We had lunch. Cubby said what he wanted to do with the new Bond film and asked if we wanted our Lotus to be in it.' Renoir decided white would be the most effective for the car's scenes in Sardinia.

The deal for such an iconic car as the Lotus was simply done on a handshake. The company supplied two cars, seven bodyshells and various spare parts. McLauchlan estimated the cost to be around £17,500 (about £105k today), a drop in the ocean given the publicity value that was generated when the film was released, and which continues to accrue. Production designer Peter Lamont remembers having to push for the second road car. 'I called Don,' he recalled, 'and asked for another car. "But we don't have a second car, we only build so many per week…" I said, "Well, the Chairman's got one." "But he's the Chairman!" "Well, ask him!" And of course Colin Chapman was absolutely delighted that we wanted his car.'

Lotus's involvement didn't end there. McLauchlan himself drove one of the Esprits to Paris for *The Spy Who Loved Me*'s press announcement. He'd forgotten that it was wearing dummy '007' registration plates, which naturally attracted the attention of French law enforcement. 'The gendarme was intrigued by the car's number plates,' McLauchlan said. 'I realised I'd accidentally driven all the way to Paris with these illegal 007 plates on. In order to get me there on time, he put his blue flashing lights on, escorted me to the press call, and I turned up in the Bond Lotus with a police car. I thanked him for his help – and he handed me a speeding ticket in return for a polite salute. That was the story and and that was great PR. "Bond car done for speeding." Cubby loved it.'

Nor did the company's involvement stop at supplying the car: it also loaned one of its test drivers, Roger Becker, although that

Above: Jaws in a Ford Taunus Ghia, in a publicity still circulated following the film's release.
Opposite: A rarely seen behind-the-scenes shot shows the second unit hard at work.

Rarely seen on-set images taken during the filming of this most famous of car chases. The Esprit's engine sat low enough in its chassis to allow it to be used as a camera tracking car.

The deal for the Lotus was simply done on a handshake

wasn't part of the original gentleman's agreement. Apparently, the film's principal stunt driver was having bother getting the Esprit to (mis)behave for the camera, and when Becker stepped in and promptly delivered the appropriately balletic performance, the second unit director Ernie Day hired him on the spot. (In a neat piece of symmetry, Roger's son Matt is now Aston Martin's chief chassis guru, and clearly blessed with the same talented genes.)

Roger Moore remembered the cars being rather temperamental, prone to over-heating and flat batteries. 'Their low driving position made elegant exits from the car an issue,' he also mused.

The Esprits had to endure a variety of alterations. One was apparently cut in half to make filming Moore and Barbara Bach's in-car scenes easier. Another found itself acting as a camera car. The jump Lotus was fired off the jetty into the Tyrrhenian Sea by a compressed air cannon. Various underwater Esprits were used, one for each part of the sequence. A scale model is seen in the immediate aftermath of the jetty jump, and the other 'shell' cars were rigged to

007 SUBMARINE CAR

Wheels turn and retract

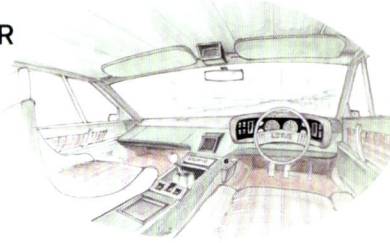

INTERIOR (Normal)

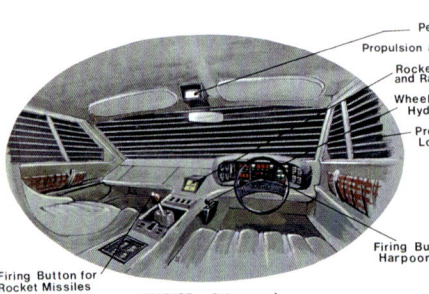

- Periscope
- Propulsion and Rudder unit
- Rocket Missiles and Radar Screen
- Wheel Covers & Hydroplanes
- Protective Louvres
- Firing Buttons for Harpoon Guns
- Firing Button for Rocket Missiles
- Harpoon Guns

INTERIOR Submerged

Eon Productions Ltd.

2, SOUTH AUDLEY STREET,
LONDON
W1Y 5DQ

Mr. F.D. Barnett,
Perry Submarine Builders Div.,
Perry Oceanographics Inc.,
Perry Building,
Riviera Beach,
Florida 33404,
U.S.A.
　　　　　　　　　　　　　　　　3rd June, 1976

Dear Mr. Barnett,

Thank you very much for the time you spent with Mr. Boren and I discussing 'The Spy Who Loved Me', our next JAMES BOND project.

I am enclosing brochures describing the Lotus Esprit which we are intending to use as our car submarine and also some drawings made by our Art Department showing the modifications to the Lotus body which they envision in order to make it an undersea vehicle.

While at your company Lamar and I also visited the division manufacturing the wet two man submarines. We would like to use one or two of the newly designed vehicles in our picture.

We anticipate being in the Miami area sometime during the last week of June and would very much like to visit your premises with members of our Art Department, in order to determine whether your company could install the propulsion system in our car submarine. We should also like to discuss arrangements for the loan of the wet submarines and possible modifications thereto. I will be calling you in a few weeks to arrange a mutually convenient date for our visit.

Yours truly,

Michael G. Wilson

c.c. A.R. Broccoli
　　　Bill Cartlidge
　　　David Middlemas
　　　Reg Barkshire
　　　Peter Lamont

EON PRODUCTIONS, LIMITED

"THE SPY WHO LOVED ME"

TO: Art Department
　　　Sp/Fx Department

FROM: DAVID MIDDLEMAS.　　DATE: Tuesday, 27th July, 76.

PRELIMINARY NOTES REGARDING EQUIPMENT
TO BE SHIPPED TO NASSAU, BAHAMAS:

The first item for transport to Nassau is:- (Approx. cost £1,500)

LOTUS CAR BODY TO PERRY OCEANOGRAPHICS: (Submarine Builders Division),
　　　　　　　　　　　　　　　　　　　　　Perry Building,
　　　　　　　　　　　　　　　　　　　　　RIVIERA BEACH,
　　　　　　　　　　　　　　　　　　　　　Florida 33404.　Tel: (305)-842-5261.

This will be packed in a crate with the following dimensions:-

　　　Length:　15'6"
　　　Width:　　6'8"
　　　Height:　4'0"

We have asked Renown Freight to collect it from Pinewood Studios on Monday, 9th August, for onward shipment to Perry. We have requested 500 Kilos of space and, at the moment, the method of shipment will be by air freight to New York, and then by truck across the States to Miami.
This will take at least one week, so that the earliest it can be expected by Perry will be during week commencing Monday, 16th August.

The remainder of the shipment consists roughly of:-

10 very large crates.　　　　　　　　　　} Approximately:
2 very heavy models: 20 x 5 x 5 Ft.　　} 10,000 cu.ft.
2 small containers to be packed at Pinewood. } £20,000.

The two most likely sailing dates are:-

　　Leave Southampton:　　Arrive Nassau:
　　26th August.　　　　　7th September. Approx.
　　15th September.　　　26th September. Approx.

Peter Lamont is to advise us of the sailing he requires and is to arrange a meeting as soon as possible with John Trafford, or Max Seeburg, of Renown to give him an idea of the size of the various items to go to Nassau. This should be done at the very earliest possible moment to enable Renown to get adequate space. It must be borne in mind that ships can be delayed by quite a few days, and dock clearance can also take some time.

Will you all be good enough to look through these notes and if you have any immediate alterations to make, I shall be pleased to hear from you.

Copies:
　Messrs. Broccoli

show the various stages of the Esprit's transformation – wheels retracting, the wheel arch fairings appearing, the fins deploying – after which it begins snooping around Stromberg's magnificently deranged submerged Atlantis lair.

'Everything was designed to operate for 30 seconds or a minute, or however long the camera is running,' Bill Cartlidge, associate producer, recalled. 'Purely for that purpose. It doesn't work before and it doesn't work afterwards.'

And of course there was a full-size submersible, as envisaged by Ken Adam and created by Florida-based marine engineers, Perry Oceangraphics. Dubbed Wet Nellie – in deference to *You Only Live Twice*'s Little Nellie autogryo – it used four propellors for forward motion, and was powered by batteries contained in a water-tight compartment. Diving and climbing were controlled by ballast tanks and, although the Lotus's dart-sharp profile naturally wanted to point it downwards, its articulated fins compensated. Inside were all the gubbins necessary for the sub's operator – a former Navy SEAL called Don Griffin – to control the craft. He rested on a platform and did the job in full scuba gear. On the roof a prismatic mirror, formerly used on a tank, offered some limited rear visibility. Perry's modifications ran to the apertures for the surface-to-air missiles, a mine hatch on the car's under-side, and a smoke screen exhaust. The conversion cost approximately $100k ($450k today).

Opposite: Concept art for the submersible Lotus Esprit, a car whose pronounced wedge shape pleased production designer, Ken Adam. Below left: Correspondence from Michael G. Wilson to Perry Oceangraphics with regard to the proposed underwater Lotus. Right: An art department memo outlines the car's movements. Above: One of the nine Esprits supplied – two cars, seven shells – is fired off the jetty, and a glimpse inside the interior of another.

The underwater scenes featuring the Lotus – now dubbed Wet Nellie – were shot in the Bahamas, where the water's clarity provided the perfect context. The unit shot the film's various submerged sequences from August 1976 until February 1977.

Rarely seen images and contact sheets of photos by Michael G. Wilson show the various stages and the complexity of the film's numerous underwater sequences. Bond films are also a demonstration of the art of the miniature.

Wet Nellie's scenes were shot in the Bahamas, the cinematography handled by 59-year-old Lamar Boren, who had overseen the dramatic underwater sequences in *Thunderball* and *You Only Live Twice*. When the Lotus makes its famous reappearance, it was winched out of the water using a cable buried under the sand. One side note here: Richard Kiel's son, RJ, is the little kid who's in shot watching its triumphant re-emergence.

Roger Moore was a man whose real-life sense of humour was on a par with his laconic incarnation of Bond, and it was his idea to drop the fish out of the Esprit's window. As he recounts in his book *Bond on Bond*, this piece of improv didn't find favour with Cubby Broccoli. 'Cubby wasn't at all happy, and said we should re-shoot; he felt it was a little too flippant and therefore not funny. I said OK, but when we ran both versions in rushes the next day my prank got a huge laugh. Cubby conceded.'

After filming, the aquatic Lotus was pressed into service by Lotus's east and west coast distributor, being displayed at various auto shows across America. Then Wet Nellie found herself in a lock-up in Holbrook, New York, and sat there for a full decade before the storage unit was sold at an auction as a complete entity, its new owners oblivious to the highly significant cultural artefact within (they paid just $100 for the lock-up). In fact, they might not even have realised exactly what it was were it not for the buzz it generated among the truckers they passed as they trailered it home; apparently they were serenaded by regular blasts of airhorn. Who knew that America's long-haul trucking fraternity were such Bond fans?

The car that Jaws and his flunkies use to chase Bond's Lotus was a black Ford Taunus Ghia, the European version of the Cortina in its most upscale form (the Ghia trim usually amounted to some

Above: Where would a Bond villain be without a monorail or specially designed pod car?

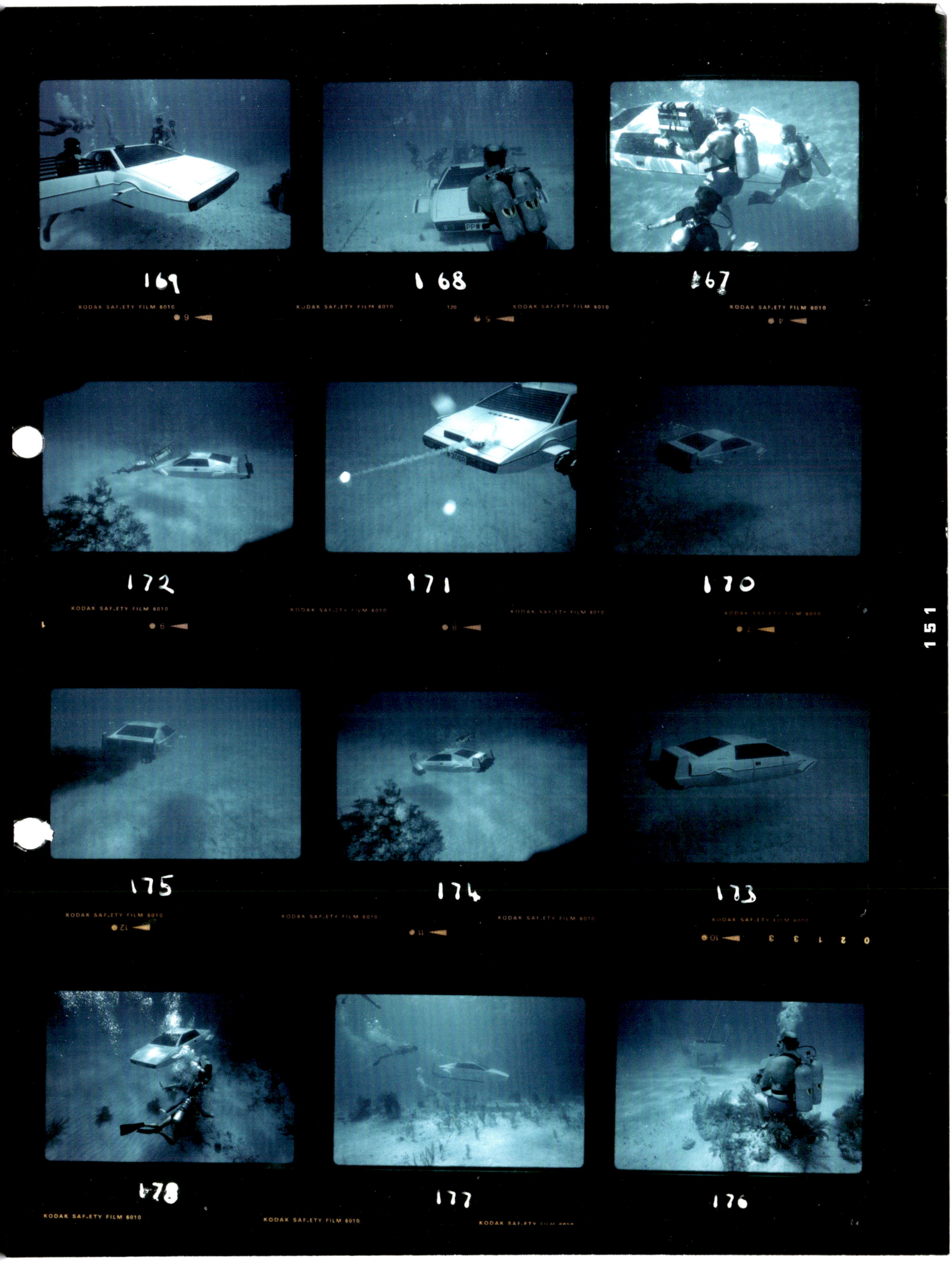
169
168
167
KODAK SAFETY FILM 6010
172
171
170
175
174
173
178
177
176
151

It was Roger Moore's idea to drop the fish out of the Esprit's window

additional brightwork outside, wood trim and an FM radio inside). The etymology rests with German mountain ranges: the Taunus mountains are north of Frankfurt, while the car itself replaced the Ford Eifel. UK buyers got the Cortina instead, named after a ski resort in Italy that would coincidentally appear in *For Your Eyes Only*, although we're spared the sight of Bond driving a Cortina in Cortina.

Then there's the Sherpa van, an utterly incongruous sight in the sequence in which Bond and Anya Amasova attempt to escape from Jaws across the Al Giza desert. Anyone familiar with British Leyland's products at the time probably wouldn't have been terribly surprised when the Sherpa overheats; it regularly did that on the M6 motorway never mind in the Eygptian desert. Credit where it's due, British Leyland's answer to the ubiquitous Ford Transit had a reputation for tremendous robustness, and was developed on the proverbial shoestring by an engineer called Stan Dews, who deserved his moment in the sun. Despite the catastrophe that was Britain's nationalised car industry in the 1970s, and the many subsequent takeovers and unwitting new owners, the Sherpa survived 31 years in production. And not even the steel dentalwork of Jaws himself could stop it.

(NB: Completists might like to note the merest of appearances in *The Spy Who Loved Me* for the Mini Moke, a pair of Chevrolets, Fiats 850, 850 Coupé and Familiare, a Hillman Avenger, VW camper van, and a Vauxhall Chevette. The 1970s in full automotive effect.)

The scenes in which the Esprit miraculously appears on the beach were shot at Capriccioli, Sardinia, on 5 and 6 October 1976. The Lotus was winched out of the sea using cables buried beneath the sand. The crew filmed two close-ups, one with and one without the famous fish, and, although producer Cubby Broccoli initially didn't approve, the fish won out…

US one sheet from June 1979, with artwork by Dan Goozee.

CHAPTER 11

MOONRAKER

1979

STARRING Roger Moore as James Bond

'Putting James Bond into orbit brought Ian Fleming into the space age,' Cubby Broccoli observed. 'Fleming's stories were tailored for the light read. They were never constructed with films in mind. Which is why we had to build on them, restyle them for the age of lasers, computers, space travel and genetic engineering. When he wrote *Moonraker* it was a little rocket that went up to destroy London. Now people have gone to the moon. It's much more scientific, much more difficult, and much more advanced.'

Moonraker, 1979's summer blockbuster, pushed the Bond boundaries to the limit – creatively, logistically and financially. Sending 007 into space was never going to be cheap, and this is a film that challenges credulity at alarmingly regular intervals, while being enormous fun. The public agreed: it went on to become the highest grossing Bond until *GoldenEye* in 1995.

Its premise also meant that, of the 25 Bond films, *Moonraker* is the one with the least automotive content. Yet the cars that do feature are all special in their own way. Hugo Drax (an amusingly saturnine performance from Michael Lonsdale) is a billionaire industrialist, Chopin enthusiast, and the sort of man who has an original

Right: Concept art for the infamous 'Bondola'.

French chateau dismantled, brick by brick, then reconstructed in California (it's actually the Château de Vaux-le-Vicomte, south of Paris). Never mind his grand plan to exterminate the human race apart from a chosen few genetically blessed examples. Now what sort of car would you cast for this megalomaniac aesthete? In the novel, Ian Fleming puts Drax in a Mercedes-Benz 300 S (indeed, a vividly written car chase sees Bond's Bentley destroyed). In the film, a fascinating trio of vehicles are briefly glimpsed outside the chateau, looking very much to the manner born. There's a 1929 Isotta Fraschini Tipo 8A, a 1936 Hispano-Suiza J12, and a Rolls-Royce Silver Shadow. Rarely in the Bond series have background cars been so acutely cast; these were some of the greatest names in the pioneering pre-war days of the automobile, with stories to match (the much later Silver Shadow is the anomaly here, a veritable daily runaround alongside the other two).

Hispano-Suiza has its roots in late 19th-century Spain, and saw its engineering prowess grow under the auspices of Swiss engineer Marc Birkigt when the company made aircraft engines during the First World War; Birkigt can claim credit for the world's first 'cast block' engine, an innovation that revolutionised the industry. Its 1920s and '30s luxury cars were advanced, powerful and highly prized by the emerging Jet Set. The car seen in *Moonraker* is a 1936 Type 68 J12 cabriolet, bodied by flamboyant French coachbuilder Saoutchik. The aviation legacy is apparent in its vast engine, a 9.5-litre V12 that bore many of Birkigt's mechanically innovative hallmarks, and was good for 250bhp.

Isotta Fraschini was formed in Milan in 1900, and its exploits in the early days of motor racing and engineering innovations saw it become fashionable among the monied elite in Europe and America during the 1920s. Clara Bow and Rudolph Valentino both owned one, and in a hugely evocative example of automotive casting Norma Desmond (Gloria Swanson) is ferried around in an Isotta Fraschini in Billy Wilder's 1950 classic *Sunset Boulevard*. She would have given Drax a run for his money… Like most of these absurdly glamorous 1920s and '30s machines, the customer had the rolling chassis clothed in a body designed by the coachbuilder of his or her choice. Drax's car was the work of the Milanese firm, Castagna, which by 1919 had 400 workers bodying 100 cars per year, and a reputation for excellent quality and good taste. This wasn't always

matched by its clientele's requests (Norma's leopard-skin interior being a case in point).

Moonraker's visit to Rio de Janeiro gathers a net around a rather different set of background cars. Aside from the long wheelbase Rolls-Royce Silver Shadow that greets Bond at the airport and wafts him along the Copacabana, the most prominent is a Brazilian curio called the MP Lafer. This is an ersatz South American homage to the MG TD (a 1950–53 quintessentially British sports car, that coincidentally garners a lot of screen time in 2019's *Once Upon a Time in Hollywood*). The company was founded in 1974 by well-regarded contemporary furniture maker Percival Lafer, and tapped into a peculiar vogue at the time for retro roadsters. Like many of them, the Lafer utilised the engine and underpinnings of the

The 'Bondola' was a motorised gondola that turned into a hovercraft

VW Beetle, while the body was made of fibreglass. What might look like a joke car at first glance survived in production for 16 years, and plenty of the 4,300 that were manufactured found an audience in other markets. Happily, Mr Lafer still makes excellent furniture to this day.

Equally special are the vehicles that *didn't* make it into *Moonraker*. As with any big film, the art department was tasked with brainstorming ideas and concepts, a process the Bond team regularly took to the next level. During *Moonraker*'s pre-production, Ken Adam and his team envisaged a whole set of vehicles for Drax, the concept art for which is reproduced here for the first time. Among them is a proposal for a sports coupé that has shades of Seventies Italian supercar, and there's also a sketch of a liveried patrol car that has the sharky feel of the Rover SD1. Most intriguing, though, are the renderings for a large RV/MPV-styled vehicle, one of which is big enough to carry a light aircraft on its roof, while the other has a small car stored under the front cabin. *Moonraker* might be the Bond film with an excess of almost everything, but it's still missing a large RV/MPV-styled vehicle with room for an entire car underneath…

The Bondola scatters the local birdlife, St Mark's Square, Venice.

Rarely seen concept art by Peter Bohanna, a former car designer who was drafted in to conceptualise and build prop vehicles for the Bond films. Here we see his sketches for a mobile HQ, an RV big enough to house a car in the front compartment.

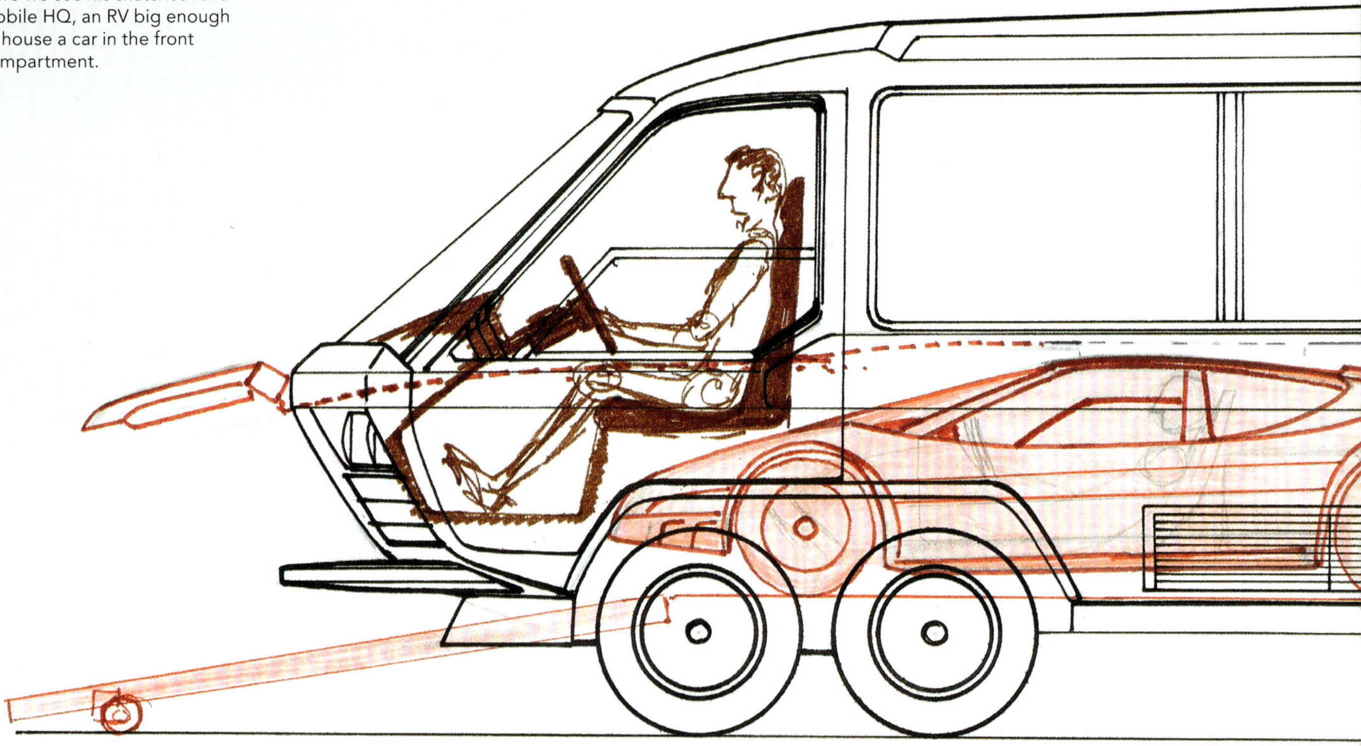

The artist responsible was Peter Bohanna, who'd returned from Colombia – where his father had been working for some years – in the early 1960s on a mission to get employment in the motorsport sector. He did what people did in those days and knocked on doors until Eric Broadley at Lola decided he liked his drawings and took him on. This gave him expertise in manufacturing car bodies and in the use of fibreglass, and he was at Lola when the company was helping Ford develop the epochal GT40. In the early 1970s, he and another former Lola employee called Robin Stables created their own car, the Diablo. The design rights were acquired soon after by British sports car company AC, and the car later made it into limited production as the 3000 ME.

By this point, Bohanna had been approached by Bond production designer Peter Lamont to work on *The Spy Who Loved Me*; you can see his handiwork in the motorcycle sidecar in the Esprit car chase, and he also designed the pod car used and seen briefly in Stromberg's supertanker HQ. And it was his Range Rover that was used to winch the Lotus out of the sea in the scene that's capped by Roger Moore dropping the fish out of the car window…

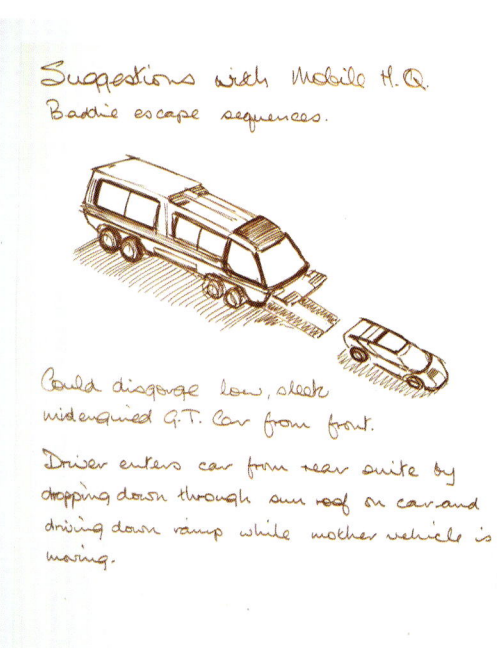

Suggestions with Mobile H.Q. Baddie escape sequences.

Could disgorge low, sleek midengined G.T. car from front.

Driver enters car from rear suite by dropping down through sun roof on car and driving down ramp while mother vehicle is moving.

Above: The MP Lafer, a rather obscure Brazilian sports car that wound up in *Moonraker*.

The Lafer was created by a well-regarded furniture designer

Bohanna also helped make the infamous 'Bondola', the motorised gondola that transforms into a hovercraft to aid Bond's escape as he zooms across the Piazza San Marco (just don't mention the double-taking pigeon). It hid a Ford Granada powertrain underneath, apparently.

According to his son, Pierre, who himself is now a top film prop-maker (and the man who created the Harry Potter wand, no less), his father was left with a *Moonraker* gondola prototype, which the landlord of his local pub, the Leatherne Bottel in Goring-on-Thames, let him store. There now follows an anecdote that will be difficult for any British child of the Seventies to process.

'He got a call one day saying a company wanted to use it. It was for Val Doonican's television show, which would always start with a contrivance where he'd be warbling away with two backing singers. They wanted to use the gondola, with him and two girls singing behind him with a gondolier as they went up the Thames. But the thing sank, and the sequence never made it onto the TV.'

As for the RV/MPV, the one with the plane on the roof and the car underneath, well that very nearly earned a glamorous afterlife. 'A very rich rock star, I can't remember who, lived near my father in Goring,' Pierre recalls. 'He was forever trying to commission my old man to build something similar for him as a tour bus.'

In the process of bringing a Bond film to life, a huge variety of concepts are explored. Design artist Peter Bohanna's sketch for an all-terrain sports coupé was intended for Hugo Drax, and may have been ahead of its time.

Japanese one sheet, from July 1981, with artwork by Hisamitsu Noguchi: "From crisis to crisis! In the middle of the series we are plunged into Bond action at its peak. Super giant spectacle!" the tagline says.

CHAPTER 12
FOR YOUR EYES ONLY

1981

STARRING Roger Moore as James Bond

'The Lotus had been a great arsenal for Bond,' Michael G. Wilson noted. 'So to take that away from him at the very beginning of the film was saying, "OK, we're making Bond more reliant on his own wits."' The producers also relieved 007 of the previous film's spacecraft, realising that a limit had clearly been reached; both Bond and the audience needed to come back down to Earth.

For Your Eyes Only was a classic adventure, a reunion of sorts for the elements that had sent the series skyward in the first place, 20 years previously: seductive hero, mysterious protagonist, a beautiful leading lady, glamorous locations. Bond redux. The plot 'McGuffin' – the search for a top-secret missile decoder called ATAC – allowed veteran screenwriter Richard Maibaum and his co-writer (and executive producer) Michael G. Wilson to anchor the action in the ever chilly hinterlands of the Cold War.

There was also a new and first-time director, John Glen, second unit architect of many of Bond's best action sequences (including *On Her Majesty's Secret Services*'s bobsleigh run and the bravura pre-credits skiing sequence in *The Spy Who Loved Me*). John was also an extremely accomplished editor, whose career had started as a junior assistant to the great cinematic polymath Sir Alexander Korda. 'And he'd been with us long enough to have Bond in his bloodstream,' Cubby Broccoli noted.

As such, Glen was no iconoclast but still happy enough to detonate a few Bond tropes, at the behest of the story. Early in *For Your Eyes Only*, Bond's car – the newly turbocharged, 207bhp version of the Lotus Esprit, whose sublime Giugiaro body somehow survived the appending of the obligatory wings, side skirts and spoilers – is blown to smithereens by one of the villain's henchmen (played by Bond stunt legend Bob Simmons), who ignores the

After a single-movie hiatus, the Lotus Esprit returned, in newly turbocharged form. This one wouldn't last long, however…

warning signs. This was topically resonant, especially in certain territories.

'There had been a spate of car thefts in New York, and insurance premiums were going through the roof,' Glen told me. 'Michael [Wilson] and I talked about it, and I said, "Why don't we start off with the Lotus, the expected James Bond supercar kind of thing." We have a notice on the car saying, "Burglar protected", and of course when the guy taps the window with his machine gun it blows up. That got a huge cheer when the film played in New York.'

As if that wasn't sacrilegious enough, the next step really messed with the audience's preconceptions. Glen explains: 'The whole concept of James Bond running out and saying, "Well, I hope you have a car..." and then seeing the little 2CV is so anti-Bond.' (This visual gag played well in the cinema in which I watched the film on release.)

Although this section of *For Your Eyes Only* was set near Madrid, filming actually took place on the Greek island of Corfu. Its topography and culture helped shape the entire film, whose tone evolved from the very first location scouting session (indeed, this has always been the case with Bond films). 'The roads weren't very good, we actually bent the front axle on the hire car,' Glen recalled of the first recce he and

Roger Moore and Carole Bouquet on location in Corfu, September 1980, receiving a little help from the locals.

Rémy Julienne was a former rallycross champion, and the maestro of car chases

Wilson conducted. 'We had a beautiful short story from Ian Fleming, which we used in its entirety but that only took care of the opening part of the movie. Michael and Dick Maibaum did the rest. A lot was based on what we saw on the recce, and helped develop the story. It was wonderful to be able to work with the writers, with a blank canvas, and to contribute the ideas. They'd say, "Leave the action sequences to John," and I loved that... Dick Maibaum was fantastic. The leading lady in his mind was always his wife. He idolised her.'

Glen worked out the rhythms of the car chase in conjunction with Rémy Julienne, the French stunt-driving maestro with whom he had worked on the *The Italian Job* 12 years previously. Julienne was a former rallycross and motorcross champion, who began his movie career doubling for Jean Marais in the 1964 film *Fantômas* and would rack up more than 1,400 film credits. The great Claude Lelouch (whose 1976 short film *C'était un rendez-vous* is a genre classic) once called him a 'reasonable madman' but, as Glen recalls, his strength lay not just in his immense skill behind the wheel, but also in his preparation. 'Rémy never really spoke particularly good English, but we somehow managed to communicate very well. He was fantastic, a stopwatch man, nothing was left to chance. He didn't do anything daring – it was all worked out meticulously.'

As the man himself concurs. 'I was a scared little boy, but I had a taste for risk. Over time, I discovered that the real difficulty is finding the right balance between doubt and self-confidence,' he told *France Dimanche* in 2015. 'You must have constant concern for perfection, precision and absolute safety while ensuring that the wishes of the director are met. My job was to calculate the risks.'

In the years that followed, he would work with a number of big names, including Lee Marvin, Harrison Ford and Al Pacino. Julienne's ability to make ordinary cars do extraordinary things

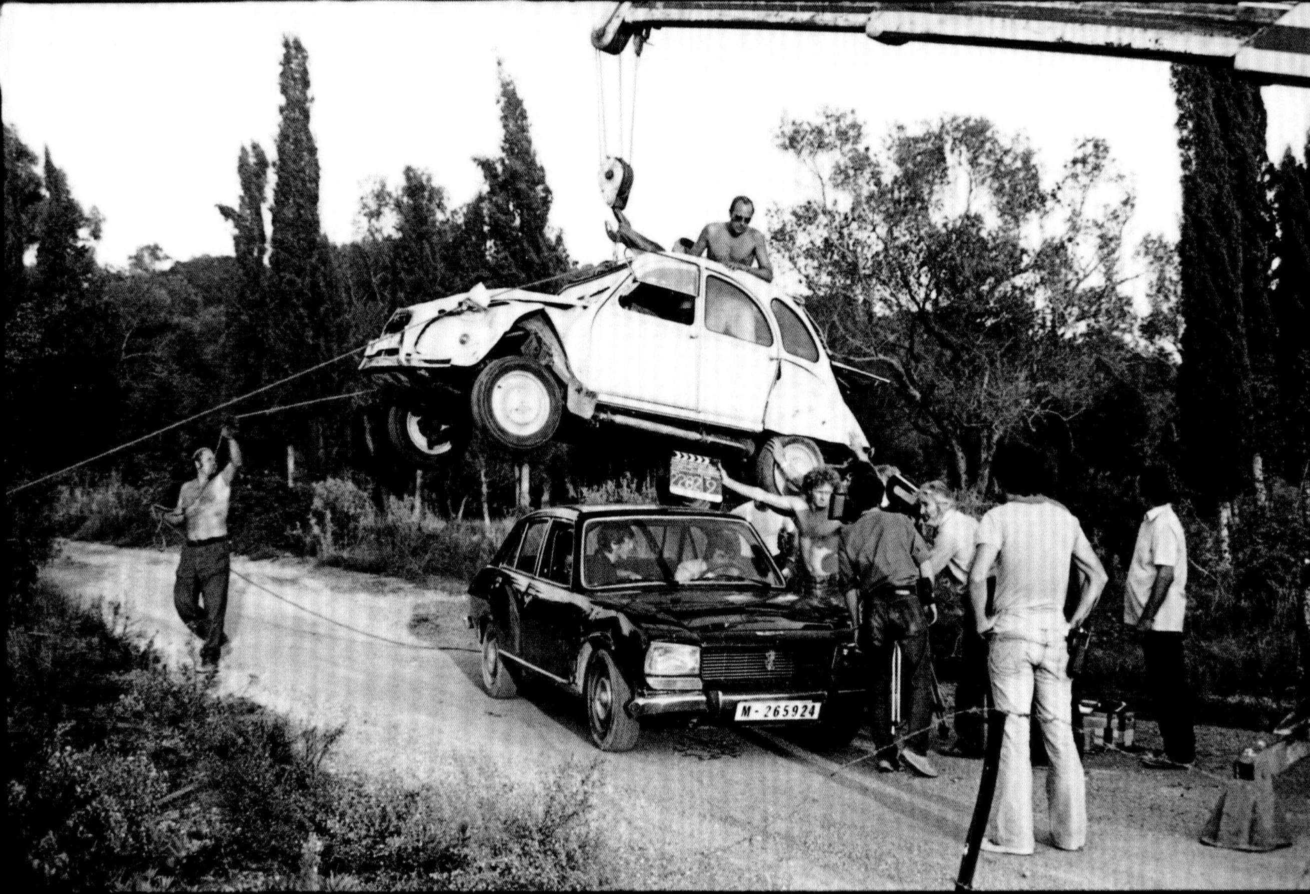

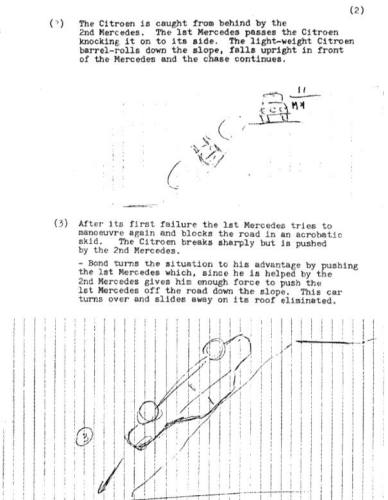

Rémy Julienne and his stunt driving team were renowned for working out a car chase in meticulous detail. Above: The 2CV is lowered into position above the henchmen's Peugeot 504. Below: Rarely seen correspondence from Julienne. Note the header on his stationery.

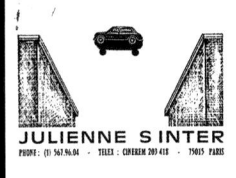

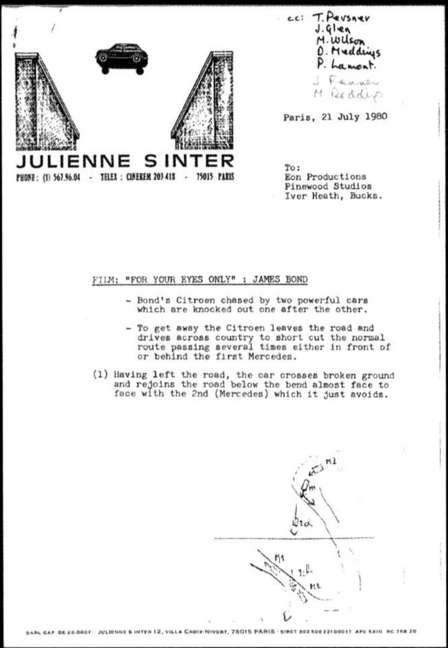

cc: T. Pevsner
J. Glen
M. Wilson
D. Meddings
P. Lamont

Paris, 21 July 1980

To:
Eon Productions
Pinewood Studios
Iver Heath, Bucks.

FILM: "FOR YOUR EYES ONLY" : JAMES BOND

- Bond's Citroen chased by two powerful cars which are knocked out one after the other.
- To get away the Citroen leaves the road and drives across country to short cut the normal route passing several times either in front of or behind the first Mercedes.

(1) Having left the road, the car crosses broken ground and rejoins the road below the bend almost face to face with the 2nd (Mercedes) which it just avoids.

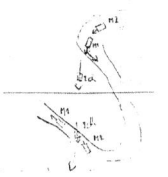

(2) The Citroen is caught from behind by the 2nd Mercedes. The 1st Mercedes passes the Citroen knocking it on to its side. The light-weight Citroen barrel-rolls down the slope, falls upright in front of the Mercedes and the chase continues.

(3) After its first failure the 1st Mercedes tries to manoeuvre again and blocks the road in an acrobatic skid. The Citroen breaks sharply but is pushed by the 2nd Mercedes.

- Bond turns the situation to his advantage by pushing the 1st Mercedes which, since he is helped by the 2nd Mercedes gives him enough force to push the 1st Mercedes off the road down the slope. This car turns over and slides away on its roof eliminated.

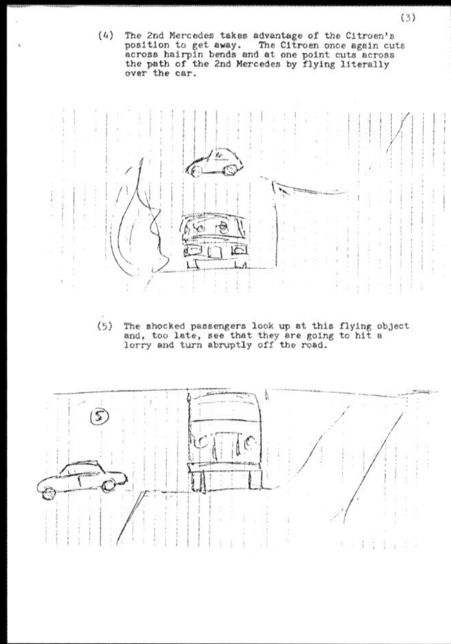

(4) The 2nd Mercedes takes advantage of the Citroen's position to get away. The Citroen once again cuts across hairpin bends and at one point cuts across the path of the 2nd Mercedes by flying literally over the car.

(5) The shocked passengers look up at this flying object and, too late, see that they are going to hit a lorry and turn abruptly off the road.

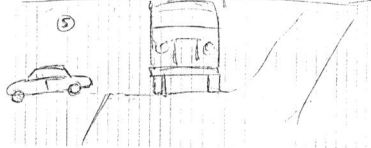

helped imbue them with unexpected character, as was the case in *For Your Eyes Only*.

The film's second unit director was Arthur Wooster, another first timer. 'He was a one-man band, he didn't need all the trappings of a feature film cameraman, and he'd done mainly documentaries. He was also a fantastic photographer, and you could dangle him off a mountain top, he was an underwater cameraman, he was everything,' John Glen noted.

The 2CV chase sequence was shot near the village of Pagoi, in northwest Corfu. Glen storyboarded all the action sequences. 'Michael and I had researched all the background, and found out about the local people. We wanted to get everyone involved with the chase sequence, otherwise the cars can look like toys. You need to be able to relate to them. It was olive-picking season, so I thought we should involve that somehow.'

Casting the 2CV might have irritated some diehards, but for those Bond fans who can see past the obvious, the sequence in *For Your Eyes Only* remains one of the most imaginative in the entire canon – not to mention one of the most improbable, for all the film's realistic intent. The Citroën had a canvas roof and the structural rigidity of a soggy shoebox, so how it survived the roll down the olive grove is an extreme example of movie magic. It did benefit from an engine that was twice the size of the 602cc, flat twin unit normally found under its funny little bonnet; the bigger, 1.1-litre engine used in the Citroën GS was shoe-horned in. Glen remains a fan to this day.

'The 2CV was a glorious little car. It's what French farmers used to drive across ploughed fields. And camera operators, too – great suspension, you see. I always saw it as a blue car, funnily enough. [Special effects supervisor] Derek Meddings came up with a model of it, and he said, "I always saw it as yellow." So we went with that. There was even a special edition 007 2CV, with bullet-hole stickers for the doors. There was one parked outside my flat one day. Its owner was perplexed when I told her about my involvement.'

Peugeot enjoyed less of a marketing uplift despite the prominent role played by the 504 saloon in the chase. Fans of French cars will know this as one of the all-time greats of its domestic car industry, and more importantly for what it achieved beyond its homeland: unveiled at the 1968 Paris motor show, the 504 was also manufactured in Argentina, Australia, Chile,

One of the most famous cars ever to star in a Bond car chase, the Citroën 2CV used in *For Your Eyes Only* benefited from a mildly upgraded engine. Mildly…

Above: Bond arrives at his hotel in the second of his Lotus Esprit turbos. Opposite: Roger Moore on location with the Lotus Esprit turbo. Below: Countess Lisl is chased by a beach buggy.

model portfolio. This first S-class was also the last car to be designed by Friedrich Geiger; his CV included the 500K, the 540K, the 300 SL 'gullwing' and the 'Pagoda' SL, four of the most perfectly realised motor cars in automotive history, so it's little surprise the W116 had such a perfectly executed elegance to match its formality.

This is also one of those cars which operates as visual short-hand for filmmakers: it evokes an era perfectly, but is such a timeless signifier of money, power and prestige that it works whatever the context. (Here's a smattering of its countless credits: Michel Gondry's *Be Kind Rewind*, Mike Leigh's *High Hopes*, Martin Scorsese's *The King of Comedy*, David Lynch's *Lost Highway*, Ron Howard's *Frost/Nixon* and Steven Spielberg's *Munich*, as well as a key role in John Frankenheimer's car chase magnum opus, *Ronin*.)

Bond pursues Locque on foot, before injuring him with a gunshot, the Mercedes coming to a precarious rest on a mountain edge. Rémy Julienne's driving was millimetre-perfect, as ever, a dummy wall and restraining leads keeping the big saloon safely in place. The question was, now that he had his adversary on the ropes, how would Bond finish the job? Bond is sometimes characterised as a thug in a Savile Row suit, but Roger Moore favoured a more nuanced approach. This led to a cliff-side debate with the film's director, John Glen.

'Being the "new broom", I wanted to make a difference,' the director admitted. 'I always admired the Connery Bonds in as much as they had a very hard edge, and I had a feeling we had lost a little bit of that. Although Roger's a completely different type of actor, I still felt we needed to put a bit of edge in it.'

As Bond approaches the stricken Mercedes, he tosses a little tie pin into the car (the insignia of the 'dove' organisation, as found clenched in his murdered MI6 contact Ferrara's hand), a symbolic gesture that might conceivably have sent the car to its doom. But Glen wanted more. 'I said to Roger, "Not only do you throw the pin at him, you kick the car off the cliff." We argued about it. I was aware that we were at a crossroads in the depiction of the character

China, Egypt, New Zealand, Nigeria, Portugal, South Africa, Spain, Taiwan and Tunisia, and was still being assembled in Nigeria in 2006. Although far less of a crowd pleaser than its automotive co-stars in *For Your Eyes Only*, it's worth noting that its design was the work of Aldo Brovarone, chief stylist at Pininfarina, Italy's premier *carrozzeria*. (A red 504 estate is seen earlier in the film outside a government building, alongside a Citroën CX and Ford Granada: this was 1981 in a nutshell.)

In terms of villainous wheels, the Peugeot also made a change from the ubiquitous Mercedes saloon, although there are still plenty of those in the background. But Emile Locque's Mercedes 280 SE (code number W116 in Mercedes parlance) has a much higher-profile presence in the film.

This was the first in Mercedes' genre-defining S-class full-size luxury line – *sonderklasse* or 'special class' – which the company has used since its arrival in 1972 to premier the new technology that it subsequently rolls out across its entire

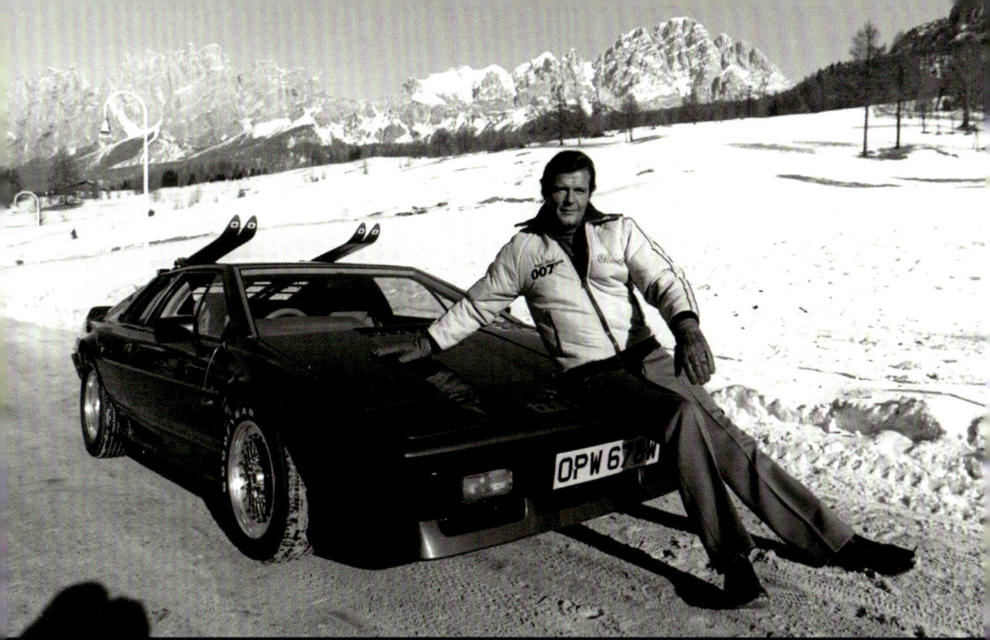
007
OPW 678W

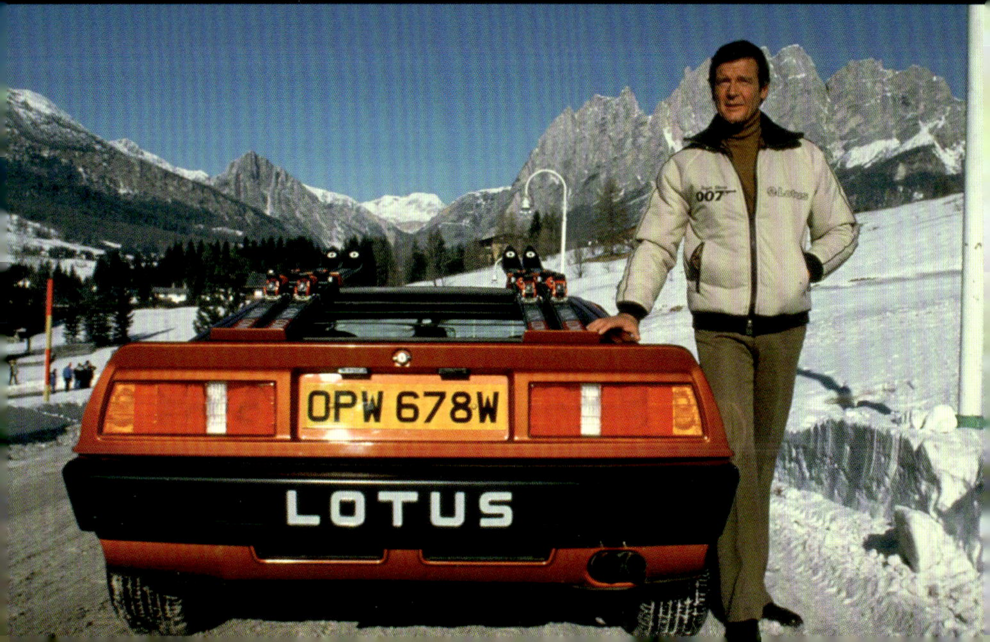
007
Lotus
OPW 678W
LOTUS

176

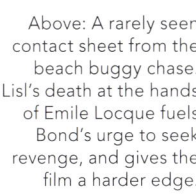

Above: A rarely seen contact sheet from the beach buggy chase. Lisl's death at the hands of Emile Locque fuels Bond's urge to seek revenge, and gives the film a harder edge.

and I fought hard to show Bond kick the car. Roger ultimately agreed it was the right decision.'

Moore recalled: 'I said that my Bond would not do that. John Glen was adamant that this man killed both Ferrara and Countess Lisl [gunned down by henchmen in Beetle-based beach buggies], and that I should show my anger and a more ruthless side to my personality. It didn't sit happily with me, so we compromised: I tossed the pin in and gave the car a not-so-hard kick to topple it.'

It's a dramatic scene, shot partly at a quarry and then on the cliff. 'The car slips a little and you can see right past the villain, through the window, and see the drop he's about to go over,' Derek Meddings recalled.

As that silver Mercedes tumbles into the rocks and sea below, the sense that the character has found an extra few gears is palpable. It's an important scene in a Bond film that's a turning point for Roger Moore's Bond.

Locque's Mercedes S-class is sent over a cliff by 007. It was a scene that prompted much debate during filming, and represented a turning point for Moore's depiction of Bond.

US one sheet from June 1983,
with artwork by Dan Goozee
and Renato Casaro.

CHAPTER 13
OCTOPUSSY

1983

STARRING Roger Moore as James Bond

O*ctopussy* was the 13th entry in the series, the franchise having become by this point the most profitable in cinema history. A pleasing situation for sure, but one that presented its own challenges. Primarily, how to avoid creative stasis and maintain relevance?

Watch the film anew, though, and its action sequences punch harder than you might remember. In particular, the sequence on the railway during which Bond runs between, and hangs off, various carriages is magnificent, and a tribute both to the second unit's art and the fortitude of the stunt crew.

That particular sequence begins with Bond commandeering General Orlov's official car – a black Mercedes 280 SE (W108) – which he proceeds to abuse in a number of typically Bondian ways. (Orlov was played by British thespian Steven Berkoff, who turned up for his audition wearing a samurai outfit; his next film outing would see him essay the role of an equally low-key villain in *Beverly Hills Cop*). The Merc is driven nicely sideways through a railyard and scatters a load of oil drums as it passes in front of a Volvo 244 and Volga M-24. These Soviet saloons were a staple of Cold War-era films and television; they were brought in by Belgian importer ScaldiaVolga minus the engine and gearbox, and were usually retro-fitted with a Peugeot powertrain in an Antwerp facility. Taxi drivers appreciated their remarkable robustness, if not their performance or aesthetics.

The Mercedes then appears unexpectedly nimble on two wheels as it slices past a Fiat 128. (Its throwaway presence in *Octopussy* underplays its pivotal role in automotive history; Dante Giacosa, also responsible for the original Fiat 500, oversaw its creation and the great Aurelio Lampredi engineered it.) The pièce de resistance occurs when 007 manages an unprecedented example of pursuit improvisation by slamming the 280 onto the railway line. As Arthur Wooster recalls, 'We did a lot of shooting from the crane on a flatbed truck on another rail. Swinging the crane out to the side and back again was quite tricky because of the tunnels and obstructions along the side of the track. Timing is the crucial thing.'

Special effects boss John Richardson also carried out some unique modifications. 'We constructed some special wheels so that the [Mercedes] could actually drive along the track. I took Roger for a test drive in it and he handled it pretty well.' The black Mercedes suffers a bleak fate when it smashes head-on into an oncoming train, its body jettisoned across a bridge and into a river full of anglers seconds after Bond has effected his escape. As with the Esprit's leap into the sea in *The Spy Who Loved Me*, an air cannon supplied the necessary propulsion.

The chase continues, and if you happen to be a child of the Seventies or have a particular love of obscure Eighties metal, then this one's for you. Bond, still disguised as a circus knife-thrower, is blanked then teased by some German motorists (in a red VW Karmann Ghia), hitches the world's slowest ride and, in his desperation to defuse Orlov's pesky nuclear bomb, resorts to stealing a car while its owner is in a callbox (like all movie scenes that feature computers or technology, anything to do with telephones now looks amusingly dated). The village set here, meanwhile, was re-purposed from another film that had just finished shooting at Pinewood.

What follows is one of the most unexpectedly satisfying car chases in the entire Bond film series, for two simple reasons: the car 007 'borrows' is an Alfa Romeo GTV6 and the vehicles the *Polizei* use to pursue him are BMW 520s (E28 era; the same model is driven by Tom Cruise in 2018's *Mission: Impossible – Fallout*). If you know your cars then you'll also know that both were resolutely rear-drive, which meant obvious potential for flamboyant

The BD jet had a wingspan of just 17ft, weighed 204kg, and had a top speed of 320mph

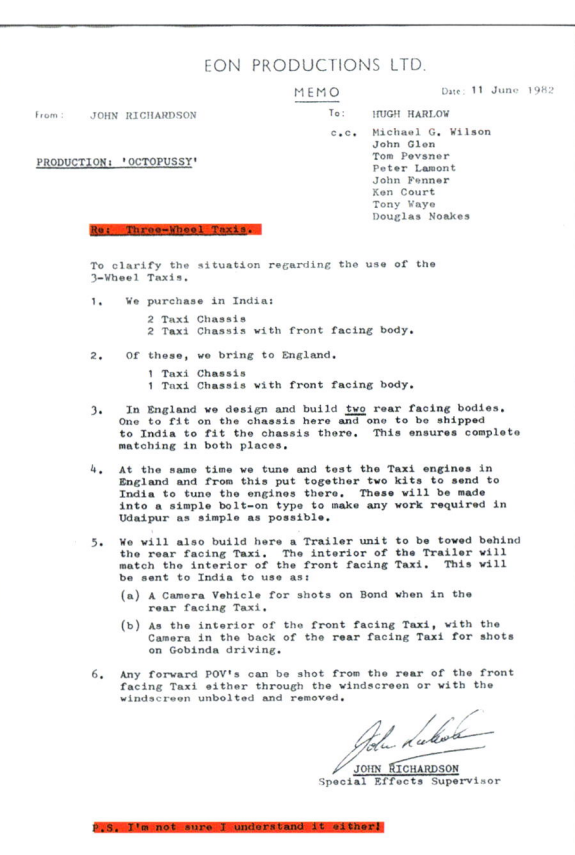

The Tuk-Tuk starred in its own chase, which commenced filming in September 1982. The vehicles required 'Bondification' in order to withstand the rigours of filmmaking, as this correspondence confirms.

oversteer out of every junction (production designer Peter Lamont clearly knew what he was doing).

Alfa Romeo is also the lifeblood of any genuine car enthusiast. A 1980 mid-life facelift managed not to ruin Giugiaro's typically graceful styling, despite the arrival of plastic bumpers and body-side trim. More importantly, Alfa dropped its sonorous 2.5-litre V6 under the bonnet, whose performance was more flexible and reliably delivered thanks to fuel injection instead of troublesome carburettors. Alfa Romeo even managed to reassert its remarkable competition pedigree: the GTV6 won the European Touring Car Championship back-to-back from 1982 through to '85.

This Italian coupé facing off against a series of BMW 5 series – most likely skinnier-tyred, less powerful 520i models – thus ensured maximum sideways / handbrake turn old-school car chase action. While the RAF base at Upper Heyford in Oxfordshire deputised for the fictional US air force base Feldstadt, the chase scenes were filmed in Germany, the combatants passing background metal that includes a lovely BMW 633 CSi, and various period Opels and VWs. (A blue Austin Allegro is also visible at one point, but we'll pass that by even faster than Bond does.) Equally nondescript but for completely different reasons is the Chevrolet Chevelle Malibu patrol car that gives chase amidst Feldstadt's circus caravans. At least it never had to endure the indignity of a quartic steering wheel.

Be in no doubt, *Octopussy* is a film with a great automotive cast of background cars. There's an illuminating Berlin-set sequence, in which Bond is briefed by M in the back of a Mercedes 200 (exterior

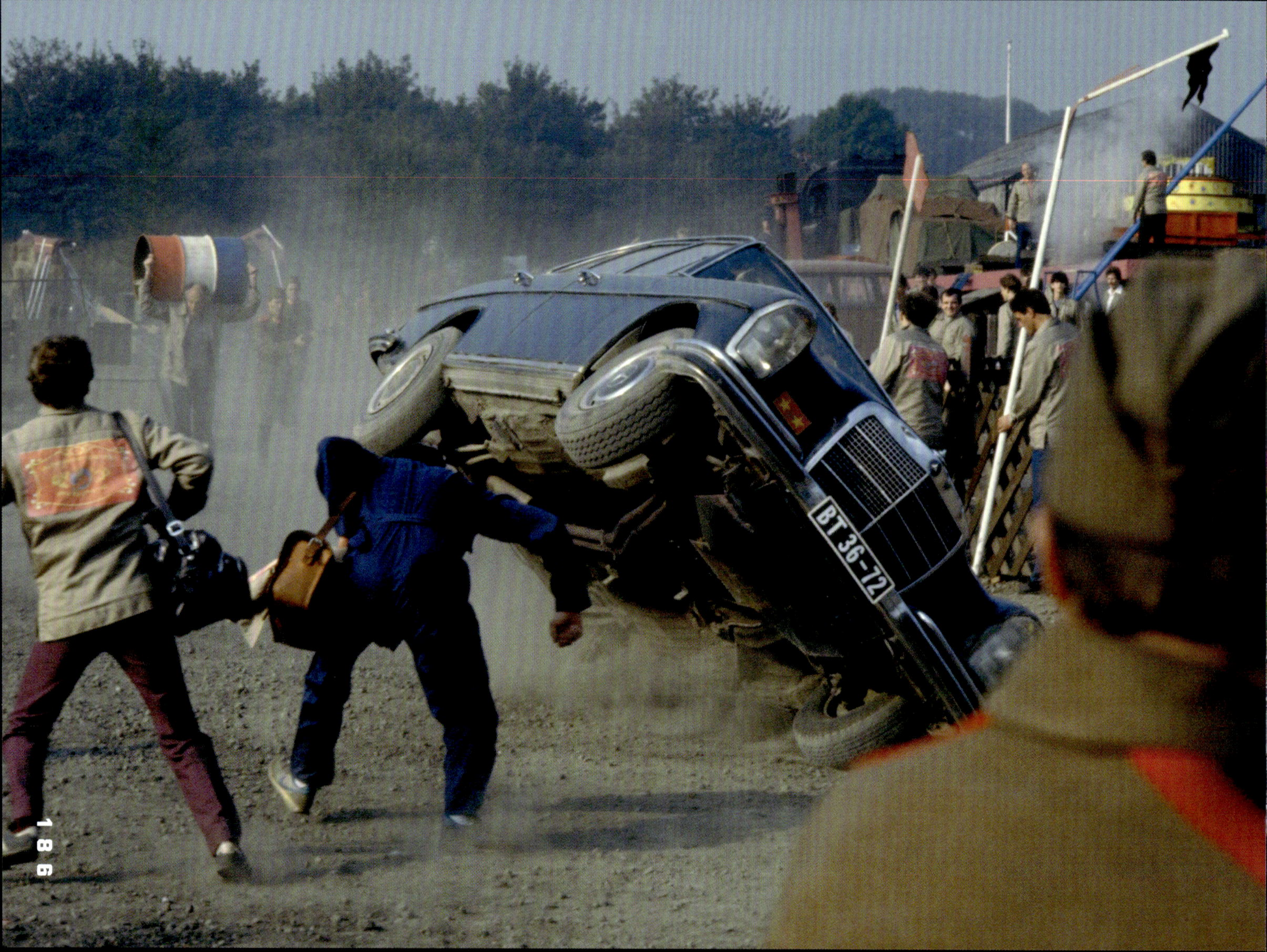
BT 36-72

NORMAL
MAX SPEED
25 MPH

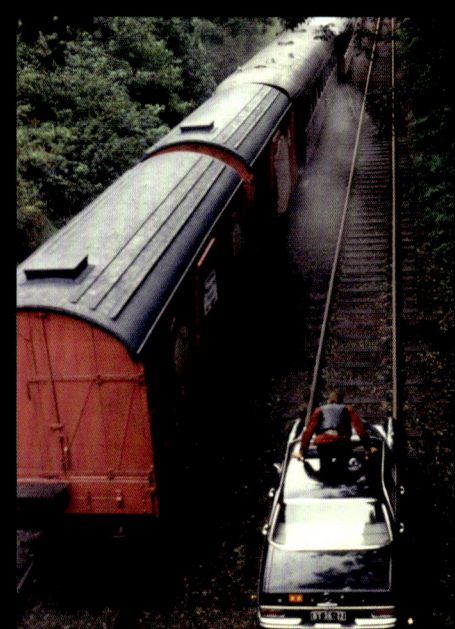

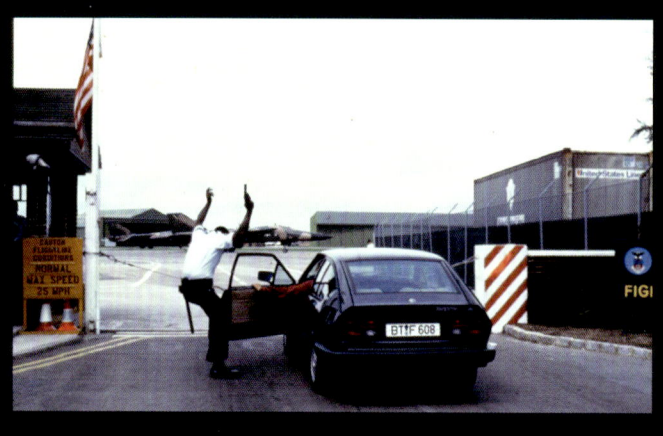

General Orlov's Mercedes saloon meets an unusual fate.

Left: Bond pursues an explosive train on two wheels, on a railway track, and in a 'borrowed' Alfa Romeo GTV 6.

shots show a black W123 – the quintessential Mercedes saloon – although some sources suggest a long wheelbase W115 was actually used for the interior shots). Look closely as they drive through the city and you'll see an Opel Ascona, a Ford Granada, Volvo 340, Simca 1300, Honda Accord, Mazda 323, Citroen Dyane, VW Golf, Golf GTI and Scirocco, a Lada, a Mk I Ford Capri, and a Porsche 928... It's all as evocative of the era as listening to Nena's '99 Red Balloons' or mainlining contemporary news footage of German Chancellor Helmut Kohl.

Equally 'of its time' is the Range Rover Convertible that stars in the film's pre-credits sequence. This conversion was done by a British coachbuilder called Rapport, who took the original Range Rover's burgeoning appeal with both Sloane rangers (as identified by celebrated style writer Peter York in the early 1980s) and more importantly in the Middle East to extravagant and taste-bothering new levels. Compared to the six-wheel Quadraporte version or the Starlight with the 'droop snoot' (which appended a Ford Granada's nose, to no good end), the Huntsman was a relatively discreet device.

It's certainly put to good use in Octopussy, towing the world's smallest jet aircraft, the Bede BD-5J Acrostar. The BD was designed by Jim Bede, who introduced the single-seat aircraft primarily in kit form. The BD jet used in Octopussy was built by John 'Corkey' Fornof and Bobby Bishop, had a wing span of just 17ft, weighed only 204kg, and had a top speed of 320mph. Although the action is set in a central American country, the sequence was shot in the altogether less balmy (and less politically turbulent) RAF Northolt, on the outskirts of London.

Director John Glen and production designer Peter Lamont cheated the hangar entrance the jet zooms through by foregrounding cut-outs of it, with the real thing in the background. But the shots of the jet flying into the hangar itself still happened for real, and some SFX trickery was required to render the shots of it in rapid transit. And this involved 'modifying' a Jaguar XJ6 saloon, as John Richardson recalled.

'One of my assistants was a very clever engineer. We got a Jaguar, cut the roof off, and made it as low as possible, built a pole-arm coming up from the middle of the car, onto which we mounted a full-sized BD jet on a little rocker. I was driving the car, and one of my assistants was in the back working the hydraulics to make the plane bank from side to side. We drove through at about 75mph. As we got close to the

Right: Correspondence from the EON archive relating to the long-wheelbase Mercedes saloon used for the briefing sequence in West Berlin.

"'I was praying that everyone else knew what they were doing. Unlike me...'"

camera, we would bank the jet over so the wing hid the pole-arm. We also had stuntmen closing the doors at the other end and I had to squeeze through.'

John Glen adds: 'We had soldiers running around in the shot to cover the pole-arm on the Jaguar. It's a great scene.' Roger Moore, meanwhile, was ensconced in the tiny cockpit. 'I was praying that everyone else knew what they were doing. Unlike me, who didn't know and was just sitting there...'

Exiting the hangar safely wasn't the end of Richardson's challenging time at the wheel of this ingenious contraption. 'When we came out [of the hangar], the road curved around quite sharply to the left. I couldn't stop the car because the throttle was jammed open. We ended up doing some interesting pirouettes across the grass before we hit one of the aircraft that was parked on the other side of it.'

Finally, a note on the Tuk-Tuk chase in Udaipur, whose filming commenced on 22 September 1982. Rémy Julienne and his team once again choreographed the sequence, as well as beefing up these charming but flimsy staples of Indian life, though even they had surely never experienced anything like it. As John Glen recalled. 'We were besieged by people. We'd ask for 5,000 extras and 10,000 would turn up. You can't actually see what you're filming for people.'

'In Udaipur,' John Richardson added, 'we had a vast number of general public, none of them used to a film unit, and *certainly* not used to three-wheel taxis with motorcycle engines that have been souped up to do 60mph through their midst.'

A prime example of this organised chaos actually made it through to the final cut. In the scene in which the treacherous Kamal Khan's henchmen are onboard a Jeep and assailing Bond's Tuk-Tuk with swords, a local on a bicycle spontaneously passes through the middle without looking left or right. 'He thought the conditions were normal,' Glen laughs.

Kamal Khan (the incomparable Louis Jourdan) uses two magnificent cars: we see him in a Mercedes 600 Pullman in London (the epic, triple-doored version, and thus even more plutocratic than the one used by Blofeld to gun down Tracy Bond in *On Her Majesty's Secret Service*), and a 1934 Rolls-Royce Phantom II Sedanca de Ville, whose bodywork was created by London-based coachbuilder Windovers. The Maharani of Udaipur had been very helpful to the producers in terms of locations and generally making things happen; this extended to the loan of one of the Rolls-Royces from the Royal Family's impressive automotive collection. It becomes embroiled in precisely zero car chases...

Eon Productions Ltd

DIRECTORS
M G WILSON U.S.A
K A BARKSHIRE
F B COOTE

2, SOUTH AUDLEY STREET,
LONDON
W1Y 5DQ

TELEPHONE
01-493 7953
CABLES BROCFILM LONDON, W.1
TELEX No 24351 CUBLON G

PLEASE REPLY:
c/o PINEWOOD STUDIOS,
PINEWOOD ROAD,
IVER,
BUCKS SL0 0NH
TEL: IVER (0753) 651700
TELEX 848091 EON G

Terry S Hogg Esq
Centurion & Merco Ltd
Cranleigh House
Cranleigh Gardens
Southall
Middx UB1 2BZ

28th July 1982

Dear Terry,

Re: 'OCTOPUSSY'

This is to confirm, as per our discussions with our Production Designer, Peter Lamont and myself, that you will supply one long wheel base Mercedes (registration number 401 MY) 1977 Model 280 LWB, with black exterior and interior, and driver for location filming in West Berlin.

We anticipate requiring the vehicle in West Berlin for approximately five days, exclusive of travelling to Berlin and return.

The charges will be at £130 per day for car and driver and Eon Productions will be responsible for all additional expenses i.e. accommodation, meals, fuel and ferry costs. It is understood that you will arrange all the necessary documents for the vehicle to travel to Berlin and that it is fully insured by you, with unlimited liability insurance.

It is also understood, that the driver you are supplying will be familiar with the Continent and West Berlin. He should report on Sunday 8th August to :-

Steingenberger Berlin Hotel
Rankestrabe 30,
D-1000 Berlin.
Tel: (010 49 30) 21080

to the Production Manager - Leonhard Gmür and/or Assistant Director, Gerry Gavigan. For additional information he can also contact the Production Assistant, May Capsaskis in the Production Office in the same hotel.

Yours sincerely
for and on behalf of
EON PRODUCTIONS LTD.

Hugh Harlow
Production Manager

copies: Tom Pevsner
Roy Barkshire
Douglas Noakes
U.A. (Teddy Joseph)
John Glen
Peter Lamont
John Richardson
Gerry Gavigan
Leonhard Gmür

US advance teaser poster, from 1985, with artwork by Dan Goozee.

CHAPTER 14
A VIEW TO A KILL

1985

STARRING Roger Moore as James Bond

Ten thousand extras in Udaipur had proved a tall order for the *Octopussy* crew and resulted in the last thing Rémy Julienne's meticulous stunt team would ever countenance: improvisation. Yet the automotive centrepiece of *A View To A Kill* was potentially even more challenging. Who other than James Bond would have the brass neck to shut down central Paris?

Loosely based on an Ian Fleming short story, Bond's 14th film outing also seems perhaps surprisingly *au courant* 35 years later, given that the film's protagonist is a wayward industrialist seeking to monopolise the global microchip market by flooding Silicon Valley ('the greatest cataclysm in human history and all attributed to natural causes'). Screenwriters Richard Maibaum and Michael G. Wilson had evidently figured out who would be pulling the levers of power as the 20th century gave way to the 21st.

A View To A Kill's first half is largely set in France, before shifting to San Francisco for the denouement. Michael G. Wilson: '[The original short story] was a French location, and we'd had some good results there in *Moonraker*. So we went back again, because it was a good place to film, and there were plenty of exciting places for us to shoot: the Eiffel Tower, the big chateaux.'

Eighties pop kids thrilled to the sight of May Day (Grace Jones) leaping off Paris's most famous building while Duran Duran seemingly starred in their own mini Bond movie, by celebrated video directors Godley and Creme.

But car geeks are also supremely well served by the film, mid-decade France and California proving equally compelling provided you're not looking for a Q-branch fettled Bond car. Instead, the

On set in Paris, August 1984. Bond stunt-driving regular Rémy Julienne was on home turf on this occasion.

Left: Singer, fashion model and artist's muse Grace Jones was a memorable Bond villain. Above: Rarely seen images from the Paris car chase shoot. Note the camera tracking car. Stunt driver boss Rémy Julienne is holding the walkie talkie.

hero here is a humble Renault 11, the unlikeliest star car since the AMC Hornet a decade before (AMC and Renault had by now forged a Stateside product alliance). According to the film's director, John Glen, the Renault was chosen chiefly because it was a common car in Paris at the time, especially among the taxi-driving fraternity (Bond commandeers it from a cabbie). That said, the car's blue exterior paint wasn't taxi appropriate for the time, and indeed its top-spec TXE trim – which ran to an early LCD instrument display and a talking dashboard – would have baffled the average Parisian driver. (Upscale versions of the contemporary British Austin Maestro were similarly equipped, in a doomed bid for modernity.)

This sequence isn't a car chase so much as a showcase for the talents of Rémy Julienne and co (his equally gifted sons Michel and Dominique were now part of the family business). It combines the balletic qualities seen in *The Italian Job* with the breathtaking and relentless panel-beating that occurred in the brilliant *La Casse* (Paris now the location rather than the Greek port of Piraeus). During his pursuit of May Day along the Seine, Bond is seen sliding the Renault backwards and forwards down two flights of steps, launches off a transporter onto the top deck of a bus, and slices the roof off on a traffic barrier, before finally splitting the car in two and abandoning it on Pont Alexandre III (it's front-wheel drive, but let's not quibble about the fuel line…) It is, by some margin, the most ambitious car chase ever seen in a Bond film, and of course hugely enjoyable for the same reason. And because it dares to take place at the heart of one of the world's most spectacular cities.

OK, so it's not pause-button-friendly; the car that collides with Bond is a BMW 323i from the POV angle, but mysteriously turns into a Renault 20 in the wide shot, and when the roof goes so does any pretence

Opposite (top): Roger Moore on set in an eviscerated Renault 11. Opposite (bottom): Julienne worked out all his driving stunts with precision, as can be seen in this image he sent to director John Glen, from a 1984 test run. Far left: Actress Alison Doody with a Renault Fuego turbo. Left: A rarely seen image of a ministerial Peugeot 604 limousine, with clapperboard.

that it's Roger Moore at the wheel. Although in fairness, he would probably have happily performed the stunt himself. 'Roger was a fantastic driver,' John Glen says. 'When you're driving you don't move all that much, although if you're acting you try to make it look dynamic. In terms of "acting" driving, of getting the body language right, you can't honestly equate it to real life.'

Visual effects boss John Richardson prepared the Renault for its evisceration by doing what dodgy car dealers used to refer to as 'cut-and-shut', ensuring that the two halves would splinter on cue. Both Glen's main unit and Arthur Wooster's second unit worked on the sequence, from 30 July to 15 August 1984, because so many of the shots needed Moore.

For all its bravado, Glen also cites the sequence as a quintessential example of how well-oiled the Bond machine had become by this point. 'On a Bond film, you've employed the best people. And in the industry, *everyone* wants to do a Bond film. So you get lots of help, they're ahead of you, they know what's required, they've done their homework. Pre-production is vital. Bond is a long-running series, and to an extent the patterns are set. People know what's expected. Before you turn over a foot of film everyone knows what they're doing.

'But we also had very good relations with the mayor of Paris. The Bond films had a reputation for doing things honorably. When we said we'd do something properly, then we'd do it properly. We assured him we wouldn't do anything embarrassing or stupid.'

The film's other highest profile car is also one with an important owner: the silver 1962 Rolls-Royce Silver Cloud II which Sir Godfrey Tibbett (Patrick Macnee) uses to chauffeur Bond to Zorin's estate – shot at Chantilly, in Hauts-de-France north of Paris – was Cubby Broccoli's personal car, driven to the location by the great man himself. Its performance was more spirited than its predecessor could muster thanks to the new 6.2-litre V8 engine.

Poor old Sir Godfrey is extinguished by May Day while he puts the Rolls through a car wash (an unconscionable act but surely

Old friends and sometime rivals on British television, Patrick Macnee and Roger Moore during filming at Chantilly, August 1984. Producer Cubby Broccoli's 1962 Rolls-Royce Silver Cloud II looks on.

Rarely seen images from *A View To A Kill*. Below: That famous EON Rolls-Royce, which is still used today for Bond premieres. Opposite, clockwise from top: San Francisco's Golden Gate bridge is the location for the film's spectacular climax; a Corvette as used by KGB agent Pola Ivanova; mayhem during the fire engine chase; Mayday and Max Zorin (Christopher Walken) watch as the Rolls submerges; Roger Moore, actress Tanya Roberts and a fire hose; Walken and the Broccoli Rolls-Royce.

not on pain of death), and the car is later pushed into a lake with Bond inside; he escapes and survives by sucking air out of the tyre. That sequence was shot at a flooded gravel pit in Wraysbury, Berkshire, using a stand-in vehicle. Cubby Broccoli's car, wearing the famous CUB 1 registration plate (but replaced in the film with 354 HYK) is still a key part of the EON car collection, and is regularly used for Bond film premieres.

The transfer of the action to San Francisco, the highlight of which is a genuinely gob-smacking chase through the city with Bond variously at the wheel of and hanging off a 1964 American LaFrance 900 fire truck, involves a sea of largely forgettable mid-1980s US vehicles. A few handsome old Cadillacs pop up, and the Corvette C4 driven by KGB agent Pola Ivanova (Fiona Fullerton) offers some proof that not all of America's automotive icons went to hell in a handcart as their makers grappled with the demands of a difficult new decade. Much the same could be said for the Jeep Cherokee driven by Stacey Sutton (Tanya Roberts). And indeed the '82 Ford Bronco XLT that keeps a steely watch outside her house.

Who doesn't love a Bronco?
(NB: We can't list them all here, but as well as being an amazing piece of film-making, the Paris chase sequence is a great throwback to forgotten gems of an era that's increasingly popular with car fans. These include the Citroën CX, in saloon and vast estate forms, the Fiat Panda and Ritmo, Ford Escort cabriolet and Granada estate, Opel Kadett, Peugeots 104 ZS, 304 saloon, 505, Renaults 4 van, 5 and 9, Talbot VF3 van, and VWs Beetle, Golf and Jetta. But the winner here is the Matra Murena, a pretty, affordable mid-engined coupé with three-abreast seating, of which just 10,680 were made by the automotive offshoot of the noted French aerospace, defence and technology company. We also see Bond leave a ministry building in Paris with M and Sir Godfrey Tibbett in a stretched version of Peugeot's 604 saloon (filmed on 24 August 1984), as fabricated by noted French coachbuilder Heuliez, though this particular one is a US-spec car. It's also not as elegantly boxy as the Pininfarina-designed original. Finally, an approving nod to Jenny Flex's Renault Fuego Turbo, another affordable and pretty French coupé now thoroughly lost to the mists of time.)

Japanese one sheet, from December 1987, artwork by Brian Bysouth. 'Commemorating its 25th year, the brand-new 15th instalment of the series! James Bond – living for danger' is the tagline translation.

CHAPTER 15

THE LIVING DAYLIGHTS

1987

STARRING Timothy Dalton as James Bond

The Living Daylights was a film that reflected changing times. Casting began in January 1986, an era that was newly defined by *glasnost* in the Soviet Union and a growing societal paranoia given the terrible realities of the Aids crisis. The Cold War was shifting into a fascinating new phase, and life in general suddenly seemed a great deal more serious.

'The story had a complex central relationship where Bond falls in love with a woman who falls in love with him, and she betrays him, and then she has to come back and help him. It required a greater romantic focus, so we couldn't have too many other distractions,' producer and screenwriter Michael G. Wilson later observed.

Timothy Dalton, who became the fourth actor to be awarded the role of James Bond in the franchise, had been on Cubby Broccoli's radar for a while. Now the stars and zeitgeist had aligned for this most serious-minded and thoughtful of actors. He was clear about how he perceived the character. 'First and foremost I wanted to make him human. [Bond] is not a superman – you can't identify with a superman,' Dalton noted. 'I wanted to capture that occasional vulnerability. And I wanted to capture the spirit of Ian Fleming.'

It was an approach that certainly resonated with the producers. 'When we met Timothy in 1986, we saw that during these intervening years he had added poise, experience, self-assurance. He was excited by the idea,' Cubby Broccoli remarked. 'He saw Bond as being more serious, just as ballsy as Connery's 007, but carrying his own imprint. He wanted to play the character closer to the way Fleming wrote it – which was in line with the sort of Bond we had in mind.'

And it's all there in the film's terrific opening sequence. Arthur Wooster's second unit began filming in Gibraltar on 17 September 1986, with Bond as one of three 00 agents apparently on a training mission to infiltrate an SAS-guarded radar station. There's an immediate sense of jeopardy. When it goes wrong and his two colleagues are taken out by a KGB assassin implementing its *Smiert Spionam* ('death to spies') policy, Bond gives chase by leaping onto the canvas roof of a Land Rover 88 Series III as it hurtles along a vertiginous road.

As with many of the 1980s Bond films, this is a beautifully edited sequence that packs a fast-moving and impressively visceral impact,

Actress Maryam d'Abo with 007's Aston Martin V8 Volante.

Two lesser spotted 007 cars. Above: A Rover 800 as seen in the Blayden House scenes. Below: Bond's Audi 200 in Tangiers.

Rover, and I said, "All we want are some nice big close-ups of you." But he was keen and threw himself around. I couldn't get rid of him quick enough – I was terrified.' Dalton remembers it a little differently. 'They put me on the Rock of Gibraltar, on the top of a cliff, a 700ft sheer, damned cliff, and I hate heights,' he reflected during an interview with *Entertainment Weekly* in 2010.

The scene itself culminates in Bond and the assassin spearing off the mountainside, 007 parachuting to safety as the Land Rover explodes below. It's an amazing stunt, and it took considerable planning. Special effects supervisor John Richardson and his team had gone to the Mojave desert, in California, and dangled a Land Rover off a winch beneath a Sikorsky H-34 helicopter, before dropping it 2,000ft. Producer Michael G. Wilson recalled: 'You can't just start dropping cars out of the sky and hope that they land safely. We were planning to use a parachute so that we could do two takes with the Land Rover.'

It didn't go well, as Richardson remembered. 'We attempted it twice and on the second occasion the parachute inside didn't open – it got wrapped around the Land Rover. [The car] had been about six feet high and was reduced to about four inches. It had just flattened completely when it hit the ground.'

The finished scene was shot at Beachy Head on the Sussex coast in December, and used that Bond stunt staple the air cannon to achieve the necessary trajectory. The parachute was deployed by radio control, with a dummy attached. Insert shots were done at Pinewood but the overall effect remains impactful; credit is also due to the film's editors, John Grover and Peter Davies.

When the action moves to Iron Curtain-era Bratislava, in Czechoslovakia, it's a reminder that not all Communist-era cars were a disaster. In the midst of sundry Ladas and Skoda 105s – which were regarded rather unfairly as joke cars in the West during the 1980s – there's a glimpse of something altogether less derivative: a Tatra 603. Tatra was the third oldest car-maker in the world, and much of its success was down to its chief engineer Hans Ledwinka (he knew Ferdinand Porsche, whose concept for the Nazis' 1930s Kdf-Wagen owed more than a little to Ledwinka's thinking). Post-Second World War, however, the Soviet Bloc's COMECON (Council for Mutual Economic Assistance) insisted that Tatra stick to truck manufacture despite its history in innovative, streamlined rear-engined cars. Some of its top engineers ignored the edict, so the 603 was actually conceived and developed covertly; that is until a return to car-making was later approved, mostly so that the socialist government's apparatchiks had something decent to travel in. Between 1957 and 1975, just 20,422 were made, and it remains an outstanding automotive curio thanks to its outré looks and unusual engineering. (Also for knowledgeable film production designers: a Tatra 603 plays a prominent part in 2004's under-appreciated *Lemony Snicket's A Series of Unfortunate Events*.)

a legacy perhaps of director John Glen's experience helming the second unit and his faith in Arthur Wooster as his successor.

Both also benefited from Dalton's willingness to get truly stuck in. 'Tim's very good at action. He was a good mover and he was very keen to do as much of his own stunt work as possible. He's always a little uneasy when someone else is impersonating him,' Glen recalled. Dalton arrived alone in Gibraltar not long after completing work on another film. 'I had a message from Cubby saying, "Don't damage him",' Wooster recalled. 'We got him on top of the Land

The Living Daylights is an excellent showcase for the original Land Rover's near unstoppability. Below: A brief cameo for a Chevrolet Impala.

Left: Scenes from the chase to the Austrian border. Special effects man Chris Corbould is pictured with the Aston Martin V8. Above: A rarely seen storyboard for the sequence in which the Aston Martin sprouts skis.

Back in *The Living Daylights*, Bond heads to the Austrian border in a quintessential though now rather forgotten 1980s car, the Audi 200 quattro. This is one of two Audis he drives in the film (we also see him in a 200 Avant in Tangier). This third generation of Audi's large executive saloon was a key car in the brand's evolution: it arrived in 1982 at a time when the automotive industry was in thrall to aerodynamics (in marketing as well as practical terms), its slippery shape and flush-fitting glazing marking it out as an innovator in a category that remained generally conservative.

The 200 quattro turbo was the pinnacle car, embellished in the film with split-rim BBS alloy wheels and then fashionable bodywork mods by well-regarded German tuner ABT Sportsline (which has an esteemed history in the DTM race series and more recently Formula E). If *The Living Daylights* is an unfairly overlooked 007 film, then the Audi is a rare-groove Bond car appreciated by fans who like to look a little deeper. (There's also a notable cameo for a 1959 Chevrolet Impala, a car with previous Bond form.)

Not least because it inevitably played second fiddle to a returning hero: Aston Martin. Absent for eight films and almost 20 years (if we set aside the brief glimpse of a DBS in Q's workshop in *Diamonds Are Forever*, a scene that was actually filmed in Aston Martin's Newport Pagnell base), the marque most associated with James Bond was now firmly back. 'It was a great positive,' Michael G. Wilson observed.

The positivity worked both ways: manufacturing and selling high-performance cars is a capricious business, and Aston Martin's priceless association with James Bond has seen it through some difficult times. By the 1980s, the company was in the hands of charismatic businessman, car enthusiast and aviator Victor Gauntlett, whose success in the petrochemical industry led him to invest in Aston Martin at a time when recession threatened to finish it off. There's little doubt that Aston Martin might have disappeared altogether were it not for his commitment, and the deal he brokered with Ford in 1987; there's absolutely no doubt whatsover that it was Gauntlett who got the brand back into Bond, dealing directly with Cubby Broccoli.

Indeed, he even loaned his personal V8 Volante to the production, which is the car we see Bond driving as he arrives at the fictional Blayden House MI6 stronghold (filmed at Stoner Park near Henley-on-Thames in Oxfordshire; note also the Rover 800 and a pair of Daimlers) for a debriefing with M and KGB defector Georgi Koskov (Jeroen Krabbé). Effectively an evolution of the DBS V8 that had appeared in 1969, the V8's continued existence may have been proof of the company's lack of development funds, but for many it still epitomised the great British sports car.

Gauntlett's Volante was fitted with a Vantage engine, but neither it nor any of the other three cars used in *The Living Daylights* were technically Vantages. And although we see Q 'winterising' the Aston by fitting a hard-top, the V8 (which Aston Martin refers to as a saloon, despite its coupé silhouette) that Bond then drives to Bratislava is categorically not a Volante with a roof.

The producers bought three V8 saloons, all of which were prepared for filming by Aston, and seven fibreglass mock-ups were also constructed for the more brutal parts of the sequence. While Bond and Kara Milovy (Maryam d'Abo) are pursued as they head to the Austrian border, the Aston's extensive suite of gadgets is revealed: there are lasers in the wheel hubs, retractable outriggers, heat-seeking missiles with head-up display, bulletproof glass, a jet engine hidden behind the rear number

Right: Preparing for a take with the Aston Martin V8, Austria, January 1987.

plate, a self-destruct mode, and a radio that scans for the local police frequency.

At one point, the car also turns into a fishing hut, a (non-Q branch) disguise it quickly sheds; two barns were made, one of balsa wood that the car could drive straight through, the other on a frame that the Aston could effectively 'drive'. 'Unless you've got an unlimited supply of action vehicles, which you rarely do, they have to be nurtured and caressed, as they suffer constant abuse,' John Richardson recalled.

The sequence on the lake was shot at Weissensee, southern Austria, but as it was January it was also perilously cold. This was a problem for both equipment and crew, as long-standing Bond special effects wizard Chris Corbould remembered: 'It was 30° below out there. We had to fire the Aston Martin up a ramp to go over the top of a hut. Because of the extreme cold, we fired the car with compressed air but, instead of opening up quickly, the valves had contracted and opened slowly. Instead of firing off like mad, the car just went "blump" and straight into the hut. It was a total disaster. I went over to Cubby and said, "I'm terribly sorry." "Don't worry, we'll come back tomorrow and do it again," he said.'

Having tried to heat the valves up and insulate them, the crew found that Cubby had already paid for their drinks at the hotel bar when they got back that night.

Above: Concept art for the Aston in ski mode. Opposite (top): The V8 prepares for take-off. Opposite (bottom): Due to the sub-zero conditions, the stunt car initially didn't achieve the trajectory the special effects crew were expecting. The following day, things went more smoothly.

The next day they regrouped. 'Cubby sat in the same seat, we fired the car and it flew like a dream,' Corbould recalled. '"Was that better?" I said to him. He said, "Yeah, that's exactly what I knew would happen…"'

Cubby Broccoli had surely seen it all by this stage of his incredible producing career. Although initially unsure that the idea of Bond and Kara escaping in her cello case would work, John Glen proved it was viable after they both visited an MGM sound stage in LA to try one out. Mind you, the film version had to be fitted with skis and steering gear. (That's Timothy Dalton throwing the cello in the air for real as they pass beneath the security barrier.)

As a Land Rover starred in *The Living Daylights*' pre-credits sequence, so another capped the film's stunning Afghanistan-set climax (actually shot in Ouarzazate, Morocco). Although its body is modified to resemble a Russian UAZ-469 military SUV, it's definitely a Land Rover 90 that Kara drives up a ramp and into the Hercules Bond is flying (the aircraft was borrowed from the Royal Moroccan Air Force). As Hercules aren't legally permitted to taxi with their loading ramps down, the producers had to improvise – and did so ingeniously. The team sourced the biggest furniture truck they could lay their hands on, and mocked up a cowling at the back of the trailer to resemble the tail of the Hercules. When the plane runs out of fuel, forcing Bond and Kara to bail out using the Land Rover, John Richardson and the model unit got to work once again.

'The vehicle coming out of the plane was a model, and the tricky thing was getting it to a predetermined altitude: it had to be something like two feet off the ground, which is very low. We had a radio-controlled drogue parachute connected to a full-size parachute connected to a model of the car.'

When the vehicle hits the ground, there's a brief excursion through a wall, and the small matter of the Hercules exploding behind them, before the duo arrive at a fork in the road. 'I know a great restaurant in Karachi. We can just make dinner,' Bond says impishly.

Aston Martin apart, where would he be without a Land Rover?

Japanese one sheet, September 1989. 'Even when he loses his licence... he'll put his life on the line for friends in peril' is how the tagline is translated.

CHAPTER 16
LICENCE TO KILL

1989

STARRING Timothy Dalton as James Bond

Above: Desmond Llewelyn as Q makes a sortie beyond his gadget bunker and finds himself in the fictional Isthmus City chauffeuring Bond in a Rolls-Royce Silver Shadow II. Below: Lupe Lamora (Talisa Soto) with a Willys Jeep M38. Although she's the mistress of the film's central villain, Franz Sanchez, the relationship is abusive and she becomes an ally of 007.

The action movie came of age in the Eighties. 'High concept' script ideas – delivered in what became known as the elevator pitch – rendered nuance increasingly redundant, while huge one-man brands such as Schwarzenegger and Stallone rode rough-shod like human juggernauts over the cinematic landscape. Once again, 007 changed gears, and in *Licence To Kill* the result was a darker Bond film. Another sign of the times, perhaps: just as the world was reeling at medieval behaviour in Latin America, so the villain of this 16th Bond movie was a Central American drug baron.

This was also a film in which screenwriters Michael G. Wilson and Richard Maibaum (who was sidelined by a writer's strike for a time) purposely tailored the story to suit Timothy Dalton's approach, allowing him to play to the darker side of Ian Fleming's Bond. Robert Davi, who portrayed the drug lord who sets Bond on a vendetta that prompts the revocation of his licence, noted that 'Sanchez is a character Shakespeare would be writing about if he were alive today.' Michael G. Wilson also had noble inspiration: Sanchez's hubris and paranoia owed something to the antagonists in Akira Kurosawa's majestic 1961 classic *Yojimbo*, which stars the incomparable Toshiro Mifune.

Not even a master like Kurosawa ever dreamt up a sequence like the tanker chase and interception that provides *Licence To Kill* with its climax, however. As director John Glen, shooting his fifth consecutive Bond, told me, he is a big fan of Henri-Georges Clouzot's 1953 classic *The Wages of Fear*, in which four mercenaries are paid to transport nitroglycerine along a hazardous road; the influence is palpable. 'That was probably the most complicated and dangerous sequence I ever devised,' he recalled. 'I drew the whole thing up, and it's a major part of the film. I had to leave Churubusco studios [Pinewood's replacement for *Licence To Kill*] and go to the location with the actors for a week or so [from 3 to 7 October 1988]. I used a Mexican editor to assemble [second unit director] Arthur Wooster's material as he went along, and even had a mobile cutting room in a truck.

'It was a six-week job for Arthur. Maybe even two months. We were in a remote area of Mexico, at an altitude of 7,000ft above sea level, and we had to build an airfield up there. Barbara Broccoli was in situ producing it. It was her first major production job, and she did an excellent job.'

Kenworth stepped up and supported the production on Rémy Julienne's recommendation. 'These trucks are very big,' Julienne observed with Gallic understatement. 'Bigger than French trucks.'

Meanwhile, special effects supervisor Chris Corbould found himself in Mexico City tasked with finding the trailers and tankers to go with the tractor units. 'That was an ordeal in itself. One of the biggest jobs we had to do was make them all look the same, because they didn't all look the same… The tankers were different sizes, some had handrails and some didn't. And the people who had them soon cottoned on that somebody was going around buying up these old used trailers and the price started going up and up. So I had to go around incognito.'

Rémy Julienne and his team proceeded to make them dance: on their back wheels, driven precariously on nine wheels, sideways across gravel and off cliff edges, into walls, alongside steep drops… you name it, they did it. Kenworth's chief engineer Larry Orr recalls the initial discussions. 'When Rémy told me of his needs, the first thing I thought was, "Where do we get the resources?" The second thing was, "This is going to be a lot of fun."'

Once the vehicles had left Kenworth's Seattle production line, the engines received upgraded turbos and new injectors, while a local firm called Truckweld beefed up the suspension on the designated 'wheelie' stunt trucks. One of the company's retired engineers, Moe

Buringrud, was also tasked with rigging a dual steer system for the scenes in which Pam Bouvier (Carey Lowell) is seen behind the wheel. 'That was a monumental job,' Orr recalled. 'Nobody knew for sure whether you could work the engine with two throttle pedals independently. All the linkages were new. Moe even published an instruction manual to send to Mexico with the truck.'

There were 16 vehicles in all, the stunt trucks named Pamela One, Two and Three in honour of the film's heroine. One of the trucks was producing 1,000bhp, far in excess of its standard power output. 'We learned that trucks could do all sorts of things we never knew,' Orr observed. 'But perhaps Rémy knew…'

There wasn't much Rémy didn't know, but this sequence tested him and his team like nothing before, for often unusual reasons. 'Driving the rig on two wheels was one of the biggest challenges,' John Glen recalled. 'Rémy had an airfield in France, and he told me, "I've got this guy in Paris, if anyone can do it he can."' Stunt drivers, by their very nature, are often unusual characters. 'Well, this guy flew into Mexico City and promptly disappeared; he'd met a girl on the flight and gone off with her, so I thought that was that. But on the

'The tanker chase was the most dangerous sequence I ever devised'

morning of the shoot he duly turns up, we do take one, he did it perfectly, and came down bam on top of the Jeep in front. Then he was straight off to the plane back to France, or perhaps to see his new friend.

'We were prepared to use some trickery if we needed to, but the guy did it *perfectly*. The truck could have turned over… We had 16 of them on set, a million dollars' worth or more. In the end, we wrote off all but one of them.'

The second unit was using a road called La Rumorosa, which connects Mexicali to Tecate and Tijuana just over the border with California. It's spectacular but also dangerous, notorious in local folklore for having claimed the lives of many unwitting travellers and widely thought to be haunted. Already struggling with the intense heat, high altitude, and a lengthy commute from their hotel to the

Rigging exploding tankers high in the Mexican mountains proved to be one of the toughest challenges Bond special effects supremo Chris Corbould tackled during his long career.

947

950

948

951

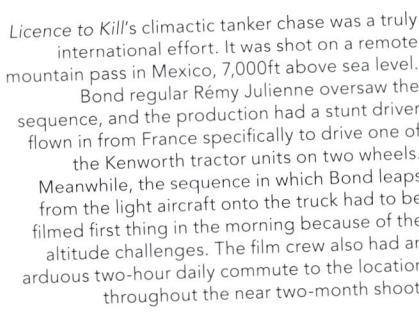

Licence to Kill's climactic tanker chase was a truly international effort. It was shot on a remote mountain pass in Mexico, 7,000ft above sea level. Bond regular Rémy Julienne oversaw the sequence, and the production had a stunt driver flown in from France specifically to drive one of the Kenworth tractor units on two wheels. Meanwhile, the sequence in which Bond leaps from the light aircraft onto the truck had to be filmed first thing in the morning because of the altitude challenges. The film crew also had an arduous two-hour daily commute to the location throughout the near two-month shoot.

952

Above: A rare example of a big-screen outing for a Maserati Biturbo 425, unusual but insightful casting.

location, the Bond crew now found themselves spooked by a series of unexplained events. Vehicles burst into flames in the middle of the night, and one started moving of its own volition. A special effects rocket managed to hit a telephone linesman up a pole two and a half miles away.

Chris Corbould vividly remembers the challenges of this particular shoot, many of which went beyond the expected realm. 'All kinds of things went wrong up there. We couldn't explain a lot of them. We were dealing with tankers that weighed in excess of five tonnes, and doing weird things with them. Sending them over the edges of cliffs, front wheelies, and some huge explosions. Probably some of the biggest explosions I'd ever done. To have a 4,000-gallon tanker blowing up, you have to create something pretty immense. Two of the tankers were meant to be smashing into one another, but the driver overcooked it a bit and sent one of the trucks into the wall. I was in that truck letting off spark effects, and thought, "That was an extra hard bump," and suddenly I was looking at sky. Not planned, but it looked so spectacular they actually wrote that part of the sequence around the crash. So there was some improvisation there, but it all worked out. It's definitely something I'll remember. Everyone likes a bit of intrigue, but the spooky stuff didn't get to me. I don't think I'll go back there for a holiday, though.'

Not that *Licence To Kill* is completely devoid of cars. The quixotic Maserati 425 is well cast as the bad guys' transport (complete with rocket launcher in the boot). A four-door evolution of the Biturbo, a modish-looking coupé originally conceived as a more accessible entry point for this most aristocratic of Italian car-makers. The mid-1970s turnaround plan was presided over by another famous name, Alejandro de Tomaso, who was entreated by the Italian government to rescue the company. It worked, up to a point, insofar as Maserati is still with us today and almost certainly wouldn't be if it hadn't been for the Biturbo.

Q pops up in chauffeur's uniform behind the wheel of a Rolls-Royce Silver Shadow II in the fictional Isthmus City, and there's plenty of screen time for a Rolls Phantom V. We also see Bond briefly driving one of the few good-looking US cars of the era, a Lincoln Mark VII, in LSC spec (rather than the Versace limited edition, thankfully), whose venerable 5.0-litre V8 was making a whole 225bhp by this stage in its career. But it's Timothy Dalton sawing at the wheel of a vast 18-wheeler for which *Licence To Kill* is perhaps best remembered. 'If you believe it's me, it's me. If you can see it's me, it's me,' as he once noted.

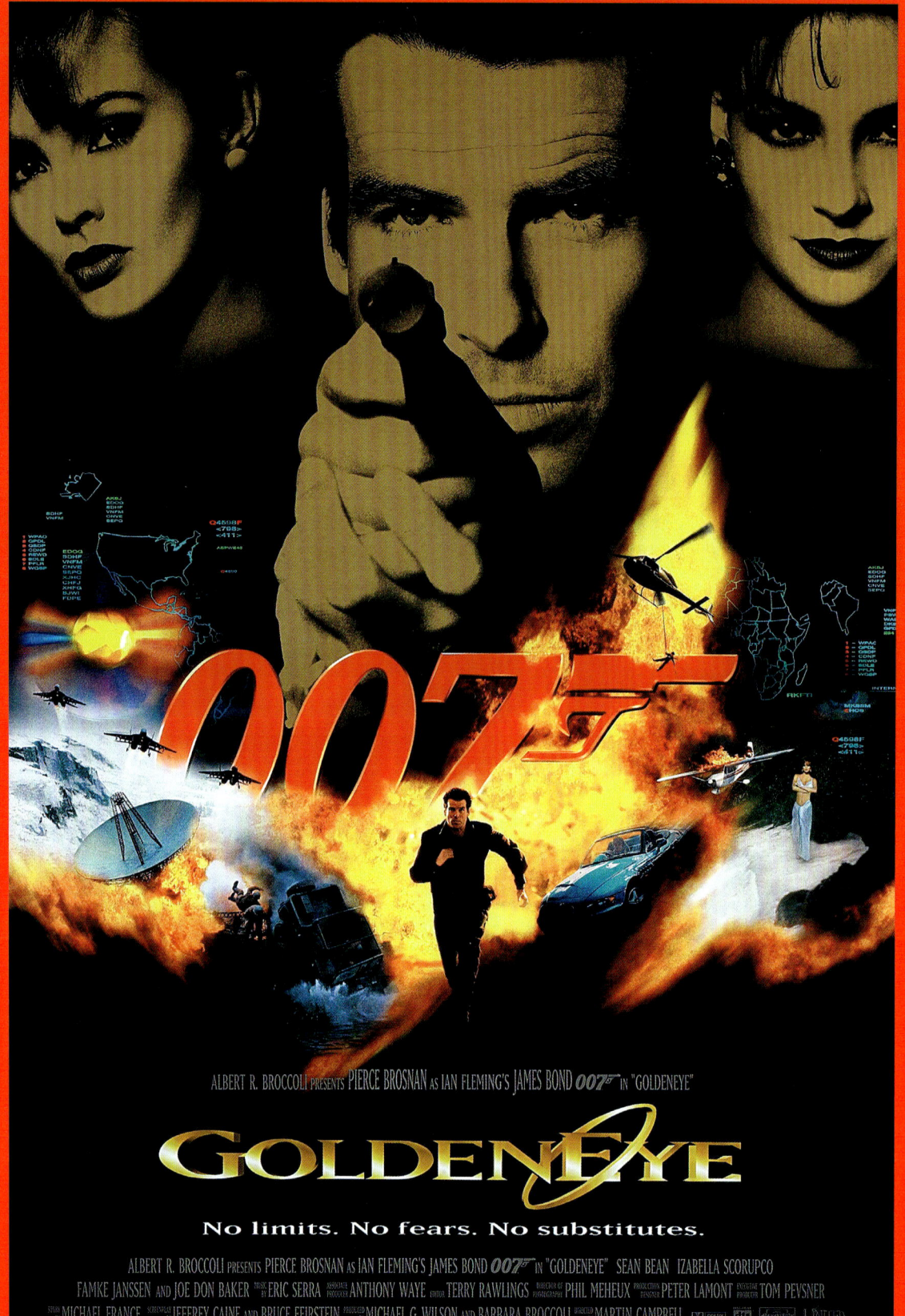

US one sheet, November 1995. Photography by Terry O'Neill, Keith Hamshere and George Whitear, with art direction by Earl Klasky and Randi Braun. The American image added a small inset of the light aircraft and Natalya compared to the British one quad.

CHAPTER 17
GOLDENEYE
1995

STARRING Pierce Brosnan as James Bond

The six years that elapsed between *Licence To Kill* and *GoldenEye*, caused by a complicated legal battle surrounding the acquisition of MGM/UA by Giancarlo Parretti, was the longest gap between films since the series started. Timothy Dalton would have resumed the role of 007 if the usual distance between instalments had been observed, but in April 1994 he announced that he was signing off. The search was on for his replacement.

'We looked at younger people and different kinds of people who were available. I think we all came to a conclusion early on that Bond is a veteran. You need a person who is experienced. Pierce Brosnan was just the right age,' producer Michael G. Wilson summarised. Having been in the frame since meeting Cubby Broccoli on the set of *For Your Eyes Only*, 41-year-old Brosnan was now, at last, officially Bond. 'The first film I saw when I came to London as a boy was *Goldfinger*. In Ireland, I had been brought up on a diet of Old Mother Riley and Norman Wisdom, so it was a bedazzling moment, seeing this lady covered in gold paint. I ended up getting the toy car with an ejector seat, but I didn't really have any aspirations to be James Bond. The character who really captured my imagination was Oddjob,' he told *The Guardian* in 2019.

With Martin Campbell at the helm, *GoldenEye* pulsed with a renewed sense of purpose. The pre-credits leap from the dam, which experts at Oxford University determined would be like 'jumping into the unknown', was one hell of a statement of intent, and a new high point even for the Bond series.

'With Bond, we used to say: "What's never been done before action-wise?"' Campbell told *The Guardian*. 'It's quite difficult after

16 films. For the bungee jump off the dam at the start of the film, we used the Contra dam in Switzerland. There was no digital manipulation: the stuntman Wayne Michaels just did the 700ft jump. As they were doing the countdown, he saw the guy on the crane crossing himself. He did it perfectly the first time. I guess he didn't want to do a second.'

Bond was also a legacy commodity so, as well as reintroducing a certain sophistication and a sly sense of humour, a few other key elements returned. The Aston Martin DB5's reappearance marked the first time 007 had found himself behind that famous three-spoke steering wheel since 1965's *Thunderball*. On one level, of course, it worked as a huge crowd-pleaser, but it also established an important narrative through-line.

The DB5 chase also comes straight out of the opening credits, an unambiguous automotive salvo: welcome home, Bond fans. In the story, the location was the famous hills that twist and turn high above Monaco, but the sequence was actually shot on the Route de Thorenc and Route de Gentelly in the Alpes-Martimes, some 47 miles from the Principality. Filming of this sequence commenced on 20 February 1995 with second unit director Ian Sharp in charge, while the driving was under the command of local hero and Bond action regular Rémy Julienne.

Three Astons were used during filming:

'The Ferrari is a racing machine, an animal. The Aston Martin is a dream car, something mythical'

a 'hero' car in pristine condition, and two rather more loved examples that were restored by main Aston Martin dealer Stratton Motor Company before being sent to France.

Given that these films pretty much wrote the template for international high living, *GoldenEye* set a surprising precedent: this was the first Bond film to feature a Ferrari. The F355 GTS is a suitably flamboyant way of introducing the film's femme fatale, Xenia Onatopp (Famke Janssen), who engages Bond in what can only be described as automotive foreplay, much to the chagrin of the MI6 operative who's beside him in the Aston attempting to conduct a psychiatric evaluation. (Bond later assuages her doubts in classic 007 style when he reveals a bottle of Bollinger in a chiller between the seats.)

'There's a very subtle race between the two protagonists, one in a Ferrari F355 which is a real animal, and the DB5 which is a relatively ancient vehicle,' Julienne noted during filming. 'We're afraid to hurt it when we drive such a venerable machine. Each time we force it my heart becomes weak because this vehicle for me is something mythical. Superlight in structure, the shape… it's a dream car. It's different with the Ferrari. It's a racing machine, it can

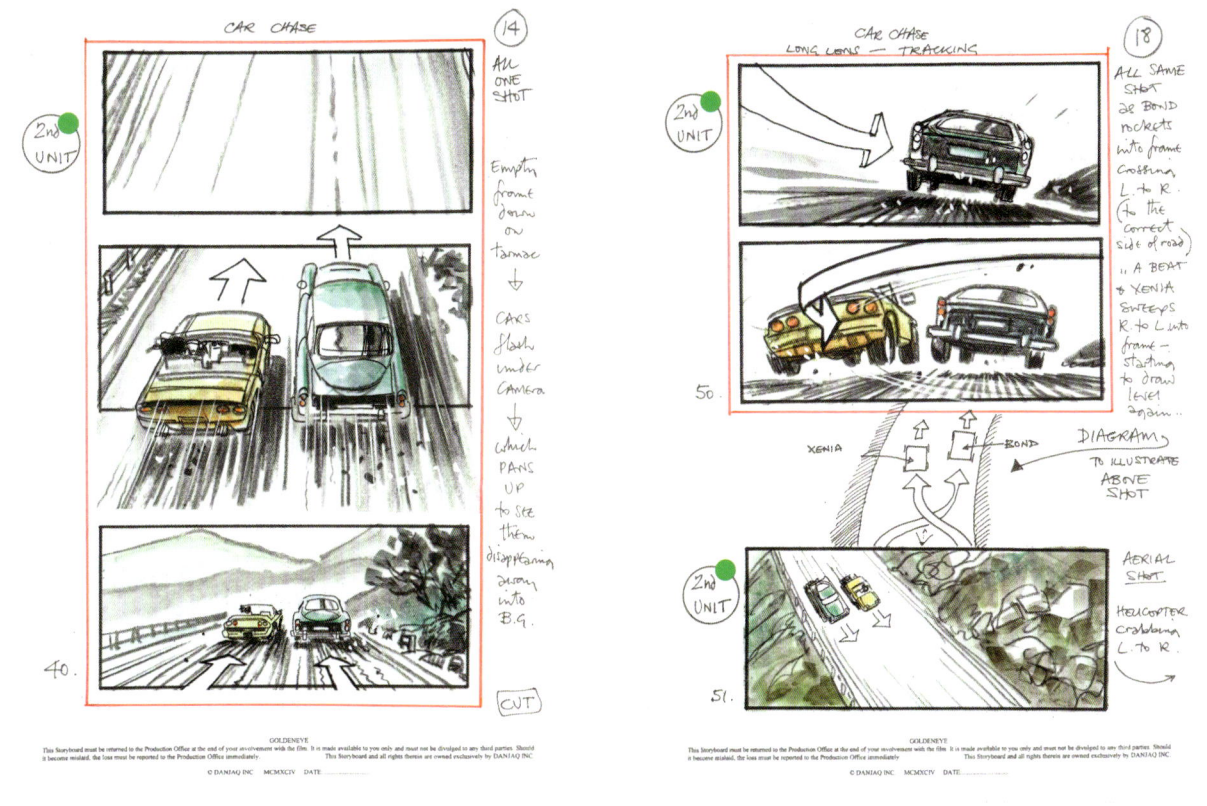

Above: Storyboard for the chase between Bond's Aston Martin DB5 and Xenia Onatopp's Ferrari F355 GTS. The sequence was filmed during February 1995 in the Alpes-Maritime, and coordinated by long-standing Bond stunt-driving supremo, Rémy Julienne. It also marked the first time a Ferrari had appeared in a Bond film. The car is later pictured in Monte Carlo's Casino Square, where it's revealed to be wearing false registration plates and thus presumably stolen.

On location in Puerto Rico, the crew setting up for Bond's first outing in his latest car, the BMW Z3.

Above: New Bond Pierce Brosnan with series legend, Desmond Llewelyn. Below: Brosnan on set with BMW Z3 and actress Izabella Scorupco. Opposite: With Roger Moore during a set visit to Leavesden Studios.

be brutalised. The Aston Martin, we are always worried about.'

The F355 represented something of a reboot for Ferrari. When the company's founder Enzo Ferrari passed away in 1988, this most celebrated of Italian companies endured an identity crisis that coincided with the weakest new cars in its then 40-year history, compounded by a dip in its Formula One fortunes. In 1991, the Fiat group boss and paterfamilias Gianni Agnelli appointed Luca di Montezemolo – one of the most suave figures in the global automotive industry – as the new CEO, and there was a rapid return to form. The F355 was launched in mid-1994, based on the outgoing 348 but benefiting from a sublime visual makeover from Pininfarina and an extensively reworked 3.5-litre V8 engine that remains one of Ferrari's greatest mechanical jewels today.

It certainly has one of its best-sounding engines, as you can hear momentarily in *GoldenEye*, the Ferrari's operatic wail contrasting with the Aston's more restrained six-cylinder burble. Rémy Julienne's son Dominique was at the wheel doubling for Famke Janssen (wig and all), and takes full advantage of the Ferrari's propensity for car-chase-friendly oversteer. The two cars are separated by three decades of technical progress, so in reality the Aston wouldn't have seen which way the Ferrari went, but that's hardly the point. This did present Rémy Julienne with some head-scratching, though.

'To match the performance of two cars that have nothing in common is very complicated,' he recalled. 'We use tricks, like spikes in the tyres, to make it slide. It's the opposite of what we were used to doing, but this is why this job is so fascinating. The chase scene – it's not a stunt scene – has to be subtle to adapt to the actors' performance. It requires a lot of skill to be precise in relation to the camera.'

Assuming one maintains complete concentration at all times, of course. 'Famke was seated in the Ferrari, and I had to drive the Aston so as to remain next to her. She was smiling at me with a smile that would blow the buttons off one's shirt, and on the first bend I was foolishly looking at her, and I almost missed it.'

When the Ferrari briefly lost control and pirouetted right in front of the Aston as it exited a hairpin, both cars suffered cosmetic damage. Aston's support team repaired the DB5 overnight, while the Ferrari was sent to the Monte Carlo dealer. Brosnan, meanwhile, later confessed to having had his own issues with the DB5. 'I got to drive it outside of the casino in Monte Carlo. I actually screwed up the handbrake on it. Really. We did about eight takes, and they said, "What *is* that smell?" And I said, "I don't know." I had the handbrake on, and I had been driving up the mountain, and reversing.'

No such problems befell *GoldenEye*'s other star car, the BMW Z3. EON had signed a three-picture deal with BMW, which led to some sniping in the press about Bond 'defecting' to a German brand. A quarter of a century on, it's easy to forget that BMW was riding a wave of mid-1990s technological, creative and commercial success, and the Z3 roadster was one of the hottest new cars of the year.

Much of the action in *GoldenEye* takes place in St Petersburg, a city whose magnificent architecture was in contrast to the Soviet cars that beetled about in it. CIA point man Jack Wade (Joe Don Baker) stoutly defends his ZAZ 965 A to a notably unimpressed Bond. This 1960s tiddler was designed to mobilise the proletariat but still commanded a huge waiting list. Its basic mechanicals could also be fixed with a sledgehammer, as Wade demonstrates.

One of the three decommissioned Soviet tanks bought by the production's special effects team. This one was nicknamed Metal Mickey by the crew.

Its introduction by Q to 007 (one of just eight vehicle handovers he carries out in the films) is also a highly endearing outing for actor Desmond Llewelyn, one of the pillars of the extended Bond family and an actor with whom Pierce Brosnan clearly enjoys sparring on screen. 'Right, now pay attention, 007. First, your new car: BMW, agile, five forward gears, all points radar, self-destruct system, and naturally all the usual refinements. Now, this I'm particularly proud of: behind the headlights, stinger missiles!'

There's also a parachute, which we see being deployed in the workshop, though its purpose would have had little to do with retarding the BMW's performance (unless it was being dropped out of a plane); these first Z3s were underpowered, the 1.9-litre four-cylinder engine only making 138bhp (which was on the weedy side even in 1995). Aside from the scenes with Q, Bond is seen driving the Z3 with Natalya Simonova (Izabella Scorupco), while CIA contact Jack Wade (Bond returnee Joe Don Baker) lands a light aircraft inches above their heads; they swap modes of transport with Bond warning Wade not to touch any of the buttons. These scenes were filmed in Puerto Rico (doubling for Cuba), with lead stunt man Simon Crane supervising. (BMW's US marketing wing commissioned a special edition Z3 007 James Bond in tandem with retailer Neiman Marcus; 100 cars were finished in Atlanta-306 Bond blue, with taupe leather interior, 007 floor mats, a rear luggage carrier and fitted luggage, a plaque on the dash, and wood accents on the steering wheel and gear-lever. As with all things Bond, they're now very sought-after collector's items – if not in the DB5 league.)

GoldenEye's other big setpiece is, of course, the tank chase in St Petersburg. Preparation was afoot to shoot the whole sequence in the magnificent Russian city, and although the second unit did shoot there in April, the original plan came unstuck amid red tape and concerns about potential damage to historic buildings. (Chris Corbould's team constructed a tank that weighed six tonnes rather than the real thing's 28 tonnes, to minimise damage to the roads they filmed on in the city.)

Demonstrating their customary resolve,

The armoured train used by the treacherous Alec Trevelyan (Sean Bean). The Soviet Union used these to transport their nuclear warheads, keeping them constantly on the move and their exact location a mystery.

production designer Peter Lamont and his crew had a remarkable facsimile constructed on an old airfield at Leavesden, Hertfordshire in less than seven weeks. 'We got the money shots in St Petersburg and intercut them with the tank doing real damage when it careens down an alleyway,' Lamont said, with an understandable degree of satisfaction. 'That way we can actually smash down buildings.'

As ever, preparation was critical. Three tanks – two Fifties T-54s and a T-55 – were purchased by Chris Corbould's special effects team and made over to look like T-80s. 'I'm very fond of that sequence,' he says. 'It was originally a motorcycle chase and Michael [G. Wilson] and Barbara [Broccoli] asked me how we could make it different. Bond was in a military area, so I said, "Why doesn't he take a tank?" It was a lot of work but it paid off. If we shot every idea that came out of the tank conversation, we'd still be shooting it now!'

A driver was hidden, allowing Brosnan to pull the levers in a dummy turret. There were some unexpected challenges. 'I got a call at 2 a.m. from one of the guys saying we had a problem… one of the tanks was still active, and could technically still fire a shell,' Corbould continues. 'We needed to deactivate it, by welding a great big billet of steel into the barrel. A guy came down from Birmingham to sign it off. We spent quite a few weeks going through walls and crawling over cars. The tank could take short-cuts no car could. The scene where it explodes through the wall had to be timed to perfection; it took the tank a quarter of a mile to get up to speed on the other side.'

Amidst the chaos, a truck carrying 90,000 cans of Perrier was destroyed (two crew members spent a week emptying them all), and Corbould had to contrive a scenario in which a statue of Tsar Nicholas on a horse ended up on top of the tank. 'The tank is like Frank Sinatra,' Ian Sharp joked. 'He only does one take.' Stunt man Gary Powell was the man in control (most of the time: like Les Dawson playing the piano, looking out of control is a skill).

The tank chase also wiped out what must have been every remaining Lada in the UK. 'We got through a few,' Corbould recalls. 'They don't take a lot of destroying.' Meanwhile General Ourumov (Gottfried John) has kidnapped Natalya and his GAZ 31029 Volga saloon – a hardy perennial of Bond movies – is being pursued by 007. Soviet cars are routinely rubbished for being crude copies of more sophisticated Western vehicles, but the Volga's fondness for getting totally sideways is a stunt driver's dream. (Along with the BMW 320i that makes an appearance, while the film is peppered with the expected retinue of Mercedes saloons.)

And finally, to the ZAZ 965 A 'Zaporozhets', 'the little blue box Wade calls a car', as the *GoldenEye* script has it. In the St Petersburg square where we meet it (in reality London's Somerset House), this tiny contraption is played strictly for laughs. But like the Citroen 2CV, Mini and Fiat 500 and 600 – which the Soviet automotive ministry *Minavtroprom* pinpointed as a template – the rear-engined, air-cooled 965 was conceived to be a people's car. Given the weather conditions and the rudimentary state of the roads, its lack of engineering sophistication was deliberate: it could be repaired with the most basic set of tools at the roadside. It's a truth honoured by Wade in the film, when we see him set about the car with a sledgehammer.

Who says Bond films aren't realistic?

One of the film's setpiece action sequences saw the production transform three 1950s Soviet tanks, two T-54s and a T55, into the ultimate Bond getaway vehicle. Bond special effects supervisor Chris Corbould, whose involvement with 007 goes back to 1977's *The Spy Who Loved Me*, rates the tank chase in *GoldenEye* as one of his all-time favourites. Dummy controls enabled Brosnan to feign control while stunt driver Gary Powell did the driving. Many Ladas and Volga saloons were destroyed, but the BMW 316 (above) escaped.

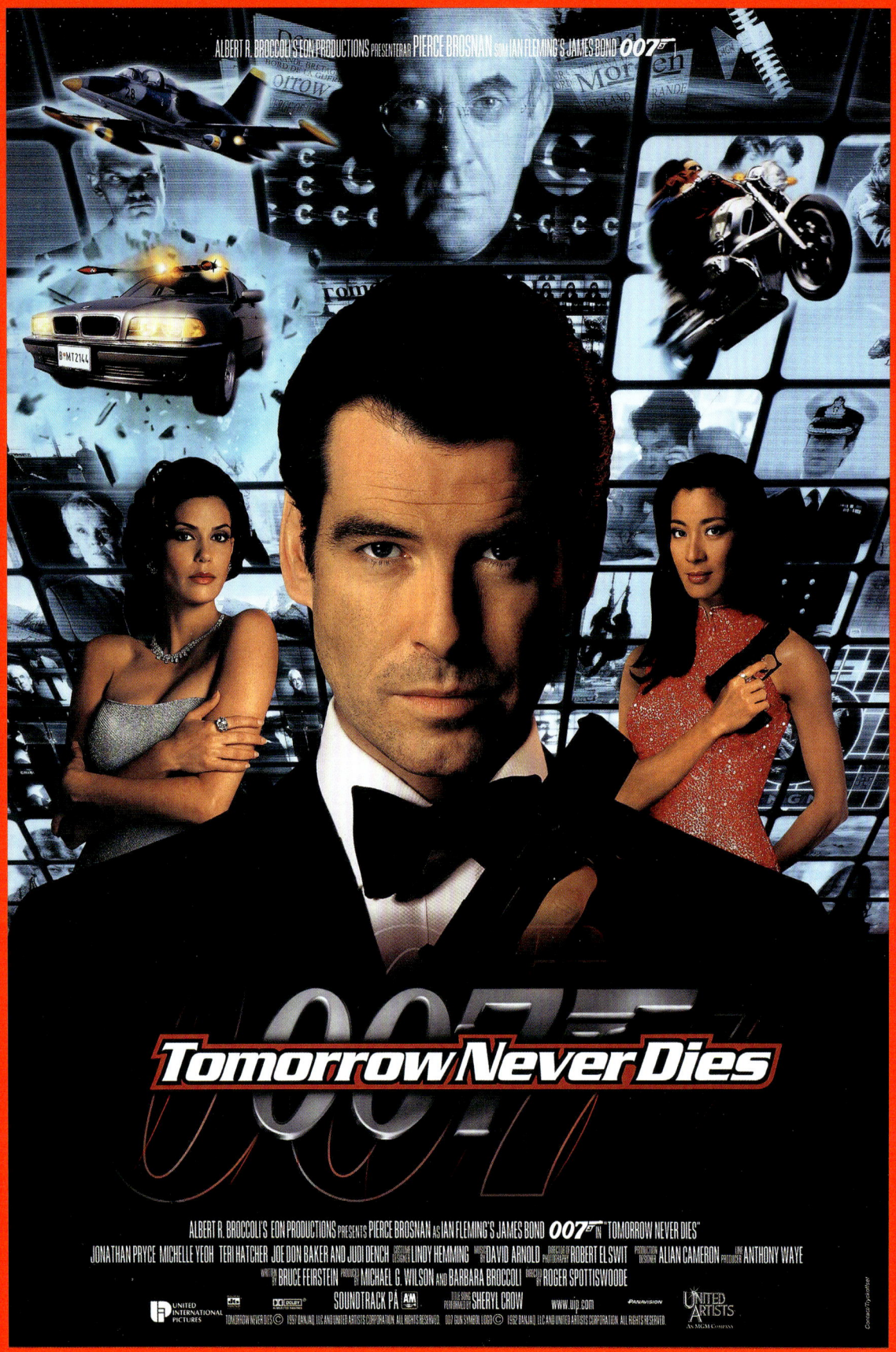

UK one sheet, December 1999. The art director on this campaign was Randi Braun, and the photography was by Keith Hamshere and George Whitear.

CHAPTER 18
TOMORROW NEVER DIES

1997

STARRING Pierce Brosnan as James Bond

'If you'd just sign here, Mr Bond. It's the insurance damage waiver for your beautiful new car. Will you need collision cover?' Pierce Brosnan greatly enjoyed the scenes he played opposite Desmond Llewelyn, pictured here with the BMW 750iL.

With the internet still in its infancy, and social media not yet a glimmer in someone's eye, the idea of a media mogul manipulating world events to sell newspapers and to promote a satellite television network was timely.

An early script draft posited a power-mad media baron called Elliot Harmsway (later renamed Shroudway then Carver), a gold-smuggling subplot, an underwater drill and a plan to destroy Hong Kong. Later versions added the villain's stealth boat, the remote-controlled BMW, the Chinese security services character Lin Tse Pao (later changed to Wai Lin, as played by Asian cinema superstar Michelle Yeoh) and the corrupt General Chang.

Leavesden studios was being used for the new *Star Wars* film, so location manager Richard Sharkey had to find a suitably vast space; he opted for an old supermarket warehouse in Frogmore, Hertfordshire, a stone's throw from the M25. 'The biggest concern I had was the lack of time. I had the luxury of eight months' preparation for *GoldenEye*, compared to two for this one,' special effects supervisor Chris Corbould observed.

Roger Spottiswoode, who was the editor on Sam Peckinpah's 1971 cause célèbre *Straw Dogs* and had directed 11 films prior to *Tomorrow Never Dies*, was hired to oversee Bond 18. It would be a challenging job: there would be some script alterations during production, and plans to film in Vietnam were nixed by the local authorities at the last moment. (A fortnight later the production confirmed a move to Bangkok, a prime example of the phenomenal

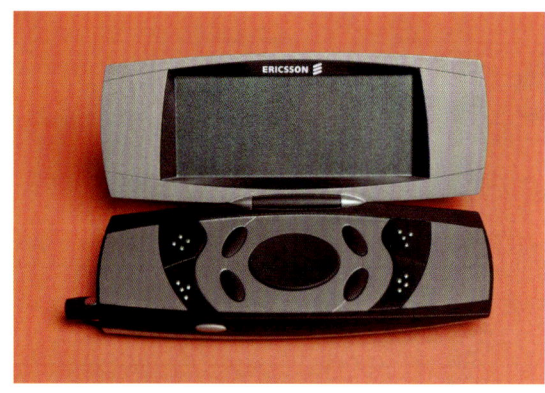

Below: The Ericsson hand-set used by Bond to drive his BMW. Not for the first time, a Bond gadget was predicting a piece of techology that would become reality – if not quite as extreme in execution.

power the Bond machine wielded.)

Other locations were more pragmatic. Although there's a titillating cameo for the Aston Martin DB5, the automotive focus was elsewhere. On 21 and 22 April 1997, Desmond Llewelyn and Pierce Brosnan filmed one of the most amusing car hand-over scenes in the series at the Business Aviation terminal at London Stansted airport. Q is off camera initially, in red Avis corporate apparel. 'If you'd just sign here, Mr Bond. It's the insurance damage waiver for your beautiful new car. Will you need collision cover?'

In the handover alone, BMW benefited from more screen time for the 750iL (an E38 model in internal parlance – the most elegant-looking of the 7 series' six generations) than the Z4 managed last time out. 'All the usual refinements,' Q continues. 'Machine guns, rockets, GPS tracking system… this I'm particularly proud of – a remote control for your car.' The E38-era 7 series was a major statement for BMW. When it was launched in 1994, it was the first to market in Europe with an integrated television screen that doubled as satellite navigation: Bond gadgetry made real. The 5.4-litre, 354bhp V12 was as silken as it was powerful, in the way only 12-cylinder engines can be. (For complete accuracy, we should note that, despite the badges, the car used in *Tomorrow Never Dies* was actually the less powerful 740i V8; given the size of the registration plate – itself a nod to the original DB5 – it was also in US-spec.) Other innovations included xenon headlights, side curtain airbags and dual zone climate control; by 1997 standards, the 750iL was unimpeachable.

But it's also an illustration of how fast the car industry moves. Sat-nav is obviously commonplace now, and most modern cars offer an impressive degree of autonomous functionality (best appreciated on the motorway). The current BMW 7 series even has the ability to park itself remotely, though not quite as Bond later interprets it. However, we're still waiting for the roof-mounted rocket launcher, caltrops, wheel arch tear-gas dispensers, the cable cutter (hidden in the BMW bonnet roundel), re-inflatable tyres, and the fingerprint-protected safe where the front passenger airbag is usually positioned. The film's prized encoder is stashed in there.

The customary comic interplay between Bond and Q ensues, with 007 demonstrating his touch with the car's rotary pad controller. The car's OS is female-voiced; 'I think we understand each other,' Bond says. The sequence was originally longer, with Q mistakenly revealing a flesh and blood Jaguar ('wrong assignment,' he says), in a scene that didn't make the final cut.

The BMW goes on to star in what's surely one of the best and most imaginatively executed car chases in the entire series, driven by the filmmakers' relentless desire to top what's gone before – *GoldenEye*'s tank chase having raised the bar to an intimidating degree. 'In every car chase the driver is stuck behind the wheel and that's all he can do. Because of this great Q device, Bond spends the entire chase in the *back* of the car,' Spottiswoode noted.

> 'I wanted the car park chase to be different. Rather than go bigger, it's better to add some canny little twists to it'

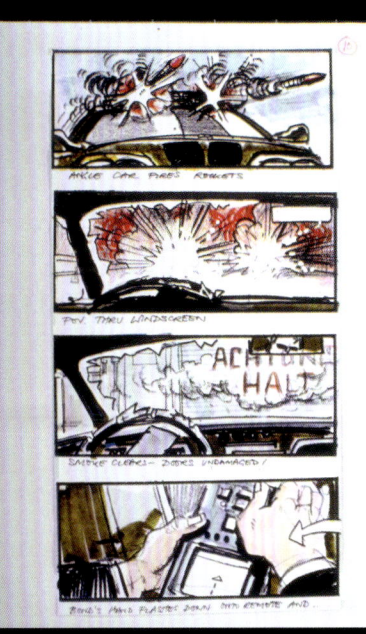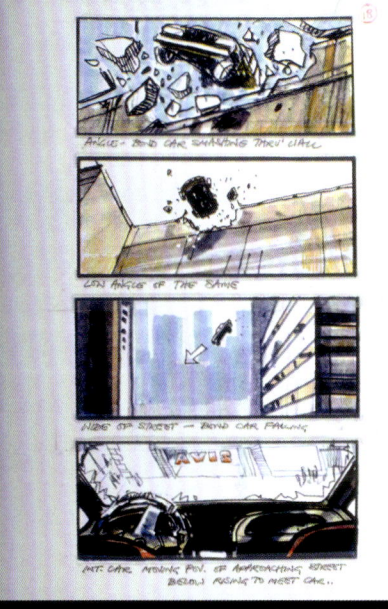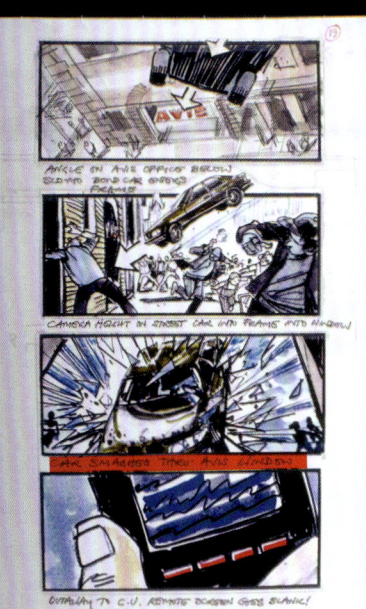

Rarely seen storyboard for the car park chase sequence. It was shot in a north London retail park during the course of three weeks in June 1997. Many BMWs were hurt during the course of filming.

Rarely seen images from the contact sheet of the car park chase. Note the unusual camera tracking car, based on a 1980s TVR 350i. The stunt car was specially converted so that the driver could operate it out of camera shot from a position on the rear seat, using a set of monitors to see where he was going. In all, 17 BMW 750iLs were supplied to the production.

The sequence is set in the multi-storey car park of the Hotel Atlantic Kempinski in Hamburg, overlooking Aussenalster lake. Ironically, the hotel's rooftop attic is called the Spectre Chamber, a ploy back in the day to deter children from playing there rather than an homage to Bond. In *Tomorrow Never Dies*, 007 escapes via the roof after disposing of Carver's assassin Dr Kaufman. ('I could shoot you from Stuttgart and still create the proper effect,' Dr Kaufman foolishly informs Bond, shortly before failing to create the proper effect.)

The BMW, meanwhile, is being set upon by henchmen with sledgehammers, despite first electrocuting several of them. When Bond arrives, he triggers the tear gas, starts the car from his Ericsson hand-set, and manages to leap through the rear side window as it passes. What follows is an impressively intricate chase sequence. Shooting started on 9 June 1997 for three weeks on level four of Brent Cross shopping centre's car park, a monolithic retail park sandwiched between the A1, the end of the M1, and London's North Circular. Such was the scale of the shoot that Roger Spottiswoode was on set alongside second unit director Vic Armstrong. 'I wanted to make the car park chase scene different to what you normally see. Rather than go bigger, it's better to add some canny little twists to it,' Armstrong noted. 'Here, the saving grace is the humour. At the same time, you must have it within the realm of believability. It's a difficult line to walk.'

BMW had supplied an array of cars, four of which had been

Bond sends the BMW off the top floor of the car park, across Mönckebergstrasse in Hamburg, before delivering it back to the rental store with a typically Brosnian flourish. An air cannon jettisoned the real thing, while a scale model was used for the mid-air element. Several were made, showcasing the production's continued commitment to the art of the miniature in the face of increasing CGI.

'This I'm particularly proud of – a remote control for your car'

adapted to what special effects supervisor Chris Corbould calls 'hidden driver' spec: the stunt drivers were able to pilot the vehicles around the confines of the car park while positioned more or less recumbent on the rear seat, with small monitors relaying the view ahead from cameras installed in the exterior door mirrors. No stunt car is ever particularly pretty to look inside, and this is no exception: like a single-seater racing car, the main part of the seat is made of lightweight Kevlar moulded to fit the driver perfectly, but the beige lower cushion looks like a charity shop reject. There are wires and control units everywhere, yet it all worked perfectly.

'We had 17 at our disposal. Tremendously fast, those cars. We probably totalled four or five. It added to the excitement because you never see anyone's head in there unless it's Bond and he's in the back seat so he can't be driving,' Armstrong added.

Behind the scenes, a specially modified TVR 350i was used as the POV camera car. On camera, Carver's henchmen use a pair of Mercedes S-classes (W126 era, rather than the later and then-current W140), an Opel Senator 3.0i, and a Ford Scorpio. The last two were their makers' entries in the Nineties luxury saloon segment; in another sign of the changing times, no equivalent car exists in their respective line-ups 23 years later. Both the Opel and Ford meet spectacularly fiery ends, the latter when the villain's rocket passes through the BMW's cabin. An Audi 80, Citroen BX, Peugeot 205, Renault Fuego – another US-spec interloper – and Volvo 265 estate suffer as collateral damage elsewhere in the sequence. Car-spotters, meanwhile, have much to identify, including an E12 BMW 5 series, E30 3 series, a W124 Mercedes E-class, a Mercedes 500 SEC, Opel Kadett, Honda Civic, two Rover Metros and an Austin Maestro. (Casting the background cars for this chase must have been a headache, but only the most Anglophiliac Hamburger would have bought either of these.)

The BMW's return to the rental shop, on Mönckebergstrasse in Hamburg's Lange Mühren, goes beyond the usual parameters of a waiver. Having abandoned ship, Bond sends the car off the top floor of the car park, across the street, to smash straight through the shop window. An air cannon jettisoned the real thing, a scale model was used for the mid-air element, and it returns to a full-size 750iL back on ground level.

'It's a cool piece, actually. It's very, very slick,' Pierce Brosnan noted of the completed sequence with more than a little understatement. (He's also made to look very good indeed later in the film's jaw-dropping bike chase, in which stuntman Jean Pierre Goy jumped a BMW R 1200 C between buildings in downtown Saigon – in reality Frogmore – above the whirling blades of a helicopter. These were added in post-production.)

Tomorrow Never Dies also features supporting appearances from the mid-1990s Range Rover (P38A), the successor to the celebrated original whose allure saw it survive in production for 24 years. This

Bond brings the BMW back. Not in one piece, admittedly, but still... thoughtful.

Range Rovers have become the archetypal villains' cars in recent Bond films, and they definitely have a certain cool factor.

The original plan was to film in Vietnam, but that was nixed at the last moment. Within a fortnight, the production was moved to Bangkok

one has achieved a fraction of the affection that model still generates, and its complex electrics and air suspension put buyers off. But time is being kind to its imperious form and presence and, although it – and the generation that followed, along with the Sport spin-off – have become archetypal baddies' vehicles, these are cool cars that can go on forever if looked after properly. Needless to say, this is not the case in *Tomorrow Never Dies*, as they get embroiled in the Saigon chase.

Finally, a respectful nod to the Daimler limousine, which we see conveying Bond, M, the Deputy Chief of Staff and Miss Moneypenny with a police escort through London. It's an interesting venue for some plot exposition, but a reminder of the role the DS 420, as it's known, has played in so many films. In production from 1968 until 1992, Daimler was by this point part of Jaguar, and the car itself was based on the Jaguar 420G, the result being a purpose-built limousine that offered a huge degree of personalisation for significantly less money than vehicles like the Mercedes 600 Pullman or Rolls-Royce Phantom V. It's arguably the most famous ceremonial vehicle in the world, a staple of the British Royal Family's fleet – the Queen Mother in particular was a devotee – and is still in use by the Courts of many European royal families despite being long out of production.

Famously, though, it didn't have much leg-room for the poor chap behind the wheel.

UK quad, November 1999. Designed by Brian Bysouth, it featured photography by Nigel Parry, Keith Hamshere and Jay Maidment.

CHAPTER 19

THE WORLD IS NOT ENOUGH

1999

STARRING Pierce Brosnan as James Bond

250

'You're always trying to do variations on the formula, but the most important thing is to come up with a good villain,' screenwriter Neal Purvis observed. 'You have a choice: either you're aware of who the villain is and you can cut to the villain doing villainous things, or you reveal things in a more Hitchcockian way,' co-writer Robert Wade added.

Cinema's greatest master of suspense was proposed by Ian Fleming in 1959 as his choice of director for the first Bond film, a version of *Thunderball*. That it never came to pass is one of those 'what-ifs?' that attach themselves to big film franchises (the longer-running the franchise, the greater the number of what-ifs). Now, with work beginning on the 19th film, Bond's newest writing team were invoking Hitch's memory in their search for a fresh creative twist.

It worked, and the film benefits greatly from oil heir Elektra King's (Sophie Marceau) seductive duplicity alongside her lover and co-conspirator Renard (Robert Carlyle), a more traditional Bond bad guy whose malice intensifies according to how much pain the bullet lodged in his head is causing him. A neatly sadistic device that brings on a migraine just thinking about it.

The film's title riffs on the Bond family motto, as referenced in *On Her Majesty's Secret Service*: 'Orbis non sufficit.' If the world wasn't enough for James Bond, imagine the challenge the filmmakers had keeping him – and the audience – happy. *The World Is Not Enough*'s pre-credits sequence focuses on powerboats rather than cars – including a magnificent Q-branch special – audaciously conducted on the River Thames right through the heart of London, and filmed over a six-week period. There's an irresistible moment of comic relief in there, too.

Opposite: Bond outwits the Russian Parahawks in a sequence set in the Caucasus Mountains but filmed in Chamonix. Below: 007 and Q with new boy R, played by John Cleese. The film's star car was the BMW Z8, although it wasn't quite ready.

Images taken on set at the Bibi-Heybat oilfield, near Baku in Azerbaijan. A Land Rover Defender appears briefly, but Bond's BMW Z8 is pictured in a long establishing shot. It would also enjoy an afterlife in various 007 computer games.

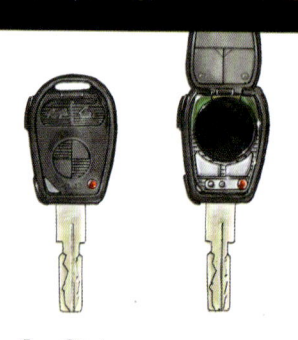

BOND'S BMW REMOTE CONTROL KEY (LIFE SIZE)
BOUDIN ITALERY 98

Michael Apted was a director whose reputation was forged more in character-driven drama, another indication of the tonal shift that was occurring. But verisimilitude was still paramount. 'It's hard to find new stuff, and not repeat what Bond has done before,' he admitted. 'There's a reality about the Bond action we're very keen to hang on to. You don't get the feeling it's been constructed by a wizard on a computer.'

Pierce Brosnan, meanwhile, was now firmly in the Bond groove, though scarcely complacent. 'They come around so frequently it feels like I never left the shop, the rest of life just falls away. You can't go thinking about icons and stuff like that, it's what's the work, what's on the page, what's the character, what's the story, who is this man, and how do you make it real for yourself and as an actor, so that it's believable.

'For me, Q's like Merlin. The last person Bond sees before he goes out on a mission. "Pay attention Bond, these are your tricks."'

In his last 007 appearance, Bond's legendary Quartermaster is joined by R (not his official title, played by John Cleese) for the handover scenes. The bumbling R attracts more of Q's ire on this occasion, and manages to be even more supercilious. The Z8, he explains, has 'the very latest in intercepts, countermeasures, and six beverage holders.' (The last one may not be strictly accurate.)

In an aside, Q reminds Bond that he has always tried to teach him two things – 'Never let them see you bleed' and 'Always have an escape plan' – before disappearing slowly out of shot on a lift. It's poignantly done, all the more so because Bond mainstay Desmond Llewelyn was injured in a car crash in Sussex in December 1999, and later died in hospital. Things would never be the same.

Top: Valentin Zukovsky (Robbie Coltrane) and Bull (Goldie), with a doomed Rolls-Royce Silver Shadow.
Middle: Pierce Brosnan on set.
Above: The Aston Martin DB5 making a cameo appearance.

Renard (Robert Carlyle) expresses his unhappiness with Davidov (Ulrich Thomsen), while the redoubtable Lada Niva and a henchman look on.

A scale model of Zukovsky's caviar farm.

This isn't a film suffused with cars, but the automotive star is one whose status has actually risen over the years: the BMW Z8. Yet the best BMW ever used in a Bond film – other than perhaps the elegant 633 CSi that has a blink-and-you'll-miss-it cameo in *Octopussy* – was actually only partially a BMW. The new Z8 roadster was in the final stages of development when *The World Is Not Enough* was in production and, in contrast to the 750iL in the previous movie, BMW was unable to supply any completely finished cars – never mind the fleet of 17 that had been made available for the car park chase sequence in *Tomorrow Never Dies*.

Two prototypes were supplied, but even that was a stretch for the company given the car's status at the time. This presented the producers with an interesting logistical challenge. 'Two cars was nowhere near enough to safeguard our schedules, especially when we were filming in so many different places,' Chris Corbould remembers now. The solution was unorthodox: his team were tasked with manufacturing three more themselves.

'BMW gave us components and we fabricated the chassis from scratch, and moulded our own body panels. They sent a couple of guys over from Germany to check what we were doing, and we walked them round a car.'

The set for the showdown in the caviar fishery was so elaborate that the paddock tank in Pinewood had to be enlarged to accommodate it. It was designed by Peter Lamont and earned the nickname the 'city of walkways'. The scenes required main and second unit participation, and required massive cooperation across the board.

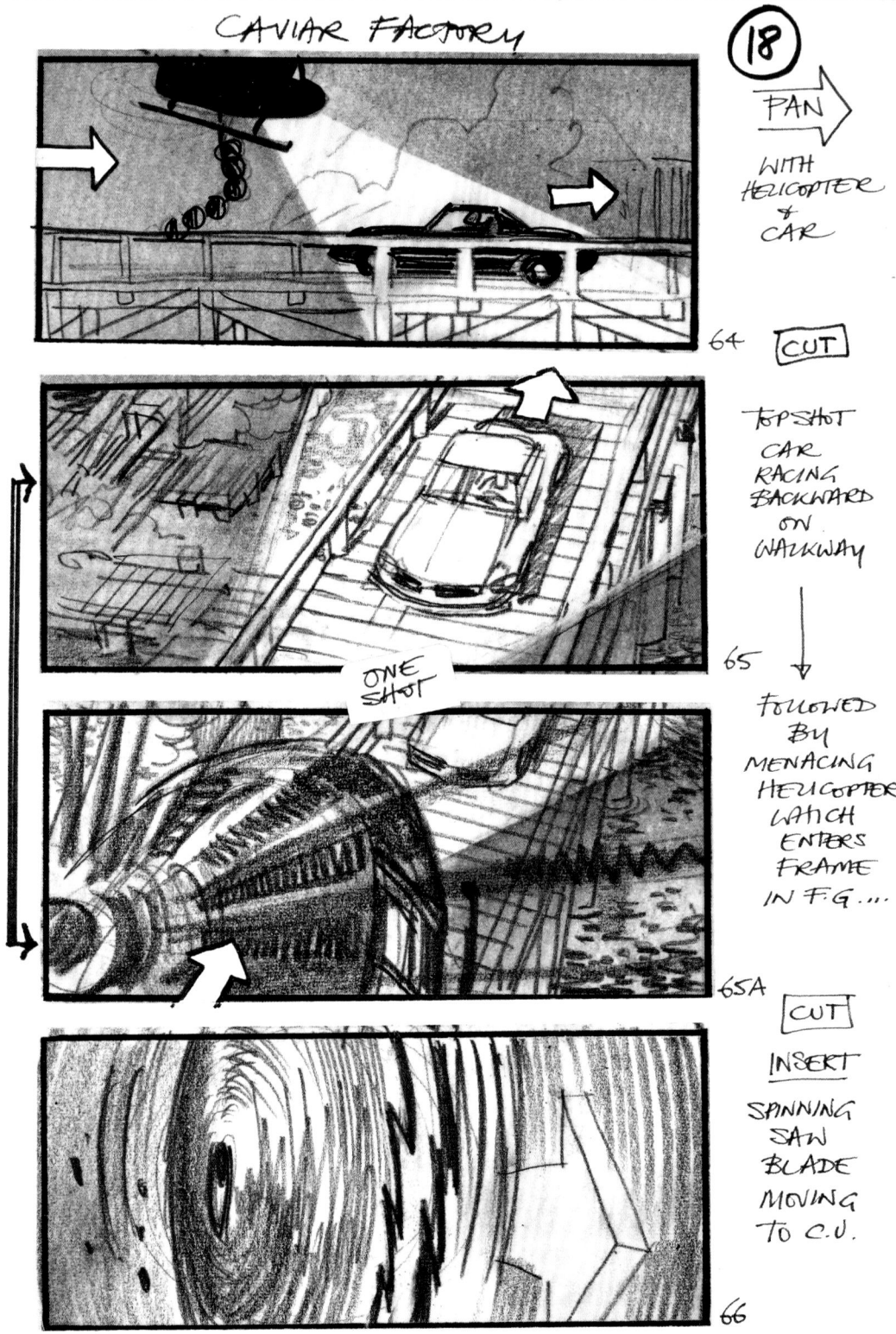

A rarely seen storyboard for the caviar fishery setpiece in *The World Is Not Enough*. Filmmakers use these and 'pre-vis' techniques to map out the flow of a sequence, and decide on camera angles. In this instance, including close-ups of spinning buzz-saws…

Fortunately, no real BMW Z8s were hurt during the filming of this sequence.

The engine used by the effects cars was a 350 cu in Chevrolet V8, the gearbox an off-the-shelf Tremec five-speed manual, the suspension from a Jaguar. The body was in two pieces, so there were fewer shutlines than you'd find on the real thing. Plus some decidedly non-standard additions: titanium armour, an advanced head-up display, surface-to-air missiles launched out of the side vents with a targeting display integrated into the Z8's wire-spoked steering wheel hub, and a reprise for the remote-control operation.

This improvised and ingenious but ultimately makeshift solution may have limited the screen time BMW's new roadster received, although we do get to see it in the unusual environs of the Bibi-Heybat oilfield south of Baku, Azerbaijan. At least the car's brutal demise – evisceration by a series of tree-cutting circular saws attached to a helicopter – didn't necessitate the death of the real thing. That would have been unpleasantly gratuitous.

The Z8 was under-appreciated at its launch in 2000, dismissed by some as an overly retro millennial update of the effortlessly elegant Fifties 507. Two decades on, the Z8 now looks equally lissom. In a world of impressively powerful but increasingly anodyne 'digital' performance cars, its naturally aspirated 4.9-litre V8 and six-speed manual gearbox offer enough sensory overload to compensate for a chassis that's more GT cruiser than sports car.

Only 5,703 were made, few enough to seal the Z8's status as a bona fide collector's car, with values to match: you'll need at least £150,000 ($195,000) should you be interested in getting your hands on one now. An appreciating asset, for sure. And of course... it's a Bond car.

(NB: honourable mentions go to Davidov's Lada Niva, the Russian farmer's car that refuses to die. As you can imagine, a vehicle that was tested and developed in Siberia and the Ural Mountains would be pretty hardy, and the Niva is almost indestructible. It's also still in production 43 years after first appearing. Zukovsky's Rolls-Royce Silver Shadow is less fortunate, and suffers a watery fate when his caviar farm is attacked by Elektra King's merciless sawing helicopters. As do the traffic wardens we see clamping an Escort Mk IV as Bond blasts past on the pre-credits powerboat. The Aston Martin DB5 was due to appear in the film but ended up on the cutting-room floor.)

UK one sheet, November 2002. Photography by
Keith Hamshere and Ron Stenzak.

CHAPTER 20

DIE ANOTHER DAY

2002

STARRING Pierce Brosnan as James Bond

'It's very hard for as an actor to show up for six or seven months and try and have some kind of emotional through line without it just being about explosions,' Pierce Brosnan opined. 'The idea that Bond falls victim to torture and then, instead of being hailed as a hero, is basically fired from his job, gives him both internal and external problems to overcome and therefore makes him a much more complex hero than we've ever seen before.'

Principal photography on *Die Another Day* began on 14 January 2002, on Pinewood's B stage. The 20th Bond film had grand ambitions at the outset and, for his fourth appearance as 007, Pierce Brosnan wanted to amplify the character. So things were changing, as they invariably did in the Bond universe. One of the scenes filmed that first week had a sadness for all involved: 007's Quartermaster (John Cleese) was handing over his new car, the Aston Martin Vanquish, in the absence of the late Desmond Llewelyn. Cleese's haughty high-mindedness cloaks a different sort of despair with Bond's inability to be serious. Although, since he's initially confronted by an empty platform, perhaps Bond does have a point.

'Your new transportation,' Q says.

'You've been down here too long,' Bond replies.

'The ultimate in British engineering.'

'You must be joking.'

'As I learned from my predecessor, Bond, I never joke about my work. Aston Martin call it the Vanquish, we call it the Vanish.'

Die Another Day's 'invisible' Aston was a step too far for some people but the technology was inspired by work being done by (the now defunct) Defence Evaluation and Research Agency. 'Tiny cameras on all sides project the image they see onto a light-emitting polymer skin on the opposite side,' Q explains. Co-writers Robert Wade and Neal Purvis dreamt the idea up, and defended its appropriateness. 'When we suggested it originally, we weren't sure anyone would go for it,' Wade said. 'The idea is that in Iceland or in the desert, when there's not much contrast in the background, it's invisible, but in an urban environment you'd be able to see it.' Adds Purvis, 'Q says it's "as good as invisible". It's a camouflage, not a cloaking device.'

Amusingly, John Cleese himself confessed to being a fully paid-up Luddite. 'I despise technology in all its forms. I can make very few things work. I've had trouble with pencils sometimes.'

Bond in full attack mode. Aldershot was doubling for North Korea here.

Clockwise from top: On set in Spain with the Ford Fairlane Sunliner; the 'invisible' Aston Martin Vanquish; Jinx (Halle Berry) and her Ford Thunderbird; 007 with the '57 Ford, the slippery Gustav Graves (Toby Stephens) and a Range Rover.

The film's director, Lee Tamahori, explained that because it was the 20th Bond movie and the franchise's 40th anniversary, the Q scenes amounted to a gadgety greatest hits. The Vanquish was no exception, being equipped with an ejector seat, torpedoes, target-seeking shotguns, bulletproof bodywork, tyre spikes, remote-control operation, and thermal imaging (and more besides, according to the instrument display).

It was the sort of Aston Martin that Ian Fleming would have envisaged for Bond – a brute in a suit, no less. It was also a major reboot for the brand after years of treading water. Ford had acquired the company and launched the DB7 (never a Bond car) in 1994, its lovely body clothing a chassis that owed much to the Jaguar XJS, which had been around almost two decades by that point. Aston Martin was gearing up for a big Noughties renewal under new CEO Ulrich Bez, with a handsome new HQ and a wave of fresh technology, but needed a halo car in the interim. The result was arguably the best car James Bond ever got himself into, and certainly one of the best-looking.

'When I started working on the DB7, I was determined to get what I call the Aston "grin" onto the car,' car design legend Ian Callum says. 'There's always been a self-awareness and knowingness to Astons, you can see it in the DB5, and it's a quality they share with Bond himself. The brief for the Vanquish was to create a two-seater with a real toughness to it. I spent days looking for the atmosphere on the car, but it ended up being spontaneous – I attacked the clay model we'd done with a knife, with a certain delicacy I should add. The Vanquish is confident, self-assertive but not vulgar. I was lucky enough to attend the film's Royal premiere. Seeing it on the big screen was definitely a "wow" moment for me.'

If it looked like a fighter, it was also a machine that needed respect and discipline from the driver. The original Vanquish was powered by a 5.9-litre, 460bhp V12 that made a noise like Tom Jones stubbing his big toe when you gave it the full beans. Such is the rate of progress in the automotive world that anyone jumping into a Vanquish now and expecting the sort of electronic safety net most contemporary high-peformance cars have would be in for a surprise. Yes, there's traction control, but its software is the equivalent of a sundial, and on a damp road it's easy to find yourself very sideways indeed, whether you asked for it or not. That plus a rather idiosyncratic automated six-speed manual gearbox makes this a car that doesn't suffer fools gladly. Again, you can imagine Ian Fleming approving of that.

The Vanquish you see in *Die Another Day* is a different beast altogether. The script posited a substantial chase across a frozen lake, and the production had found a frozen lagoon near Vatnajökull in Iceland, a spot with unique cinematic properties because icebergs get trapped within it when the lagoon freezes over. After some concerns about its viability, the coldest February in 60 years ensued, giving the production a three-week window to film from 25 February. In addition, art director Peter Lamont and his crew constructed a vast exterior of the ice palace on an airfield near Burford, Gloucestershire, while the interiors were done at Pinewood. All this icy business meant that special effects supervisor Chris Corbould had to employ some typically lateral thinking. With Bond in a Vanquish and the villain's henchman Zao (Rick Yune) in a Jaguar XKR, not even the finest stunt drivers in the world would be able to keep things under control on a frozen lagoon in -35°C.

'[Second unit director] Vic Armstrong and I agreed we'd need four-wheel drive. So I went to Aston Martin and JLR, and of course there were no four-wheel drive versions of the Vanquish or XKR. We had

The Vanquish is arguably the best Bond car of them all – a brute in a suit

four examples of each car [for the ice chase] and we modified the front end on both to make them all-wheel drive. Because we were filming on ice we had to think about safety, too. So we built airbags into the bonnet and boot areas that would inflate automatically, to stop the car sinking too quickly into the water if the worst happened, and give the stunt drivers a chance to get out. We had to work out what sort of buoyancy we'd need to keep the vehicle afloat.'

Thus the *Die Another Day* Vanquish, though not invisible, was closer to a real-life Bond car than first appeared. The V12

was replaced with a Ford 302 cu in (5.0-litre) V8, set as far back as possible in the engine bay to make room for the driven front axle. Then the cars were fitted with the running gear from Ford's 1990s Explorer SUV, including a simple but robust three-speed automatic transmission geared for a maximum speed of 120mph. Some way off the real Vanquish's performance potential admittedly, but it was sufficient for filming purposes and also enabled the car to do things the real McCoy couldn't, such as climb stairs. Corbould's team also fitted the cars with a Quaife torque-sensing differential, a vital component in the pursuit of perfect oversteer. Which is what Bond car fans and more importantly the film's stunt drivers really want.

Top left: Zao (Rick Yune) in his modified Jaguar XKR convertible. Top right: Original concept art. Above: On set in Iceland.

Given the gruelling nature of filming, repeatability was also vital; during filming in Iceland, and despite the seriously sub-zero temperatures, overheating proved to be the only problem. Meanwhile, each of the eight Vanquishes had a specific job; the weapons car was the star and housed machine guns and four missile launchers behind its grille, along with bonnet-mounted motion-sensing mini-guns.

Zao's XKR is also quite the machine, finished in the same metallic light green used by Jaguar's Formula One cars at the time. As with the Aston Martin, the production crew created four special effects cars (there were four other XKRs), working closely with the engineering geniuses at Jaguar's SVO department. They replaced

A

ANGLE ON ZAO HE OPENS UP THE GATLING GUN, BEHIND HIM..

B

EX LOW ANGLE - HIGH SPEED TRACK IN FRONT OF VEHICLES..

WIDE - (PANNING FROM JAG TO ASTON

C

D

HELICOPTER TRACKING?

TILT UP FROM JAG TO ASTON.

Rarely seen storyboard for the car chase set on the frozen lagoon in Iceland. Filming on that sequence began on 25 February 2002 and took three weeks, during the coldest temperatures there for 60 years.

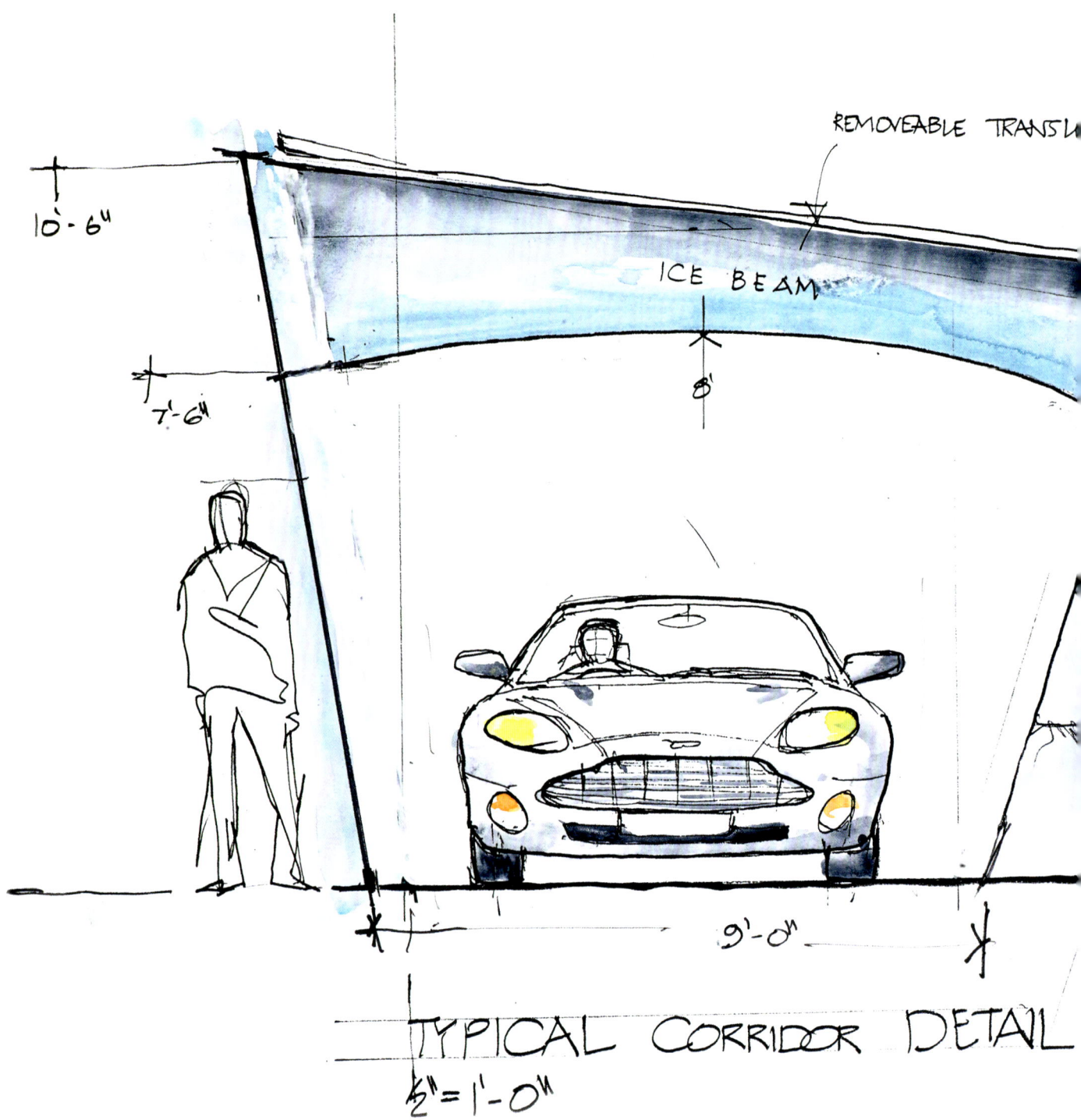

TYPICAL CORRIDOR DETAIL
1/2"=1'-0"

Left, concept art for the ice hotel. The real thing was constructed on an airfield in Gloucestershire. Below, the Vanquish on set.

the standard car's supercharged 4.0-litre V8 with the same Ford V8 and hardware, and installed stunt-friendly hydraulic handbrakes. Having watched as a minion's skidoo T-bones the camouflaged Aston, Zao uses his thermal imaging gizmo to track Bond, then disables the camouflage by unleashing a rear-mounted M134 minigun on it. He and Bond exchange fire – Bond performs a J-turn to face-off against the diamond-studded Zao – using a front-mounted rocket launcher, before side-mounted missiles put the Vanquish onto its roof. Bond uses the ejector seat mechanism to right the car again, an improbable-looking scene that Chris Corbould's team did for real.

'We shot that sequence at Bovingdon Airfield. The art department painted a big section of tarmac white,' Corbould remembers. 'You need a fair amount of force to flick a car like that over, then flick it back again. We also built a rig with a car in it that we put Pierce into and we rolled over, then towed behind a Range Rover. We rotated the whole thing round.' It's another great example of the improvisational skill and ingenuity needed to realise a scene.

The chase culminates in a climb through a rapidly defrosting ice palace, as Bond races to the aid of Jinx (Halle Berry). By this point Zao's Jaguar has unpacked a bootful of mortars (the display suggests he has nine at his disposal) and a battering ram, but the camouflage flickers back into life in time for Bond to dodge it, sending Zao – and car – to a watery doom (though it takes an ice chandelier to finish him off). Note that in this particular Aston Martin the 'traction' button doesn't configure electronics, it triggers a set of impressive looking tyre spikes. Never mind being bulletproof, the car is also

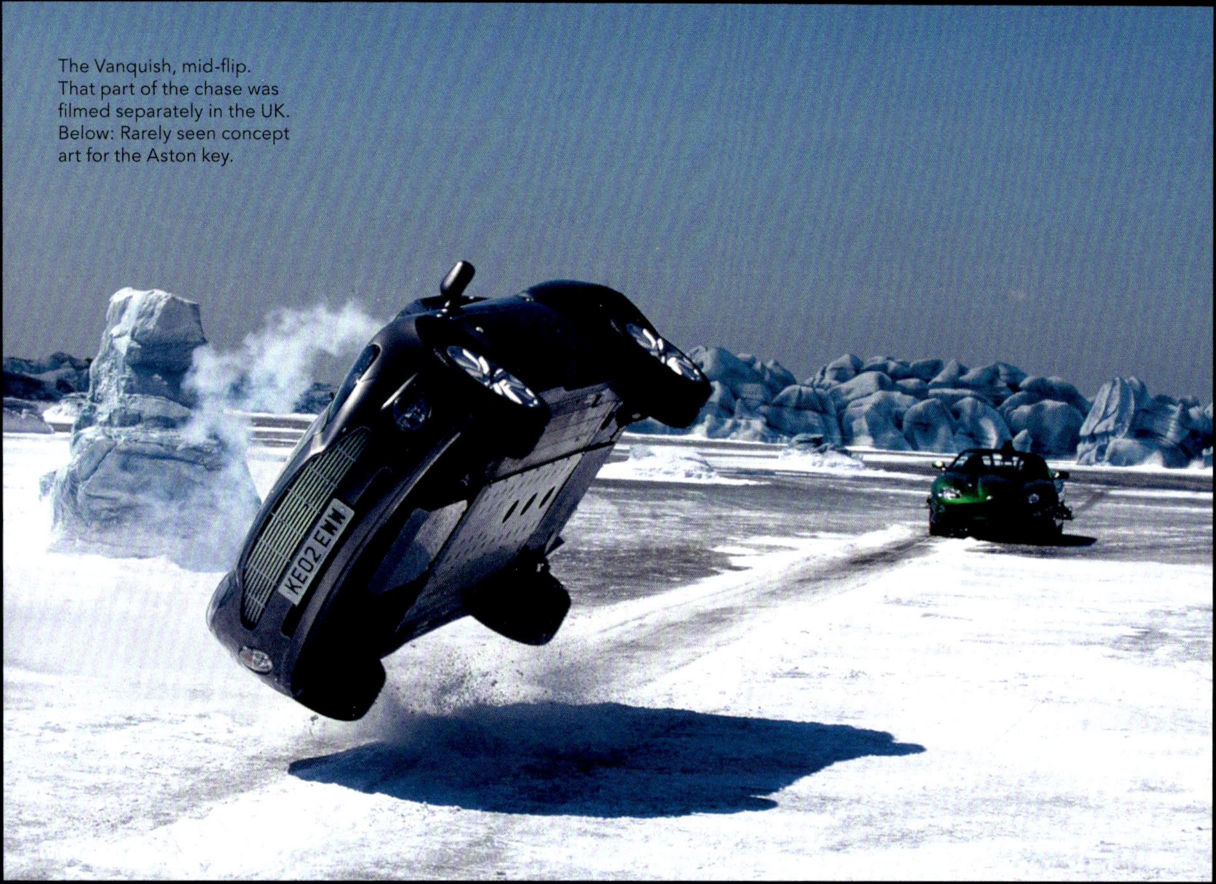

The Vanquish, mid-flip. That part of the chase was filmed separately in the UK. Below: Rarely seen concept art for the Aston key.

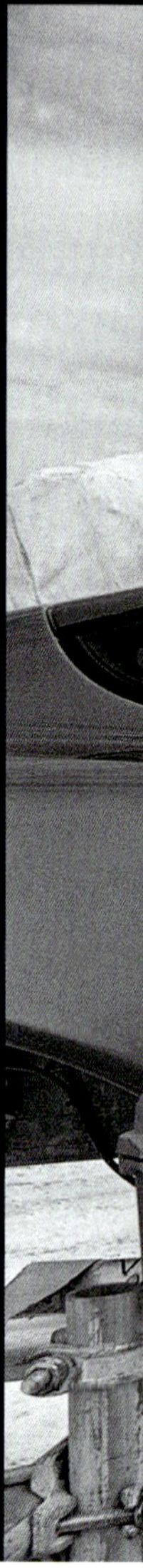

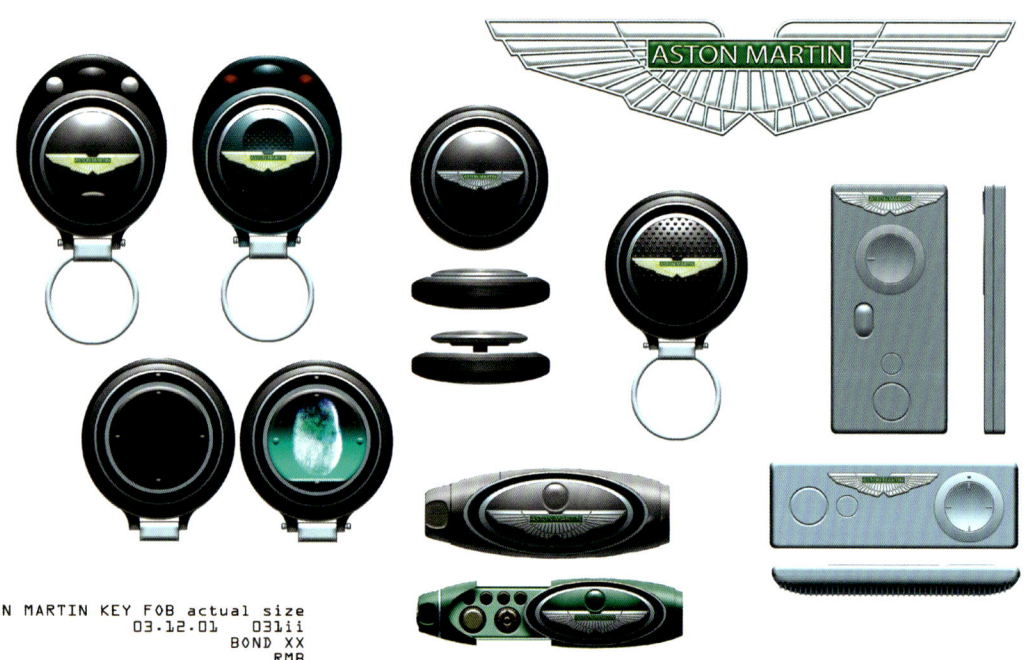

ASTON MARTIN
ASTON MARTIN KEY FOB actual size
03.12.01 031ii
BOND XX
RMB

Pierce Brosnan gets ready for an Aston Martin-assisted close-up.

Icebergs became trapped within the lake when it froze over

seemingly fully waterproof, which gave anyone who's ever owned a classic British sports car something to mull over. Despite the debate about CGI that followed *Die Another Day*'s release, the fact is the Bond special effects team made the cars work incredibly well, and kept them working in a hostile environment, enabling the stunt drivers to do what they do so brilliantly.

There's an interesting array of background cars in *Die Another Day*, too. A visit to Cuba (in reality Cadiz, in Spain) allowed the production designers to indulge themselves – and us – in a variety of old American cars, frozen in time following Fidel Castro's import ban on new metal in the wake of the 1959 revolution (the local slang for the estimated 60,000 US cars still in use on the island is *máquina*). Bond uses a Ford Fairlane 500 Sunliner (very similar to the car destroyed by Fiona Volpe in *Thunderball*), and we're treated to a 1958 Chevrolet Bel Air, a 1941 Chevrolet Special de Luxe, a 1938 Chrysler Royal Six, and a 1952 Mercury Custom. There's also a more recent US car, a 2002 Ford Thunderbird, that rode in on the fashion for retro design that gripped the car industry in the late 1990s. This generation played with the design cues of the very first T-bird. A limited edition 007 commemorative version was created, painted the same Coral red as the car Jinx drives in the film, with a plaque inside in the glovebox; only 700 were made.

We also get a glimpse inside the mind of the film's villain, Gustav Graves, casting some light on the automotive tastes of a maladjusted megalomaniac. He's obviously a fan of classic racing cars, because there's a Ford GT40, seen sporting a paint job that was close to its famous Gulf livery (that version of the car won the Le Mans 24 Hours race in 1969). The real thing is effectively priceless, so the production used a pair of replicas from a company called MDA, who had a month's notice to paint one of their cars in the requested finish. The other got involved in the shoot-up, and ended up covered in bullet holes.

Alongside it is a Porsche 911 (993-era), another very informed choice because this was the last of the air-cooled 911s (perhaps Graves disavows the arrival of water cooling in Germany's most famous sports car). Look closely and what appears to be a Turbo S is actually an accident-damaged Carrera 4 with no interior, tidied up for filming. Only for it to be shot to bits. Worse still, perhaps, is the fate meted out to the Ferrari F355 GTS and 1992 Lamborghini Diablo, both of which are sent plunging out of Graves' Antonov cargo plane somewhere over North Korea and into a paddy field. Happily, we can reveal that the production's excellent model unit did its work again here, and the scale miniatures of those two Italian classics are stored in EON's magnificent archive in a (top secret) location in London.

A rarely seen storyboard, drawn up during pre-production. Above: A still from the finished scene.

UK one sheet, November 2006, with photography by Greg Williams. The new era is exemplified by the reduction in the number of images, and there's an almost noir-ish quality to it.

CHAPTER 21

CASINO ROYALE

2006

STARRING Daniel Craig as James Bond

Casino Royale is the first of Ian Fleming's 007 novels, and James Bond's origin story. The movie rights had evaded EON for some time, but now that they'd finally secured them the tale could be told, and in dramatic style. The film's pre-credit sequence – shot in black and white – sees Bond earning his 00 status, establishing not just the fictional character but also the latest of the six actors to play him on the big screen.

It was a move that would rejuvenate the franchise in mesmerising fashion, a newly emboldened Bond for the troubling realities of life in the 21st century. Daniel Craig, shrugging off ludicrous early internet-led criticism, delivers a 007 who is in the process of working out who he is, rough edges and all, as physically impressive as he is emotionally vulnerable. It's a magnificent performance, and earned Craig a BAFTA nomination for best actor.

'*Casino Royale* is a coming-of-age film. It explains why he is who he is,' producer Barbara Broccoli told me during principal photography in Prague in spring 2006. 'There's a realisation that this is a dangerous world, that people have a more serious, measured view of world events. The Bond films reflect the times, and James Bond means different things at different times. Right now there are worries about world order and global security, but people have always loved the idea of heroes on the ground. In *Casino Royale*, we'll really uncover the Bond character.'

That same day saw the world debut for Bond's latest car, the Aston Martin DBS, a car created and developed at least partially with Craig's 007 in mind. Barbara Broccoli was delighted with the synergy. 'It's an emotional thing. Bond and Aston go way back,' she told me. 'Even when we were using other cars we tried to maintain the link. Bond's personal car in *Goldfinger* was a DB5. It's great now to have an Aston management that recognises the love affair.'

Filming was taking place at Barrandov studios in the outskirts of the Czech capital, where director Martin Campbell – who had helmed *GoldenEye* – turned his attention to a pivotal poker game. Maximising the tension between Bond and the film's primary antagonist, Le Chiffre (played by the wonderful Danish actor Mads Mikkelsen) was key. The internalisation of a poker game meant that it was this, as opposed to the film's magnificent parkour sequence, that really tested his movie-making skills. 'The card game was probably the most difficult scene I've ever had to film,' Campbell admitted. 'When you're playing Texas hold 'em poker with 10 players around a table, that's tough because it's a more complex game and, with 10 players all looking at each other, it's very tricky to film.'

Co-producer Michael G. Wilson happened to be an accomplished player himself and tutored the cast on process and technique, adding the necessary jeopardy by playing with real cash (though not the $115m that's at stake in the film). 'I'm sure there was a lot of money lost on that set,' Daniel Craig recalled.

Meanwhile, the actor's total commitment to the role of 007 wasn't just manifest in poker training or a punishing physical regimen, he was also working hard preparing for *Casino Royale*'s driving sequences. While the film was in pre-production, Craig had extensive stunt-driving tuition at Millbrook Proving Ground, a giant industry test facility in Bedfordshire, and also got time at the wheel of a BMW M3 (excellent for honing your ability to control oversteer).

Like many people, the actor became more interested in cars as his career developed and the opportunities arose. We talked briefly about his car history – he missed his first driving test because he had a late night and didn't make it, while the first car he owned was a Datsun Cherry. He also played the getaway driver in Steven Spielberg's superb 2005 thriller *Munich*.

Casino Royale was a step up on that front. The DB9 helped familiarise him both with the demands of a high performance car on the limit, but was also a taster of what was coming down the pipeline. The DBS succeeded the last Bond Aston Martin, the lovely Vanquish, as the halo car in the company's already seriously starry model hierarchy. It helped amplify the technological

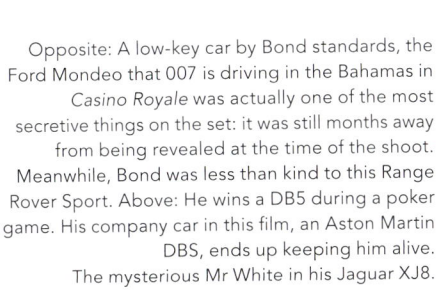

Opposite: A low-key car by Bond standards, the Ford Mondeo that 007 is driving in the Bahamas in *Casino Royale* was actually one of the most secretive things on the set: it was still months away from being revealed at the time of the shoot. Meanwhile, Bond was less than kind to this Range Rover Sport. Above: He wins a DB5 during a poker game. His company car in this film, an Aston Martin DBS, ends up keeping him alive. The mysterious Mr White in his Jaguar XJ8.

SC·167 13 JUN 2006 ⑥

19 — ANGLE OF THE SAME — ASTON JUST MISSING HER..

20 — TOP SHOT — ASTON LEAVING ROAD.

21 — C.U. VESPER — SHAPE OF CAR WIPES FRAME IN F.G.

22 — ANGLE ASTON LEAVES ROAD — CRASHES INTO UNDERGROWTH.

END OF SEQUENCE

Opposite: The storyboard for one of the film's most memorable sequences. Right: Vesper Lynd (Eva Green) is spotted in time for Bond to take suitably dramatic evasive action.

attributes whilst evolving the car's brutally beautiful looks. 'We started sketching in May 2005 and had a full-size clay buck by early October, and that's when the Bond team visited the factory,' Aston Martin's chief creative officer, Marek Reichman, told me. 'You know, there was curiosity on both sides. We wanted to meet the new Bond, work out whether it was a good associaton for us. But Daniel's a very cool guy, and it was only when I met him that I began looking beyond the character and really looked at how we'd make the car for him, too. Then there's the premise of the new film, which is much darker. And that absolutely fits with the car.

'The DB9 is a beautiful car,' he continued, 'with a softness and fullness to its surfaces. It's feminine without being effeminate. But the DBS is definitely masculine.'

Aston Martin didn't launch the production car until 2007, so effectively manufactured two hand-built prototypes for the hero shots in *Casino Royale* and supplied a further three stunt cars. The DBS used the same VH-bonded aluminium structure as the DB9, for improved structural rigidity. The DBS's fat 20-inch wheels and huge carbon ceramic brakes meant that its front wheel arches were pumped, and it was significantly wider at the back too. The bonnet, front wings and boot-lid were all reworked and made of carbon fibre, a race-bred material which is lighter yet also stronger than aluminium or steel. The DBS's bodywork also underwent a substantial aerodynamic reprofiling, with spoilers, ducts, sill extensions, diffusers and splitters. It's a truly magnificent looking car. The tyres were bespoke Pirelli P-zeroes.

The DBS we saw in Barrandov had a few other interesting refinements. The rear seats had been junked in favour of carbon fibre pods to store crash helmets, there were skeletal race-car seats with four-point harnesses and a memory foam that 'remembers' the driver's shape. The cabin was swathed in a specially treated leather, the dashboard finished in lacquered piano black wood and chrome, and the selector pattern in the gear-lever glowed red to white according to gear. That was the concept car. Bond's iteration added a sliding tray in the place of a glovebox, containing his gun and a defibrillator, an item that would play a significant part as *Casino Royale* unfolded.

As startling as the DBS looked, the most seductive element was its engine. This was a 5.9-litre, 510bhp V12 (40bhp more than the DB9) that made a noise like controlled thunder, a truly captivating sensory experience especially as the needle in the rev counter arced past the 3,500rpm threshold. If you lifted that sculpted, artful bonnet, it even looked good, too, which not all modern engines do. The 2007 DBS was an aristocratic performance car, and its six-speed manual gearbox was a wonderful anomaly in a time when semi-automatic gearboxes were becoming the norm at this level. But it was also a car firmly in the lineage that Ian Fleming envisaged for his creation.

Needless to say, it also became another high-profile automotive sacrifice to the demands of a Bond plot. In June 2006, second unit director Alexander Witt and his crew used the sweeping hill route at Millbrook to shoot the sequence in which Bond finds himself narrowly avoiding an imperilled Vesper Lynd (Eva Green). She's tied up in the middle of the road; his lightning-fast reflexes save the day, but leave the Aston's carbon fibre body panels with damage that was unlikely to polish out. The stunt driver was Adam Kirley, who had prepared for the scene using two BMW 5 series, having spent two months calculating the eventualities alongside stunt coordinator Gary Powell. The crew had also done practice runs in a white Aston Martin DB9. But when it came to shooting the real thing, there were unexpected problems. 'We couldn't get the Aston to roll over with the six-inch ramp as we had with the BMW,' he recalled. 'The Aston literally took off into the air, levelled, and landed on all four wheels. No chance of rolling whatsoever because of the stability of the car.'

'The centre of gravity is lower, it's basically a race car that's allowed on the road,' Gary Powell observed. The ramp size was increased until it was a shade under two feet in height but to no avail. So the special effects team, led by the indefatigable Chris Corbould alongside Gary Powell, were forced to fit the DBS with an air cannon positioned behind the driver's seat which used pressurised nitrogen to trigger a ram on the car's floor. There would be no further problem getting the Aston to pirouette.

'We were going to be happy with a couple of rolls, maybe three at a push,' Kirley continued. 'As I hit that button the car flipped, landed on its roof, and then started to roll. It's a very violent sort of ride. As the car's going over you're anticipating the impact. I could feel that we were going for quite a few rolls, so it was just a case of holding on.'

This was an understatement. The DBS didn't come to rest until it had fully rotated seven times, which was later verified by the *Guinness Book of Records* as a new world record. Proof, if any more were needed, of just how far the Bond production crew were now prepared to go to deliver the spectacular film that fans demanded. It's a scene that still makes the car-loving viewer wince.

'When you do your first Bond film,' Daniel Craig noted, 'you discover that the action sequences take a lot of time and a lot of work.' *Casino Royale*'s big setpiece chase sees Bond intercepting a terrorist at Miami airport, causing mayhem but avoiding the destruction of a plane when

he manages to seize control of a tanker on the runway. The sequence took two months to shoot during the summer of 2006, most of it at Dunsfold aerodrome in Surrey (long-term location of *Top Gear*, coincidentally). Miami Dade police department's Ford Crown Victoria interceptors are featured prominently; this mid-size saloon was an absolute staple of US-set movies in the Nineties and Noughties. Indeed, in one fantastic scene, a Crown Vic gets blown off its tyres when it's caught in the wake of an aircraft's jet engine thrust as it aborts a landing. The fuel tanker, meanwhile, was a 1989 International 4000-series, recreated in various states of distress by the production crew.

Casino Royale also features some notable supporting cars as we arrive in the Bahamas.

The aftermath... The special effects team needed an air cannon to get the Aston to roll, but once it started it didn't want to stop.

The latest, fourth-generation Ford Mondeo was on its way, but the car we see Bond driving was a pre-production prototype, hand-built in Ford's design studio in Cologne to match the real thing, which wouldn't be formally launched to the media for another year. Bond looks more at home when he wins an old friend during a poker game with Alex Dimitrios – an Aston Martin DB5, making one of its guest appearances – before heaping further ignominy on the man by seducing his wife. There's also an amusing sequence (shot at the One and Only Ocean Club, near Nassau) during which Bond creates a distraction by valet parking an ignorant hotel guest's Range Rover Sport.

Back in Europe, Bond and Vesper check in to the Hotel Splendide in Montenegro, the exterior of which was actually the Grandhotel Pupp in a town called Karlovy Vary, in Bohemia. It evokes a suitably decadent atmosphere, with the background cars to match: a Bentley Arnage T, BMW 6 series convertible, Ferrari F430, Maserati Spyder (M138-era), Mercedes S-class (W220-era), and Porsche 911 turbo (996-era) are all seen outside. The other significant automotive presence in *Casino Royale* is the Jaguar XJ. This particular iteration of Jaguar's famous saloon channelled the original's distinctive silhouette, but was underpinned by an advanced aluminium chassis. It looked familiar, but had a genuine dynamism.

It reappears throughout, but is perhaps best appreciated during the film's denouement, in which Mr White (Jesper Christensen) parks up outside Villa La Gaeta on Lake Como, ahead of a fateful meeting. It's exactly the right car for this understated but menacing character, a man who will, of course, become a key presence in the next film (and beyond). At this point in *Casino Royale*, he's left staring up from the gravel at his assailant. And it's only now that Daniel Craig gets to proclaim the immortal words.

'The name's Bond. James Bond.'

A Japanese one sheet, November 2008. The film title is translated as
'Quantum Crisis', while the tagline says, 'There's only a quantum between
loneliness and cold blood.' The photography is by Greg Williams.

CHAPTER 22
QUANTUM OF SOLACE

2008

STARRING Daniel Craig as James Bond

An immovable object meets an unstoppable force: Bond and the Aston Martin DBS in the thick of a car chase, filmed in Carrara, Italy, May 2008.

'One of the main things about watching a Bond movie has always been, where does it take you? Not just where emotionally, but physically,' Daniel Craig observed during filming for *Quantum Of Solace*. 'It sets the tone, it sets the feeling, it sets the mood on the set.'

Bond films famously traverse the globe. Yet as part of the doubling down that occurs on every new production, this 22nd 007 film would see the crew spend more time on location than on any of the previous movies. Not just more places, but also some of the most challenging from a geopolitical and logistical standpoint. 'Marc wanted Bond really out on a limb, in desolate terrain, and in interesting urban environments like Colón, Panama. It's never been photographed before and it made the film visually very exciting,' co-producer Barbara Broccoli said.

Choosing a director for a new Bond film is a unique responsibility in the movie industry, given the vast scale and the sheer number of moving parts a production of this magnitude entails, but also the pressure to deliver reliably executed beats amidst acute audience expectation. Coming off films such as *Monster's Ball* and *Finding Neverland*, Swiss-German director Marc Forster represented something of a left-field choice, the closest to an art-house filmmaker that the franchise had come. 'In the beginning, I had to navigate Ian Fleming's Bond, and the framework and rules of the films,' he said. 'Once I understood them, I started breaking them. I wanted to go a little bit retro, to pay homage to the early design choices of Ken Adam and the thrillers of the Sixties and Seventies I loved so much. I went back to these movies to absorb their look so I could create their feel, but at the same time making it modern and cutting-edge.' And the cars?

285

The opening part of this remarkable car chase was shot beside Lake Garda, on a two-lane road that was closed off at a preordained time of day. This was one of the most demanding action sequences in Bond history, and required astonishing precision.

'Everything you choose, whether it's cars, boats or planes, everything has a character,' Forster noted, indicating a filmmaker who appreciates nuance. Importantly, his creative team included Academy Award-winning production designer Dennis Gassner.

Quantum Of Solace was also the first time a Bond film had been conceived as a direct sequel, with 007 on the trail of the shadowy organisation that had blackmailed the woman he loved. So it begins where *Casino Royale* left off: with Mr White now in Bond's custody and in the boot of his Aston Martin DBS. After an atmospheric pan across Lake Garda, accompanied by a soundtrack of menacing strings, we're parachuted into a car chase; at exactly one minute in, the cellos are superseded by the sonorous roar of an Aston V12 in thunderous, maximum attack mode.

The second unit on this occasion was presided over by Dan Bradley, a former stunt coordinator who had helped redefine the action genre on films that included *The Bourne Supremacy* and *The Bourne Ultimatum*. He favoured tools like the Russian arm and Ultimate arm – a five-axis gyro stabilised camera crane usually mounted on a high-performance SUV – which took the viewer closer to the action than Terence Young would ever have thought possible. You can practically taste the discarded tyre debris in this pre-credit chase.

It took Herculean effort to shoot. The second unit arrived in Lake Garda in April 2008, and began filming the sequence on the 14th. Bond is being tailed by a pair of Alfa Romeo 159s, precisely the sort of car the Italian wing of Quantum (a quasi-SPECTRE) would deploy to take out their British nemesis: cool but understated enough to fly under the radar. It's an electrifying chase, in which Bond's Aston is skewered by a DAF 95 truck that's been rammed into the tunnel concrete, forcing him into a J-turn which he manages in the face of much traffic, losing the driver's side door in the process. 'One of the big challenges was that we were on these two-lane roads,' Bradley recalled. 'It's very hard to shoot a chase with just two lanes available.'

'It wasn't the size of the car, or the amount of cars, that made it complicated, it was the locations,' stunt coordinator Gary Powell added. 'We were in a very long tunnel, only 28 feet wide in parts. When there are over 40 cars going through it at the speeds we were doing, it becomes a technical challenge.'

Lack of space wasn't the only impediment, as executive producer Anthony Waye remembered. Securing necessary permissions in a country not known for its bureaucratic user-friendliness was a problem. 'For the chase through the tunnels of Lake Garda, our local team had to negotiate with several mayors and town councils covering the area. There was only one road around the lake, so we had to reach an agreement to completely close the road at set times each day and put on a boat service between villages.'

The unit then relocated further south, to the Tuscan city of Massa, on the Ligurian coast. It lay in the heart of the Carrara region,

What's the collective noun for a group of specially prepared DBSs? A Bond of Astons?

famous throughout history for its marble: London's Marble Arch was constructed of Carraran stone, as was Michelangelo's *David*. Movie car chases belong in a different line of antiquity, and from 26 April to 12 May the second unit worked flat-out to ensure that this pre-credits sequence would be one for the ages.

'Some of the mountain roads we were on were quite high up and very narrow,' Dan Bradley remembered. 'The quarry was 3,000 feet above sea level, and we had cars coming down, doing handbrake turns, going round corners at speed with a 700-foot drop next to them. The action vehicle department did a pretty phenomenal job. Cars were being dragged off the set; two hours later they came back and they're running again. If you count the redos, we probably wrecked something like 14 Aston Martins.'

As well as the gravel that was being kicked up, the backdrop proved a formidable location for the drivers (one of whom was Ben Collins, whose work doubling for Daniel Craig meant he could temporarily hang up the white racing overalls he wore as *Top Gear*'s ultra-enigmatic Stig, although he somehow fitted a test in Ferrari's 430 Scuderia

'Where does a Bond film take you, emotionally and physically?'

into his schedule). 'It's tricky and dusty and the roads are lined by slabs of marble,' Gary Powell remarked. 'So if you get it wrong there's no forgiving.'

As well as the punishment meted out to the Aston and the Alfa Romeo, a carabinieri Land Rover almost wipes Bond out at one point. When the 159 falls off a cliff, Bond heads into Siena with his terrorist cargo still intact, for a rendezvous with M. Once again, the production had spent months securing permission to film in this most beautiful of Italian cities, Bond duly pursuing a rogue MI6 agent through the underground tunnels, across the slippery terracotta-tiled roofs, culminating in a truly mesmerising art gallery rope fight (shot on Pinewood's A Stage from 14 January to 2 February), all to the backdrop of the city's famous Palio. In order to cover the rooftop chase, four mobile cranes had to be driven into Siena, but only after a three-month geological survey determined where they could be positioned. Once again, the level of effort that goes in beggars belief. Including that demonstrated by the film's leading man, whose willingness and ability to get stuck in even on the hairiest stunts underpins his Bond.

'You know, we've done what I always wanted a Bond movie to do to me when I was a kid,' Daniel Craig told *GQ* magazine in 2008. 'Which is go and sit down and get transported somewhere. To go and see a place I've never seen before and feel what I've never felt before.'

(NB A nod to the background car cast, the most prominent of which were Fords. Dominic Greene is seen getting out of a rare supercharged Daimler Super V8 in Bregenz (it's later a landing pad for a bodyguard, post Bond meeting), his retinue use the handsome Edge crossover, Camille Montes (Olga Kurylenko) intercepts Bond in Port-au-Prince in the then-new gen II Ford Ka.

Best of all is the 1989 Ford Bronco II Bond 'borrows', a car that has become so unexpectedly iconic that its maker is preparing an all-new version after a quarter-century hiatus. Bond also drives a Range Rover Sport, whose boot contains the body of poor old Mathis (Giancarlo Giannini). Filming in Panama, meanwhile, means the presence on screen of numerous Eighties and Nineties Mitsubishis and Nissans. These cars make up in mechanical indestructibility what they lack in any sort of stylistic charm.)

Quantum of Solace took Bond on an exotic travel odyssey. Above: Camille Montes (Olga Kurylenko) at the wheel of a VW Beetle, in a sequence filmed in Panama. Baddie Dominic Greene used a Daimler Super V8, his henchmen a Ford Edge.

Daniel Craig, a Range Rover Sport, and a venerable but beautiful DC-3 aeroplane. 'Sometimes the only thing between the bottom of the plane and the ground is just the cactus,' its pilot Skip Evans observed.

UK poster, October 2012, with
photography by Greg Williams.

CHAPTER 23

SKYFALL

2012

STARRING Daniel Craig as James Bond

Skyfall was released on the series' 50th anniversary, adding an additional emotional undertow to the usual pressure to exceed what had come before. When the film emerged it had a gravitas to go with the spectacle, a sense of ambition matched by an unstoppable commercial appeal. *Skyfall* was the first billion-dollar Bond film at the global box office.

And it punched hard, from the get-go. We see Bond tumble into a watery abyss at the end of another blistering opening volley of action, then apparently confront his own demise in Daniel Kleinman's gothic credits sequence. Sometimes this spying malarkey looks utterly thankless. When 007 reappears in London, three months later according to the film's timeline (having taken to drinking with scorpions on his hand in a bar near his beach retreat), he is bloody, beaten but unbowed.

Among its many big themes, *Skyfall* is a film about loyalty, which repeatedly challenges authority before putting no less a figure than M (Dame Judi Dench) to the sword. It's also one that's painted in forbidding colours before emerging more hopefully into the light.

It was director Sir Sam Mendes' first Bond, his ability to command a huge film bolstered by the work of 14-time Oscar-nominated (and winning) cinematographer Roger Deakins. Production designer Dennis Gassner was also back, and this formidable triumvirate led a production that delivered what's arguably the most majestically cinematic Bond film ever made.

In addition to Neal Purvis and Robert Wade, screenwriter John

Right: Moneypenny (Naomie Harris) dispenses with the windscreen of her Land Rover Defender 110. Below: *Skyfall*'s pre-credit sequence took five weeks to shoot across three Turkish cities, in March 2012.

Logan (*The Aviator*, *Gladiator*) was brought on board to give the script an enhanced sensibility. 'Sam and I talked a lot about why a Bond movie is a Bond movie and not a Bourne or a John le Carré,' Logan informed the *Hollywood Reporter*. 'It has to do with that intense seriousness and a pain that hurts and also this sense of panache and elegance.'

It's all there in the story and on the screen. In addition to the customarily high-quality work done by Alex Witt's second unit, the pre-credits sequence is notable for how often Bond switches mode of transport as he pursues an assassin (Patrice, played by Ola Rapace) who has stolen a computer drive: first in a Land Rover Defender 110, then on a motorbike, before leaping onto a train. On which he also finds himself – but of course – improvising with an enormous Caterpillar digger. Two 320D Ls were manufactured specially for the film; the controls and hydraulics were re-routed to the right side of the cab so that, while Bond is clearly pictured in the driving seat, a real operator was working the machine. A bunch of latter-day VW Beetles get trashed in the process.

Eve Moneypenny (Naomie Harris) is a field agent in *Skyfall*'s first act, and manages to keep pace in the Land Rover. '[Stunt coordinator] Gary Powell and his team did a very good job in preparing Naomie to drive so it looked like Eve had been doing it for years and years,' Alex Witt said. Lead stunt driver in the highly modified Defender was Bond regular Ben Collins. 'The [special effects crew] played with the suspension quite heavily and we made it wider track and used different wheels that we kept out of shot,' he said. 'We also used standard wheels, but that gave it much more stability when we were cornering hard, because of the extra weight on the roof. They put different shock absorbers in there, stiffened up the suspension, there was much more control of the weight.'

Chris Corbould's expert team had by now become very adept with the pod car concept, wherein the stunt driver sits in a safety cage on the roof, leaving the actor beneath to concentrate on the acting and the camera able to move through a 360° angle. 'It feels very strange. You're quite disconnected in a way because it's so high up, but then again, you have more control,' Collins recalled. 'It's different because normally you have a steering rack, and it's a direct link to the front wheels. In this case we use a hydraulic system, so you have much less feedback. There's a delay in the kind of reaction.

'You have to turn the wheel twice as much to get the amount of travel in the front wheels that you get in a standard road car. And the

Skyfall sees an emotionally resonant return for the Aston Martin DB5, the original Bond car. It doesn't end well for the car but, rather than destroy the real thing, highly accurate 3D-printed models were created. The dramatic conclusion was filmed at Hankley Common in Surrey during February and March 2012. Opposite top: The Range Rover L322 and M's Jaguar XJ L also play key, if less explosive, roles.

Original concept art for the climax of *Skyfall*, proposing guns from the DB5 and interesting apparel for Silva's men.

sensations you get are exaggerated. The movement in the car is tripled by the time it's reached you. But that's the joy of it really as a stunt driver – adapting to that technology and making the most of it. And it actually outperformed the standard car in the end.'

In total, 12 Land Rover Defenders and 15 Audi A5s were used in the opening chase in Istanbul. If that seems like rather a lot, remember that multiples of every car have to be prepped for their role according to the demands of the sequence. For example, the Audi that ends up on its side slithering through a bazaar will have been fitted with a roll cage. In fact, an even more complicated rig was employed, enabling the rotation of the Audi to be controlled when it's pushed into a spin by the Land Rover. But the stunt didn't make the final cut.

'Originally Patrice's car got broadsided by Eve's Land Rover, she pushed it along and, after it hit the kerb, it went up and barrel-rolled through the air,' Corbould recalled. 'Sam thought it was a bit over-the-top, so we did a more realistic version, where the car flips on its side as it goes through the main square in Istanbul. We had a lot of time perfecting the barrel roll, and a lot less time to do the stunt where it flips on its side. It's amazing once the adrenalin kicks in how quickly you can do things.'

The second unit rehearsed for a month from 28 February and began a five-week shoot on 22 March. The action took place across three different Turkish cities, Daniel Craig finding his feet on a moving train whilst wearing a safety wire (to the ruination of many tailored suits). 'We do things for real in Bond movies, and that's just the way it is,' he later noted. 'The CGI is just to help out as opposed to creating the scene.'

Skyfall's major locations also emerge as distinct characters. Shanghai is about space, light and a certain eeriness, Bond trailing Patrice in his VW Passat taxi using that series staple, the Mercedes S-class (now in its sleekly modernist W221 incarnation). Turkey is more aggressive, chaotic, and often shot hand-held. And then there's London, a city that's been captured on film so often it's inescapably reduced to cliché while rarely capturing its restless essence. *Skyfall* aimed higher, and hit the target. 'How many times I've sat in meetings and people have said, "We're going to make London look like London,"' Daniel Craig observed post-filming. 'Yeah. So when the red bus goes past the postbox… [In *Skyfall*] we see parts of London we hadn't seen before and use the iconography more than you would be able to in most movies because Bond opens a few doors.'

That iconography extends to the cars we see. The background warp and weft of London is more generically monochrome than Istanbul's vibrancy, but the ministerial Range Rover and Jaguar XJ L have an obsidian omnipotence. Bond later spirits M away from Silva's (Javier Bardem) attack in the Jaguar, clipping a kerb on the exit. (This is a subtle example of the filmmaker's desire for pressurised verisimilitude versus the stunt driver's preference for a clean pass.)

And so to the film's third act and the arrival of an old friend, the Aston Martin DB5. Never mind that it starts first time, or that Bond and M then drive from a London lock-up all the way to Glencoe (or indeed that the Aston is part of Bond's plan to go off-grid). If you want proof that a machine has genuine character – *is* a genuine character – then here it is. 'It's a signature car for Bond, and something the audiences love to see,' co-producer Michael G. Wilson noted. This is car as movie star.

'The film is about going back home and confronting old demons'

'The DB5 is part of my boyhood,' Sam Mendes observed. 'It's part of my generation's boyhood. I had the model, I had the ejector seat, and I had the little man. I spent the rest of my childhood looking for it behind various sofas… I felt there was a thematic link. It's about the old and the new, and there's something about the last part of the movie that deliberately and very consciously could have taken place in 1962.'

The film drops weightlessly out of time at this juncture, or perhaps daringly goes through the looking glass. We know that Bond is set for a showdown with Silva, but it's bigger even than that, the DB5 now assuming a metaphorical status. 'The story is about going back home and about returning to his roots and confronting old demons,' Daniel Craig said. 'I'm sure we could have put a brand new Aston Martin in [the film] and it would have been beautiful and fantastic, but it was appropriate to use the DB5. And we got some good use out of it.'

It also has the screen very much to itself, a car that's haunted by Bond's half-century as much as it's conveying 007 and M to his ancestral home. There's nothing particularly subtle about what happens next: Skyfall (the house) and the Aston Martin get blown to smithereens. Location filming in Glencoe with the Aston took place on 9 February 2012, with the interiors shot at Pinewood between 15 February and 10 March. The exterior scenes were filmed at Hankley Common in Surrey, the explosive conclusion overseen by Chris Corbould and his special effects team. Although the filmmakers used two DB5s – one from EON's collection and another sourced and restored by Aston

The DB5 is haunted by Bond's half-century

Martin's Works Service in Newport Pagnell – clearly some movie magic was needed when it came to the car's destruction. Propshop Modelmakers were commissioned and they turned to a German company called Voxeljet, a leading exponent of 3D industrial printing (an increasingly important tool in the creation of movie props). Although a 1:3 model could have been created using one of their biggest printers, the teams involved wanted the maximum detail and functionality and decided to produce 18 individual primary components, with a further 36 ancillary ones. Propshop then assembled three models for filming. Meanwhile, Gary Powell prepared Daniel Craig for the driving sequence.

'The cars were a fortune. I had to take [Daniel] for a test drive and it was at Pinewood Studios, so the production was like, "Where are you going to take him?" We went around the studio and it was absolutely hopeless because you had trucks driving around, forklift trucks. It was dangerous there.' A five-mile countryside loop around Pinewood Studios was more helpful. 'You could see people waiting at the gate for us to come back to make sure there wasn't a scratch on it,' Powell recalled. 'I'm sure they aged ten years while we were out in this car. It was actually really funny because while we were driving along, we were in the DB5, but Daniel Craig's driving it. As we were going past people, people were looking and going, "That looks like Daniel Craig driving the Aston Martin."'

Top: Taking aim – in *Skyfall*'s third act Bond isn't just tackling the film's protagonist, he's squaring up to elements from his past. The DB5 isn't just a car in this instance, it's a metaphor. Above: Concept artwork from the final showdown posits a memorable if distressing end for the Aston Martin. These images offer tantalising glimpses into the creative process during pre-production.

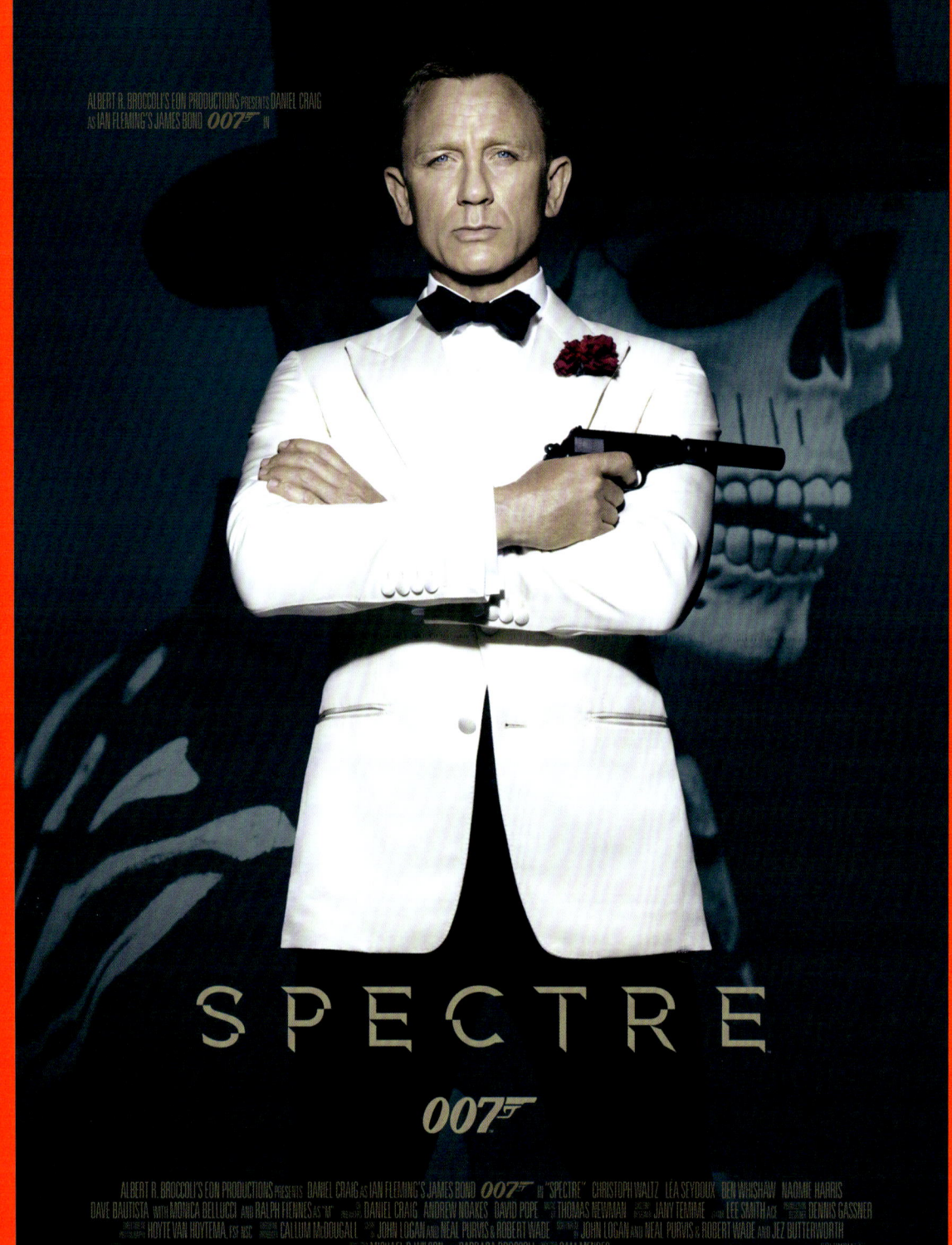

UK poster, October 2015, with
photography by Greg Williams.

CHAPTER 24
SPECTRE

2015

STARRING Daniel Craig as James Bond

One of *Spectre*'s more bravura touches was to place two remarkable vehicles at the heart of its car chase centrepiece, which was filmed in Rome nightly over a three-week period. The Aston Martin DB10 was commissioned by director Sam Mendes specifically for the film after he'd spotted a rendering in the company's design centre, while the Jaguar C-X75 was a hypercar project glamorously reincarnated.

Commission a bespoke Aston Martin for Bond? Re-purpose a Jaguar supercar concept? Film a car chase through the centre of Rome at night, past the Vatican and into the River Tiber? *Spectre* achieved a high-water mark for 007, literally and metaphorically. But then, it had its work cut out for it: 53 years and 23 films in, *Skyfall* had proven to be the biggest Bond ever.

On 11 July 2013, it was announced that director Sam Mendes would return to direct Bond 24, and he had cars on his mind from the start. 'I was looking for a way to get a new car into Bond 24. I wanted what comes with the cars: mischief, fun and speed,' he said. Mendes, with producers Michael G. Wilson and Barbara Broccoli, visited Aston Martin's Gaydon HQ late in January 2014, during which the director spotted a sketch on the design office wall and knew what he wanted. 'I was actually presenting a different car to him,' Aston Martin's chief creative officer Marek Reichman recalls. 'And he asked, "Has Bond ever had a car designed purely for himself?" No. Then he saw a sketch and said, "Could you build that?" Well, yes, but it's just a sketch. "Well there you go…" It was an incredible opportunity.'

The result was a Bond car unlike any before, and the pinnacle of a relationship that was now exactly 50 years old. But the DB10 was a rather different beast to its famous forebear. 'It's a predator, which is what I wanted it to be, because Bond is a predator,' Reichman added. The shape was the work of Aston designer Sam Holgate, whose first Bond film was *GoldenEye*. 'Essential Aston,' he told me. 'The message from Sam Mendes was that he wanted everything pared right back. It's not a retro reworking of the DB5, but it has that car's purity. Bond is an analogue sort of character, and so is his new car.'

The DB10's body was made of carbon fibre, the bonnet a huge single-piece clamshell. As per Mendes' request, it was very pure, and becomes progressively prettier as the eye runs along it. There were some Q-approved special features, though. Tucked in amidst the aero features dominating the DB10's rear was a fin that ignites a flamethrower. The lights, meanwhile, were tiny dimples lit from below by powerful LEDs. Inside, the car's carbon fibre exoskeleton is visible at various points but mostly clad in black leather. Aston's interior designer Steve Platt described it as 'deconstructed', and there's a purposefulness consistent with the man it was designed for. It's driver-focused, the main dials defiantly analogue, even the air vents reimagined. The switches are all meticulously handcrafted bespoke items, there's a button with fingerprint recognition nestled within the steering wheel, and a hi-tech compressed mesh in the seats.

Tellingly, the DB10 also rejected modish connectivity in favour of a strong simplicity. It's ironic, given Bond's long affiliation with cutting edge gadgetry, that you can't imagine him having much patience with the ever-evolving smartphone. Although the film does have considerable fun with exactly that when he calls Moneypenny midway through the car chase in Rome. (There's also a reminder that the DB10 was actually assigned to 009, and that 007 'borrowed' it, as is his wont.)

Top Gear editor-in-chief Charlie Turner was on set in the city during filming, swelling the 400-strong crew by one for a ringside seat at one of the most ambitious car chases in movie history. The sequence sees Bond flee the SPECTRE gathering (actually filmed at Blenheim Palace, near Oxford), only to be pursued by Hinx (Dave Bautista) in his Jaguar C-X75 into the Eternal City. Cue a chase that dares to homage some of the more humorous aspects of a Moore-era

307

Below: Images from the storyboard for the Rome chase sequence. Right: Not all of Q's DB10 gadgets are fully functional, but the flamethrower is certainly effective.

action setpiece, while elevating the driving to near-art. The Aston may not perform an astro spiral jump, but power-sliding past the Pope's front door at 100mph-plus is pretty punchy stuff.

The sequence continues through some narrow side streets, decapitates an Alfa Romeo, and nudges an elderly, opera-loving Italian gentleman in a Fiat 500 into a barrier. Then we descend the steps of the Scalo de Pinedo and hurtle along the banks of the River Tiber, for a flamethrowing and, ultimately, unexpectedly aquatic climax.

For *Spectre*, Aston Martin built ten DB10s: three hero cars and seven modified by the special effects team and its action vehicles department. Each of those seven were individually rigged according to what they needed to do in the car chase; the steps down to the Tiber, for example, demanded more of the suspension than the factory setting. Neil Layton, a former motorsport engineer with experience in British touring cars and the world rally championship, is now Chris Corbould's right-hand man in the highly specialised world of car prep on a Bond film. 'It's not just the maintenance side

of it, it's the re-jigging and the re-prep work between different stunts,' Layton said. 'At the moment, we've got just under 20 guys, so we do two shifts to cover 24 hours, but we've got guys back in the workshop. They're always fabricating. We've got one scene that's coming up, where the Jag comes up behind the Aston and then we hit it with a firebomb. It's in the back of that car, it's all rigged ready and we've got flamethrowers in there and the guns.' Layton's team were also tasked with supervising the background cars, ice cream vans and all.

Bond, as ever, is for real. Although the filmmaker's skill – led by second unit director and action cinema legend, Alexander Witt – and the precision of the driving is what's most obviously apparent when you watch *Spectre*, spare a thought for the logistics and planning involved. 'We've got 20 sets of hero wheels and 40 sets of stunt wheels just for the DB10; for the Jag, we have 30 sets of wheels, and then we have sets of tyres to go with each set of wheels. For the Jag, we have ten clamshells… the list goes on,' Layton said. 'I've had some pretty cool jobs in the years that I've been involved with cars, but I don't think anything will top Bond and the Bond cars.'

Above: One of the seven Jaguar C-X75s created specially for *Spectre*.

The Spectre Land Rover Defender is called Bigfoot, for obvious reasons

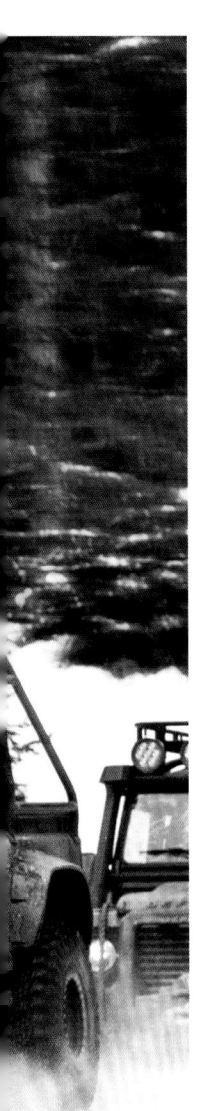

Left: Villainous intervention is facilitated by Range Rover Sport SVR and two Land Rover Defender 'Bigfoot' vehicles. They're riding on vast 37-inch wheels, hence the name.

Mark Higgins, former British rally champion turned world-class stunt driver, was the man making Daniel Craig look very good indeed in Rome. The job has some unique properties, as he told me. 'What they're looking for and what you think is cool can be totally different. It's about what the camera wants to see. I did a lovely drift, it was left to right and it felt great, but you have to make it look real, it has to be almost a bit scrappy. Bond is under pressure, so it has to look less fluid. It can be frustrating because I'll look back and think, "I can do it a lot better than that." Working on films has ruined how I watch them. I'm looking for different things now.

'I also remember going through St Peter's Square, fully sideways at 80 or 90mph, but had to drop it down to 2,000rpm in third gear, and the road narrowed as I was on the lock stops. If it had gone from narrow to wide it would have been straightforward. But we had to do it the hard way!'

Equally hard is the treatment handed out to the Jaguar C-X75. Punished repeatedly in the name of entertainment, this Jaguar's route to big-screen immortality was, if anything, even more startling than the creation of a bespoke Aston Martin. The original car arrived in concept form in 2010, a technically awesome high-performance hybrid. It was a 'go' project initially, but in December 2012 Jaguar pulled the plug, having created five prototypes, co-developed with Williams Advanced Engineering (an offshoot of the storied Formula One team). The C-X75 was powered by a 1.6-litre four-cylinder engine, turbo- and supercharged to make 502bhp, bolstered by lightweight electric motors on either axle producing another 194bhp each, and fed by a 19kWh lithium ion battery. A heap of power, altogether, enough to propel the car to 60mph in less than 3.0secs, 100mph in less than 6.0secs, and well past 200mph in terms of top speed. All while producing a quoted 89g/km of CO_2. It's a mesmerising blend of Jaguar design at its very best and ferocious hi-tech, sadly abandoned because of cool commercial realities.

But at least it was gifted with a unique afterlife, albeit in a form designed for movie repeatability. Seven C-X75s were made for *Spectre*, two in hero form with full interiors, the other five to withstand the rigours of stunt-driving brutalisation. A team of 12 Williams engineers were tasked with the cars' creation. 'First thing is, it had to be tough,' Williams' Wes Partridge told *Top Gear*'s Ollie Marriage. 'So we designed a steel frame made from 60mm tubing. It means the car isn't exactly light – I think it weighs a bit under 1,500kg although weight didn't matter too much – but what we were happy about was when the cars all came back from filming, we put them on a jig and none of the frames had moved or bent so much as a fraction of a degree.'

Jaguar's proven supercharged 5.0-litre V8 as used in the Range Rover Sport SVR was installed (rumoured to be running a non-standard 600bhp in this car), harnessed to a six-speed sequential GT3 racing gearbox from Ricardo. A WRC-style suspension set-up with fully adjustable shock absorbers allowed for a certain amount of give-and-take on the Scalo de Pinedo, the brakes were supplied by AP Racing, and fibreglass body panels meant repair or replacement was more straightforward – useful, because this was a daily occurrence. Inside, carbon fibre race seats were fitted, with five-point harnesses. The stunt driver doubling for Dave Bautista's giant henchman Hinx (and he fitted in the Jag) was Russian specialist, Martin Ivanov, a Bond regular since

When Hinx (Dave Bautista) kidnaps Dr Swann (Léa Seydoux), the ensuing chase takes place near Solden in Austria, while the helicopter shot of Bond's plane tracking the cars was done at the Rettenbach Glacier. A number of Land Rovers most definitely were hurt during this sequence.

Above: Bond fans will recognise the Rolls-Royce Silver Wraith as a callback to a previous film.

Quantum Of Solace, who's also doubled for Tom Cruise, Matt Damon, and Ryan Reynolds. His task was made ever-so-slightly easier by the fact that one paddle on the steering column was for the gearshift (push and pull), while the other operated a hydraulic handbrake. A car purpose-built to go sideways, in other words. And then some.

The supporting cast is hardly hiding its light under a bushel. A pair of Land Rover Defender SVXs – colloquially known as Bigfoot – dominate the sequence in which Bond pursues a kidnapped Madeleine Swann (Léa Seydoux) – using an aeroplane. JLR supplied ten of these beasts to the production, a modified Defender 110 crew cab originally created as a support vehicle for Land Rover events in Iceland and Morocco. Each features gigantic 37-inch wheels clad in 395/70 rubber, a reworked transmission with ultra-low ratios for rock crawling, a power upgrade to 185bhp, differential locks that use compressed air, a detachable chassis cross member, rose-jointed suspension, Bilstein steering shock absorbers, Recaro seats with four-point harnesses, and a satellite phone. Hinx is seen in a Range Rover Sport SVR, the most potent model the company makes, and a Bond regular. It gets trashed in the post-Solden showdown. M's Jaguar XJ8 meets an equally ignominious fate in a London tunnel, as the film powers towards its climax. It's a clever piece of automotive casting; somehow, this previous generation XJ fits Ralph Fiennes' nuanced portrayal of the man. He cuts a rather traditional figure, but he's resolute beneath the surface.

Back to that SPECTRE gathering. One might imagine that this emergency gathering of the world's most amoral power-brokers would necessitate a string of generic limos. Perhaps they're off-duty here, and so we're treated to a gathering of some fine contemporary supercars, as well as a few lesser-known gems: an Aston Martin Lagonda Taraf, Audi R8, Bugatti EB110 GT, Bentley Arnage T, Ferrari 599 GTO, Ferrari California, Ferrari F355 Spider, Ferrari FF, Ferrari 430 Spider, Jaguar F-type, Lexus LFA, Maserati GranCabrio, McLaren MP4-12C, Mercedes-Benz SL55, Mercedes-AMG SLS and SLS convertible, Mercedes McLaren SLR, Porsche 959, and a Rolls-Royce Phantom Drophead Coupé are all visible. SPECTRE membership presumably precludes mortal concerns such as speed cameras or parking tickets.

There are also two significant callbacks. Blofeld sends a Rolls-Royce Silver Wraith to collect Bond and Dr Swann in the desert (similar to the car used in *From Russia With Love*). And early in the film we see the DB5 in Q's workshop: 'Oh, yes. That old thing is taking quite a bit of time. Mind you, there wasn't much left to work on. Only a steering wheel. I believe I said, "Bring it back in one piece," not, "Bring back one piece."'

Happily, it's repaired in time for the film's wonderful coda:

'Good morning, Q.'

'I thought you'd gone…'

'I have. There's just one thing I need…'

UK poster with photography by Greg Williams

CHAPTER 25
NO TIME TO DIE

2021

STARRING Daniel Craig as James Bond

Daniel Craig and one of the new Land Rover Defenders, Buttersteep Woods, Ascot, August 2019.

Ardverikie Estate covers 60,000 hectares, and the 300-strong crew on Bond 25 are many miles deep within its borders. They're hard at work on a particularly brutal car chase. A group of black SUVs are carving their way through the countryside, while a helicopter hovers above. A second helicopter is in the air, too, its gimbal camera trained on the unfolding action.

It's July 2019, and *No Time To Die*, directed by Cary Joji Fukunaga, has yet to receive its official title; visitors to the set are issued with laminated passes with the famous 007 logo printed on them and a simple 'B25'. The unit base is an assembly of Winnebagos and trailers that must be ten miles or more from the nearest main road, and once you're approved you get handed a vital piece of equipment: a bug net to pull over your head. The midgies in the Scottish Highlands can detect fresh prey miles off and move in predatory, buzzing clouds.

Filming is taking place another ten-minute drive from the base and, on top of the customary secrecy and security concerns that accompany any major film shoot, there's another unusual factor today. This chase is using a handful of Land Rover Defenders, but not the familiar and unarguably iconic model that first appeared way back in 1948 (and somehow managed to remain in production for 68 years, its basic form still recognisably the same). No, we're talking *all-new* Defender, one of the most keenly anticipated cars of the decade. Its global reveal at the Frankfurt motor show is still two months away, and the car itself is entering the final stages of developmental sign-off.

Yet here it is, being pummelled by the Scottish landscape, and defending itself against the none-too-tender mercies of the Bond second unit. These Defenders are very early prototypes, the first ten to come off a pilot production line. Action Vehicles Supervisor Neil Layton

has seen and done most things with cars in his career, but he's never had to prep a car that's so new it's still technically a rumour. 'It's always exciting to get your hands on new stuff,' he tells me. 'You have to interrogate the software. But the guys from Land Rover have been amazing. They said, "If you have a problem, we'll just write new code for you."'

And there's plenty of it on the new Defender. Where you could fix the old one with a well-judged hammer blow, now it's all about 'software-over-the-air' updates, the new car's 14 electronic control modules and 85 ECUs ensuring that it's running the latest tech wherever it is in the world – assuming there's a satellite phone and suitable data connection. There's a brand-new aluminium-intense chassis, the cabin's blocky minimalism can be given a lavish 'lifestyle' makeover, and many buyers may never venture off-road. But the new Defender can still wade through 900mm of water, and during its development Land Rover's engineers repeatedly accelerated it into a 200mm concrete kerb at 25mph.

The Bond stunt team are keen to add their own tortuous tests. Stunt coordinator Lee Morrison is the architect of the Defenders' pain here in Scotland, having devised the car chase in the new film. It's set in Norway and much has already been shot on the Great Atlantic Road, but Ardverikie is standing in for this section. Which means taking the action fully off-road, including a sequence on a fast-flowing river. 'The water level has changed constantly,' Morrison tells me, 'and it's marshy and rocky. I want the vehicles to look as dynamic as possible, and

The DB5s in the new film are genetically modified superheroes, with a race-car chassis

Below and right: The pre-credits car chase was shot in Matera, Italy. The new film sees a full-blown comeback for the Aston Martin DB5.

we always try to be original. These sequences are also story-driven, and this one is pivotal for Bond. I've shot all over the world, including in the Cambodian jungle, but this has got to be the toughest chase I've ever helped put together. It's been brutal.'

A month later, we find Mark Higgins, a former British rally champion turned stunt driver, between takes for the new film's pre-credit sequence. The unit has swapped Scotland for Matera in southern Italy, and the Defenders have been replaced by a familiar, highly charismatic Bond performer: the Aston Martin DB5.

Matera is a UNESCO jewel in the heel of Italy, a location which presents a different set of challenges for the production on a hot late summer's day. Securing permissions to perform an elaborate action sequence in such a naturally beautiful place required nine months' negotiation. The Bond production prides itself on leaving many of its locations in better shape than when it arrived; in Matera, they just want to protect the ancient stone walls, which have been covered in a protective cladding. It's also illegal to over-fly the city with a helicopter, which means rethinking how they shoot. Meanwhile, the slippery stone streets have been doused with fizzy soft drink, which dries to a curious stickiness that gives the cars vital extra traction.

As to the Aston Martin, well it's the gift that keeps on giving. 'Cary really wanted a DB5 in the film, along with the DBS Superleggera and the V8 that was in *The Living Daylights*, which is a personal favourite of mine,' Chris Corbould says. 'For me, the most exciting time is at the start when I'm bouncing ideas off the director. Cary likes his bikes and his cars. It's my team's job to throw ideas at him.'

Eight DB5s have been made for the film by Aston Martin, in collaboration with Chris Corbould and the special effects crew. The new DB5s were laser-scanned so that their body panels – now made of carbon fibre – are identical to the original. But beneath them there's a bespoke racing car-style chassis, and a modern six-cylinder engine provides the motive power. They were all shaken down by endurance racing driver Darren Turner before being sent into duty. The DB10 in *Spectre* was a special car, but this DB5 is something else again: purpose-built so that the stunt drivers can maximise their

Top left: Director Cary Fukunaga in discussion with Daniel Craig and Léa Seydoux, during filming in Matera, Italy, September 2019.

potential, and to enable the support crew to repair any damage as swiftly and efficiently as possible. Yep, we're talking genetically modified superhero Aston Martin DB5.

Each of the cars has been set up specifically for different parts of the film's chase and, on closer inspection, has more in common with a world rally car than a beloved British sports car. One has a metal bar reinforcing its bodyside, another has a motorsport suspension set-up designed to tackle steps and jumps. They're all fitted with hydraulic handbrakes, roll cages, and camera mounting points, and are magnificently well-engineered.

In Matera they're also surrounded by a supporting cast that includes a series one Range Rover, several Jaguar XFs, a 1996 Maserati Quattroporte, a 2004 Lancia Thesis, and an early 1980s Fiat 127. The bad guys are in the first three, while the little Fiat adds context and flavour. Needless to say, there's nothing random about this selection, and they all fall under Chris Corbould and Neil Layton's purview.

'The art department has a storyboard wall, with images showing the look they're trying to get,' Layton explains. 'We source the cars, they get safety checked, and then we fit the stunt gear. Small capacity stunt tanks, hydraulic handbrakes, fire-suppression systems...' he tells me. 'On a lot of the newer cars we have to interrogate the software and turn off the stability control systems. Sometimes you get technical support, sometimes you don't, but it's all about getting the car to behave dynamically. Everything has to be switchable, down to seemingly silly little things. Sometimes the guys will want brake lights on, sometimes they want them off. That can be tricky on new cars, but the DB5s... they do exactly what we ask them to do.'

Then there's the Aston with the pod mounted on the roof, its steering rack extended so that a stuntperson can do the driving, and the actor gets to concentrate (as described in Chapter 23). Chris Corbould's team has actually developed a pod car that works by remote control from a range of 500m but, for now, it's down to Higgins and the other drivers to hit their marks. 'You have to be extremely precise, to understand what the camera is doing, and understand what you're trying to get across,' Lee Morrison explains. 'These guys have got four seconds to tell a story that's happening throughout the whole film. So they've got to attack that certain shot as if it's the last thing they're ever going to do. No one arrives with the ability fully formed. Mark has learnt all that and he's up there now with the best in the world.'

Higgins has worked on Bond since 2008's *Quantum Of Solace*. He recalls arriving on set for the first time to see a crew member wielding a sledgehammer and beating the life out of three Aston Martin DBSs. An unusual induction to the world of Bond, but something he quickly became accustomed to. 'It's about what the camera wants to see. You have to make it look real, it has to be almost a bit scrappy. Bond is under pressure, so it has to be less fluid.

'It's a very different pressure, because there are 200 people out there. Repeatability

Images from the pivotal car chase action sequence in the new film. Top right: Rami Malek (who plays Safin) on set and preparing himself for a take. Second row, left: Second unit director Alexander Witt with stunt coordinator Lee Morrison. Bottom right: Léa Seydoux (Madeleine Swann) in the heat of battle.

Above and below: The off-road sequence involving the new Land Rover Defender and Range Rover Sport SVR is said to be the most brutal chase ever devised for a Bond film, as the extreme tracking vehicle would suggest.

Daniel Craig enjoys a pause in filming with Bond's Land Rover Series III, on set in Jamaica.

is very important. It's totally different to competing, but it's still a buzz especially when you're doing the big scenes. It's a massive team operation; I might be doing my little handbrake number up here but somebody else is doing a big pipe ramp stunt behind me, and if I make a mess of my handbrake then that's a £20k shot that's potentially gone down the drain. Everyone has to do their bit, especially when you're writing cars off or blowing them up… And it's dangerous.'

No Time To Die's car cast list really is expansive. Fellow 00 agent Nomi, played by Lashana Lynch, gets an Aston Martin DBS Superleggera, one of the very best cars the company has ever produced. It's a suitably high-end mix of materials, and the Italian name (which means 'superlight') references the fabricating techniques used by Aston's coachbuilder of choice back in the 1960s – Touring of Milan, who designed the DB5 (Federico Formenti is the man who deserves the credit). Reworking the software on the 5.2-litre, twin-turbo V12 lifts the power output to 715bhp while torque rises to 663lb ft. The eight-speed gearbox has been reinforced to cope, while the suspension and damping have been retuned for the extra body control you need when you're on a mission to discover what an extra 180kg of downforce feels like at 211mph. There are various different modes for the engine, gearbox, and suspension, and massive 410mm diameter carbon ceramic brakes discs at the front (360mm at the rear). Zero to 62mph takes 3.4 seconds, 0-100mph a deeply impressive 6.4.

Bond dusts off another classic, the Aston Martin V8 last seen in 1987's *The Living Daylights*, which is wearing the same registration plate as that car. 'The V8 is a car I have always loved,' Cary Fukunaga says. 'Aston Martin's cars are beautiful works of art and have become a quintessential part of a Bond film.' It's also a favourite of Daniel Craig's, and the car's return elevates it to a

Left: Bond's contact in Cuba, Paloma (Ana de Armas), and her Chevrolet Bel Air, shortly before all hell breaks loose. Below left: Nomi (Lashana Lynch) with her Aston Martin DBS Superleggera. Below: the truly remarkable Aston Martin Valhalla.

point where it's almost as revered a crowd-pleaser as its DB5 predecessor. 'I'm really happy about the V8 being included in this movie,' Craig says. 'I'm such a fan of this car: it's got a muscle car attitude but with a very British sophistication.'

The still-in-development Aston Martin Valhalla supercar also makes a brief appearance. Only 500 will be made, powered by an all-new twin turbo V6, hybridised to optimise efficiency and maximise performance. Elsewhere is a retinue of Jaguar XFs and a handful of Range Rover Sport SVRs. And Bond also finds himself behind the wheel of a Land Rover Series III in Jamaica.

Daniel Craig is extremely well-regarded as a driver by the Bond stunt crew, but the insurance risks were too great for him to do much of the driving in the film. But that's actually him behind the DB5's wood-rimmed steering wheel in the scenes in which Bond donuts his way out of trouble in Matera. 'I'm lucky to have access to a brilliant bunch of experts who take me out, and we talk about it,' he tells me. 'We talk about the correct body language behind the wheel, but often when you're with really good drivers they're usually about three inches away from the steering wheel, and that's just not very cinematic. Rally drivers are practically on top of the wheel.' He pauses. 'Look cool! That's all you can do…'

As to the film itself, his last as James Bond, Daniel allows himself some satisfaction amidst the obvious sadness at surrendering his 00 status. 'When I finished *Casino Royale*, I thought, "We've made a good movie,"' he says. 'But I was quite prepared to go, "That's it, I did one movie, swing and a miss," and walk away. Because who knows what's going to happen. It was a success, and that was amazing. But I always had in the back of my mind a story I wanted to tell, and it kind of happened. We have a through line. And this movie is about tying all those ends up, about reconnecting him to *Casino*, really, and that's what we've managed to do.

'It was emotional to finish, it always is to finish something you've been working on for two years, with a bunch of people you get very close to. I'm just immensely proud of the whole thing, of the five movies. What I'll miss most is the collaborative process that goes on when you make these films. The Bond eco-system is unique.'

Finally, and inevitably, I ask Daniel if he has a personal favourite Bond car. There's a lengthy pause, and an exhalation. 'The Toyota 2000GT convertible,' he says. 'It's so unusual. It's that Japanese design thing, it's an amalgamation of so many different things. I loved that. The Aston Martin V8 that we get back into this film… and the *Casino Royale* DBS is a special car. I got to drive those quite a lot. They were a lot of fun. What do you like? Did you get a closer look at the DB5 in the film?'

We did, Daniel. We sure did.

James Bond (Daniel Craig) and an old friend, the Aston Martin V8.

ACKNOWLEDGEMENTS

This book wouldn't have been possible without the help of rather a lot of people, but in particular I'd like to order a round of Vodka Martinis for the man who designed it, Elliott Webb, and Meg Simmonds, Archive Director at EON Productions. The three of us whiled away many an hour trawling through EON's remarkable photographic archive in London, every moment of which felt like a privilege. Elliott, you are an absolute gentleman and a true artist; Meg, thank you for your supreme patience, insight and fine selection of berets.

Thanks to Charlie Turner, BBC *Top Gear*'s magnificent editor-in-chief, for his friendship, support and advice along the way, and to Stephanie Wenborn, EON's head of marketing and publicity, for inviting me to tackle such an outrageously enjoyable project in the first place. Debi Berry provided invaluable assistance when it came to sourcing images, and was endlessly patient even as I regaled her with tales of particularly obscure cars. To Yvonne Jacob, Charlotte Macdonald and production manager Phil Spencer at BBC Books – thank you all for going above and beyond. To Steve Tribe, my project editor: I would offer fulsome praise, but I won't (he'll understand why). Special thanks to John Glen, director of five of the Bond films, for being so gracious with his time, to special effects genius Chris Corbould, and to Lee Morrison, Bond stunt coordinating supremo. Dave Worrall's history of the Aston Martin DB5 was a tremendous resource, as was Paul Duncan's exhaustive tome *The James Bond Archives*. Thanks to Suzy Littlejohn, Jenni McMurrie, Rosie Moutrie, Rabia Lingemann, Greg Williams, Juliet Fairbairn and Richard Agnew at Jaguar Land Rover, Kevin Watters, Marek Reichman and Steve Waddingham at Aston Martin, Sara Bertusi at Lamborghini, Ed Byrne and Claire Walker, Greg Fountain, Mark Graham, John Cork, Pierre Bohanna, Dylan Jones and Paul Henderson at *GQ*, Rob Harris, the Webbs, the Bullmans, the Sweeneys, and the Woods (Damon, the F355 is obviously the best Bond car).

Finally, huge love to my parents and my long-suffering family, Andrea, Gracie, Willem and Doug. The last one is a daft Golden Retriever, but he kept me company while I worked my way through the Bond movie back catalogue.

NO, MR BOND. WE EXPECT YOU... TO DRIVE

01. DR. NO 1962
Alfa Romeo Giulietta Spider
Austin A55
Cadillac Fleetwood 60 Special
Chevrolet Bel Air convertible 1957
(NB The first car driven by 007 in a Bond film)
Chevrolet El Camino
Chevrolet Impala saloon
Ford Anglia 105 E
Ford Consul
Hillman Minx Series III
Jaguar XK140
LaSalle hearse
Mercedes 180 (W120)
Renault Dauphine
Studebaker Skyhawk
Sunbeam Alpine
Vauxhall Velox PA

02. FROM RUSSIA WITH LOVE 1963
Bentley 3.5-litre drophead coupé
Chevrolet C30 Apache
Chevrolet C30 flatbed
Chevrolet One-Fifty
Chevrolet Styleline De Luxe
Citroën Traction Avant
DeSoto Diplomat
DeSoto Fireflite
Dodge Coronet
Dodge Kingsway
Mercury Custom
Plymouth Belvedere
Plymouth Cambridge
Plymouth Cranbrook
Plymouth Savoy
Rolls-Royce Silver Wraith

03. GOLDFINGER 1964
Aston Martin DB5
Ford Country Squire Station Wagon
Ford Falcon Ranchero
Ford Mustang convertible
Ford Thunderbird

Humber Sceptre
Lincoln Continental
Mercedes 190 (W121)
Mercedes 220 SE (W128)
Rolls-Royce Phantom III Sedanca de Ville

04. THUNDERBALL 1965
Aston Martin DB5
Citroën DS
Ford Mustang
Ford Thunderbird
Lincoln Continental Executive Limo conversion by Lehmann-Peterson
Rolls-Royce Silver Cloud II
Simca Aronde

05. YOU ONLY LIVE TWICE 1967
Chevrolet Impala convertible
Dodge Polara
Mini Moke
Nissan Cedric
Pontiac Catalina
Pontiac Parisienne
Prince Gloria
Prince Skyline
Subaru 360
Toyota 'Toyopet' Crown Deluxe
Toyota 2000 GT convertible

06. ON HER MAJESTY'S SECRET SERVICE 1969
Aston Martin DBS
Austin Mini
DKW F12 roadster
Ford Escort Mk I
Ford Taunus 17M
Jaguar Mk X
Lancia Flavia
Mercedes 200 (W115)
Mercedes 220S (W111)
Mercedes 600 Grosse (W100)
Mercedes bus (O309)
Mercury Cougar XR-7
Rolls-Royce Silver Shadow Drophead

07. DIAMONDS ARE FOREVER 1971
Cadillac hearse
Ford Club Wagon
Ford Custom
Ford Fairlaine 500
Ford Galaxie 500
Ford LTD
Ford Mustang Mach One
Ford Thunderbird Landau
Mercedes 600 Grosse
Triumph Stag

08. LIVE AND LET DIE 1973
AEC Regent III RT246 double decker bus
Buick Skylark
Cadillac Coupé DeVille
Cadillac Fleetwood 60 Special
Cadillac Fleetwood Eldorado
Cadillac Sedan de Ville
Chevrolet Bel Air (taxi)
Chevrolet C-10 Custom Fleetside
Chevrolet Caprice estate
Chevrolet Caprice coupé
Chevrolet Chevelle Malibu
Chevrolet Corvette Corvorado Dunham
Chevrolet Impala convertible
Chevrolet Impala Custom Coupé
Chevrolet Impala Sport
Chevrolet Nova
Datsun 411
Dodge Polara (police car)
Ford Custom
Ford Econoline
Ford Galaxie 500
Lincoln Continental Mark IV
Mack AB truck
Mini Moke
Plymouth Duster
Plymouth Fury Custom Suburban
Pontiac Bonneville two-door hardtop
Rambler Marlin
Toyota Corolla
VW Beetle

09. THE MAN WITH THE GOLDEN GUN 1974
Alfa Romeo Giulia Super
AMC Hornet
AMC Matador coupé
AMC Matador saloon (police car)
BMW 2.8 CS
BMW 5 series
Datsun 120Y
Fiat 124
Fiat 850 coupé
Ford Consul
Ford Escort Mk 1
Ford Prefect van
Ford Taunus
Holden Kingswood
Holden Torana
Lancia saloon
Mazda Bongo
Mercedes 220 S (W180)
Mercedes 220 D (W113)
MG B
Rolls-Royce Silver Shadow
Simca 1301
Toyota Celica
Toyota Crown
Toyota Hiace
Triumph 1300

10. THE SPY WHO LOVED ME 1977
Chevrolet Caprice Classic
Chevrolet Nova
Fiat 850
Fiat 850 Coupé
Fiat 850 Familiare
Fiat 600D
Ford Taunus 2.3 Ghia
Lotus Esprit
Mini Moke
Oldsmobile Toronado
Piaggio Ape
Sherpa van (by Leyland)
Volvo truck
VW Microbus

11. MOONRAKER 1979
Isotta Fraschini Tipo 8A roadster
Hispano-Suiza J12 convertible
Jeep Wagoneer
Mini Moke
MP Lafer
Rolls-Royce Silver Shadow 1

12. FOR YOUR EYES ONLY 1981
Citroën CX saloon
Citroën 2CV
Innocenti Mini
Lotus Esprit Turbo (white & red)
Mercedes 200 D (W115)
Mercedes 280 SE (W116)
Mercedes SL (R107)
Opel Rekord diesel
Peugeot 504
Renault 18
Rolls-Royce Silver Shadow I

13. OCTOPUSSY 1983
Alfa Romeo GTV6
Austin Allegro
Austin FX4 taxi
BMW 3 series (E20)
BMW 5 series police car (E28)
BMW 633 CSi (E24)
BMW 7 series (E23)
Cadillac Seville
Fiat 128
Ford Escort Mk II
Ford Granada estate
Ford Taunus
Mercedes 200 (W123)
Mercedes 250 SE (W108)
Mercedes 600 Pullman (W100)
Mercedes S-class (W116)
Opel Kadett
Opel Kadett estate
Opel Rekord
Range Rover Rapport Huntsman
Renault R4 van
Rolls-Royce Phantom II Sedanca
Rover 2200 TC
Volga M-24

VW Beetle
VW Golf
VW Jetta
VW Karmann Ghia convertible
VW Passat Estate
VW Polo
VW Transporter van
Volvo 244

14. A VIEW TO A KILL 1985
Alfa Romeo Alfasud Sprint
AMC Concord
AMC Eagle
Audi 80 MkI (B1)
BMW 7 series (E23)
BMW 3 series (E21)
Cadillac Fleetwood 75 limo
Cadillac series 62 convertible
Chevrolet C-series truck
Chevrolet Corvette C4
Chevrolet Malibu
Chevrolet Monte Carlo
Citroën 2CV
Citroën C25 van
Citroën CX Safari
Citroën CX saloon
Dodge D-100
Dodge Diplomat
Dodge Monaco
Fiat Panda
Fiat Ritmo
Ford Bronco XLT series III
Ford Escort cabriolet
Ford Fiesta Mk 1 and Mk 2
Ford LTD
Ford Taunus coupé
Ford Thunderbird
Matra Murena
Mercedes 200
Mercedes S-class (W126) 500 SEL with AMG body kit
Mini 1000 HLE
Opel Kadett
Peugeot 104 ZS
Peugeot 205

Peugeot 304 saloon
Peugeot 305
Peugeot 505
Peugeot J7 Fourgon police van
Peugeot 604 limo, by Heuliez
Plymouth Reliant
Pontiac Fiero
Porsche 928S
Porsche 944
Renault Fuego turbo
Renault R4 van (F6)
Renault 5
Renault 9
Renault 11 TXE
Renault 12
Renault 14 police car
Renault 16
Renault 20
Range Rover
Rolls-Royce Silver Cloud II
Talbot 1100 VF3
Volvo 740
VW beach buggy – Sovra LM1
VW Beetle
VW Golf GTI
VW Jetta

15. THE LIVING DAYLIGHTS 1987
Aston Martin V8
Aston Martin V8 Volante
Audi 200 Quattro
Audi 200 Quattro Avant
Chevrolet Impala Convertible
Daimler Double Six
Dodge M37
Ford Granada
Land Rover series III
Land Rover series III armoured
Mercedes 240 D (W115)
Range Rover
Rover 800
Skoda 105
Tatra 603
UAZ 469
VAZ 2105

16. LICENCE TO KILL 1989
Cadillac Seville
Chevrolet Caprice
Dodge Ram
Jeep CJ-7
Lincoln Mark VII
Maserati Biturbo
Mercury Grand Marquis limo
Rolls-Royce Phantom V
Rolls-Royce Silver Shadow II

17. GOLDENEYE 1995
Aston Martin DB5
BMW 7 series (E23)
BMW Z3 1.9 (E36/7)
Mercedes S-class (W140)
Ferrari F355 GTS
GAZ 31029
Mercedes 200 (W123)
Mercedes 230 E (W124)
Mercedes S-class (W126)
Renault Fuego
UAZ 3151
VAZ 2106
ZAZ 965

18. TOMORROW NEVER DIES 1997
Aston Martin DB5
BMW 750iL
Daimler limousine
Ford Scorpio
Jaguar XJ6
Jeep Cherokee
Mercedes S-class (W126)
Opel Senator
Peugeot 504
Peugeot 505 estate
Porsche Boxster
Range Rover (P38a series II)
Renault Fuego
UAZ 369
Vauxhall Omega

19. THE WORLD IS NOT ENOUGH 1999
Aston Martin DB5
BMW Z8
Ford Escort Mk IV
Lada Niva
Land Rover Defender 90 custom
Rolls-Royce Silver Shadow II
UAZ 469
VAZ 2121

20. DIE ANOTHER DAY 2002
Aston Martin Vanquish
Ferrari F355
Ferrari 360 Modena
Ford Fairlane Sunliner
Ford GT40 (by MDA)
Ford Thunderbird
Jaguar XKR
Lamborghini Diablo
Mercedes SL (R230)
Porsche 911 Carrera 4
Range Rover (L322)
UAZ 369

21. CASINO ROYALE 2006
Aston Martin DBS
Aston Martin DB5
Ford Crown Victoria police car
Ford Mondeo
Jaguar XJ8
Range Rover Sport

22. QUANTUM OF SOLACE 2008
Alfa Romeo 156
Alfa Romeo 159
Aston Martin DBS
Audi A6
Daimler Double Six
Ford Bronco II
Ford Edge
Ford Ka
Range Rover Sport
Volvo S40

23. SKYFALL 2012
Aston Martin DB5
Audi A5
Jaguar XJ8
Land Rover Defender
Land Rover Discovery 4
Mercedes S-class (W221)
Range Rover (L322, series III)

24. SPECTRE 2015
Alfa Romeo 159
Alfa Romeo 166
Aston Martin DB5
Aston Martin DB10
BMW 7 series (FO1)
Bugatti EB110
Ferrari California
Ferrari FF
Ferrari F355 GTS
Ferrari 360 Modena Spider
Ferrari 599
Fiat 500
Jaguar C-X75
Jaguar XJ8
Land Rover Defender Bigfoot
Land Rover Discovery Sport
Maserati Gran Turismo convertible
Mercedes AMG SLS (C197)
Mercedes S-class (W222)
Mercedes SLR McLaren
Porsche 959
Range Rover
Rolls-Royce Ghost
Rolls-Royce Silver Wraith

25. NO TIME TO DIE 2020
Aston Martin DB5
Aston Martin DBS Superleggera
Aston Martin V8
Aston Martin Valhalla
Jaguar XF
Lancia Thesis
Land Rover Defender (2020)
Land Rover Series III
Maserati Quattroporte (1990s)
Range Rover Series I
Range Rover Sport
Toyota Land Cruiser

NB It's impossible to include absolutely every car seen in every Bond film, given that some are only visible for a split second or in the background. But we've tried to cover off all the significant ones… and even plenty of insignificant ones, because they're often just as fascinating.

336

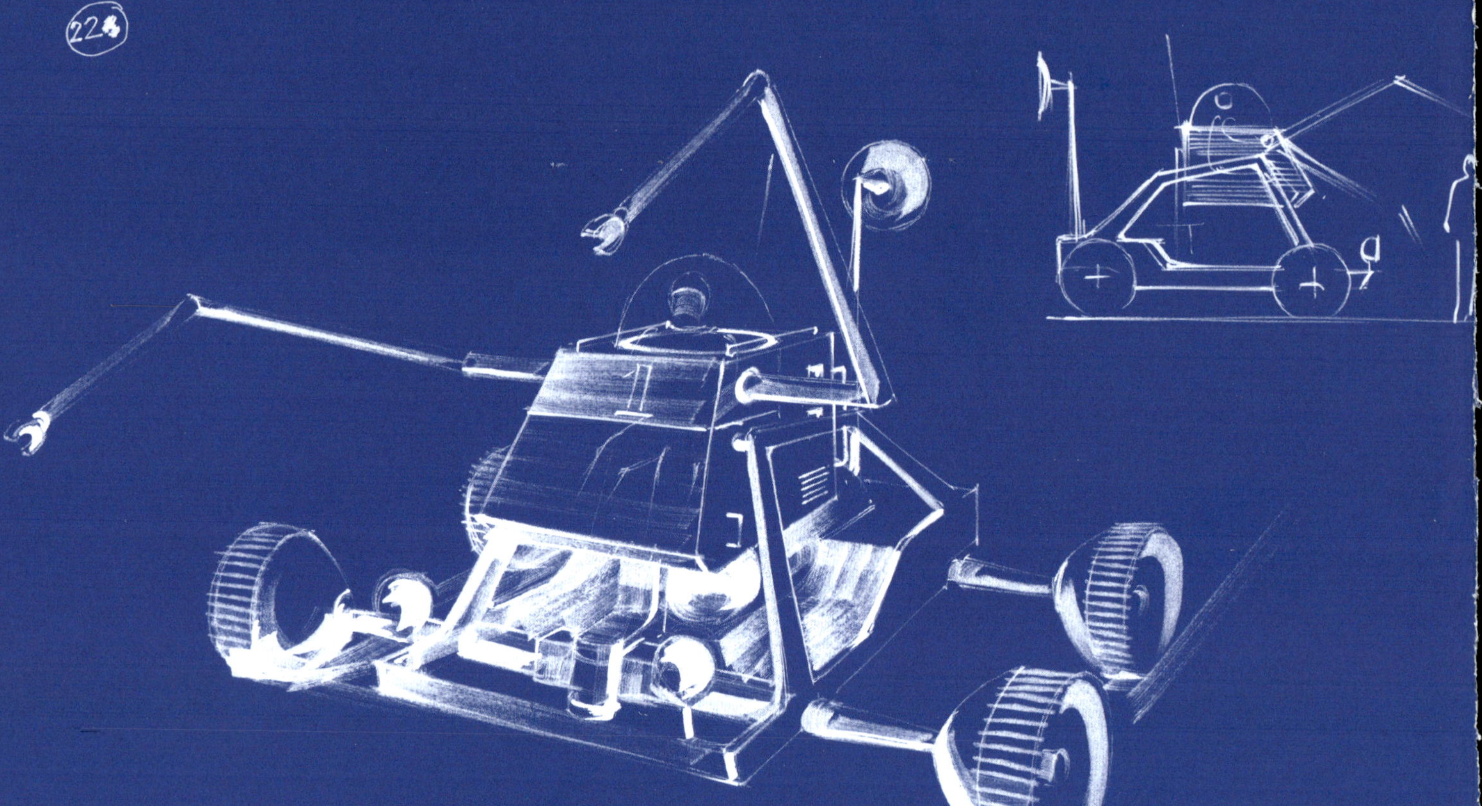

DIAMONDS FOR BUZZ "LUNAR VEHICLE"